MW00813255

Volume 2

Glorianna
"Glori" Silver is
an independently wealthy
businesswoman from Norway who has
focused her entire life on becoming the
bearer of the Ember Stone, a mystical Artifact
gifting its bearer the Dragon's form and flame.
Michael "Finn" Finnegan is a small-time criminal
from Ireland whose entire life consisted of a series
of larger events that force him into one bad decision
after another until he was bestowed the Glacier
Stone, an Artifact allowing him to transform into a
giant ice-clad warrior.
Two dramatically different people tasked with
opposing duties and fated to destroy each
other, but unknown to either Glori or
Finn, there is a third Artifact in
this Broken Trinity.

published by
Top Cow Productions, Inc.
Los Angeles

BROKEN TRINITY PANDORA'S BOX
Volume 2

Written by: : **Bryan Edward Hill** and **Rob Levin**
Art by: **Alessandro Vitti** and **Facundo Percio**
Colors by: **Sunny Gho, Arif Prianto**
and **Imaginary Friends Studios**
Letters by: **Troy Peteri**

For this edition cover art by:
Tommy Lee Edwards
Special thanks to: Ron Marz

Original editions edited by:
Filip Sablik & Phil Smith
For this edition book design and
layout by: Jana Cook

Want more info? check out:
www.topcow.com
for news and exclusive Top Cow mercha

IMAGE COMICS, INC.
Robert Kirkman - chief operating officer
Erik Larsen - chief financial officer
Todd McFarlane - president
Marc Silvestri - chief executive officer
Jim Valentino - vice-president
Eric Stephenson - publisher
Todd Martinez - sales & licensing coordinator
Sarah deLaine - pr & marketing coordinator
Branwyn Bigglestone - accounts manager
Emily Miller - administrative assistant
Jamie Parreno - marketing assistant
Kevin Yuen - digital rights coordinator
Tyler Shainline - production manager
Drew Gill - art director
Jonathan Chan - senior production artist
Monica Garcia - production artist
Vincent Kukua - production artist
Jana Cook - production artist
www.imagecomics.com

COMIC SHOP LOCATOR SERVICE
888-COMIC-BOOK
888-266-4226

to find the comic shop
nearest you call:
1-888-COMICBOOK

For Top Cow Productions, Inc.:
Marc Silvestri – CEO
Matt Hawkins – President and COO
Filip Sablik – Publisher
Bryan Rountree – Assistant to Publisher
Elena Salcedo – Sales Assistant
Erin Perkins – Intern

BROKEN TRINITY VOLUME 2 PANDORA'S BOX TRADE PAPERBACK
June 2011 FIRST PRINTING. ISBN: 978-1-60706-199-1, $19.99 U.S.D.
Published by Image Comics Inc. Office of Publication: 2134 Allston Way, 2nd Floor, Berkeley, CA 94704. Originally published in single magazine form as BROKEN TRINITY: PANDORA'S BOX 1-6. Bro
© 2011 Top Cow Productions, Inc. All rights reserved. "Broken Trinity," the Broken Trinity logos, and the likeness of all characters (human or otherwise) featured herein are trademarks of Top Cow Productions
Inc. Image Comics and the Image Comics logo are trademarks of Image Comics, Inc. The characters, events, and stories in this publication are entirely fictional. Any resemblance to actual persons
dead), events, institutions, or locales, without satiric intent, is coincidental. No portion of this publication may be reproduced, in any form or by any means, without the express written
of Top Cow Productions, Inc. **PRINTED IN THE USA.**

TABLE OF CONTENTS

•••••

Bonus Materials

•••••

BROKEN TRINITY

"PANDORA'S BOX" Part 1

{
written by: **Bryan Edward Hill & Rob Levin**
art by: **Alessandro Vitti**
colors by: **Sunny Gho of IFS**
letters by: **Troy Peteri**
}

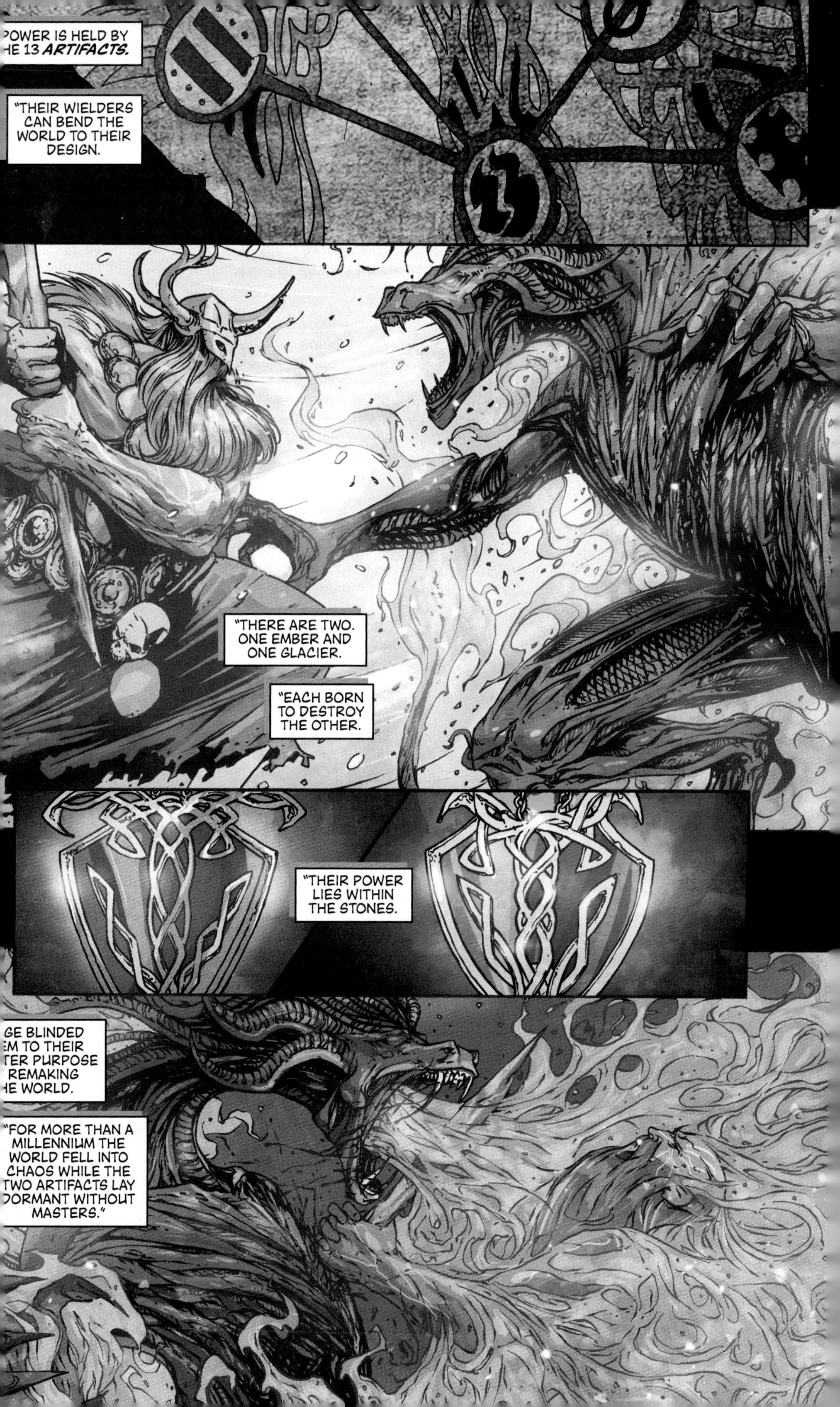
POWER IS HELD BY
HE 13 *ARTIFACTS.*
"THEIR WIELDERS CAN BEND THE WORLD TO THEIR DESIGN.
"THERE ARE TWO. ONE EMBER AND ONE GLACIER.
"EACH BORN TO DESTROY THE OTHER.
"THEIR POWER LIES WITHIN THE STONES.
GE BLINDED EM TO THEIR TER PURPOSE REMAKING HE WORLD.
"FOR MORE THAN A MILLENNIUM THE WORLD FELL INTO CHAOS WHILE THE TWO ARTIFACTS LAY DORMANT WITHOUT MASTERS."

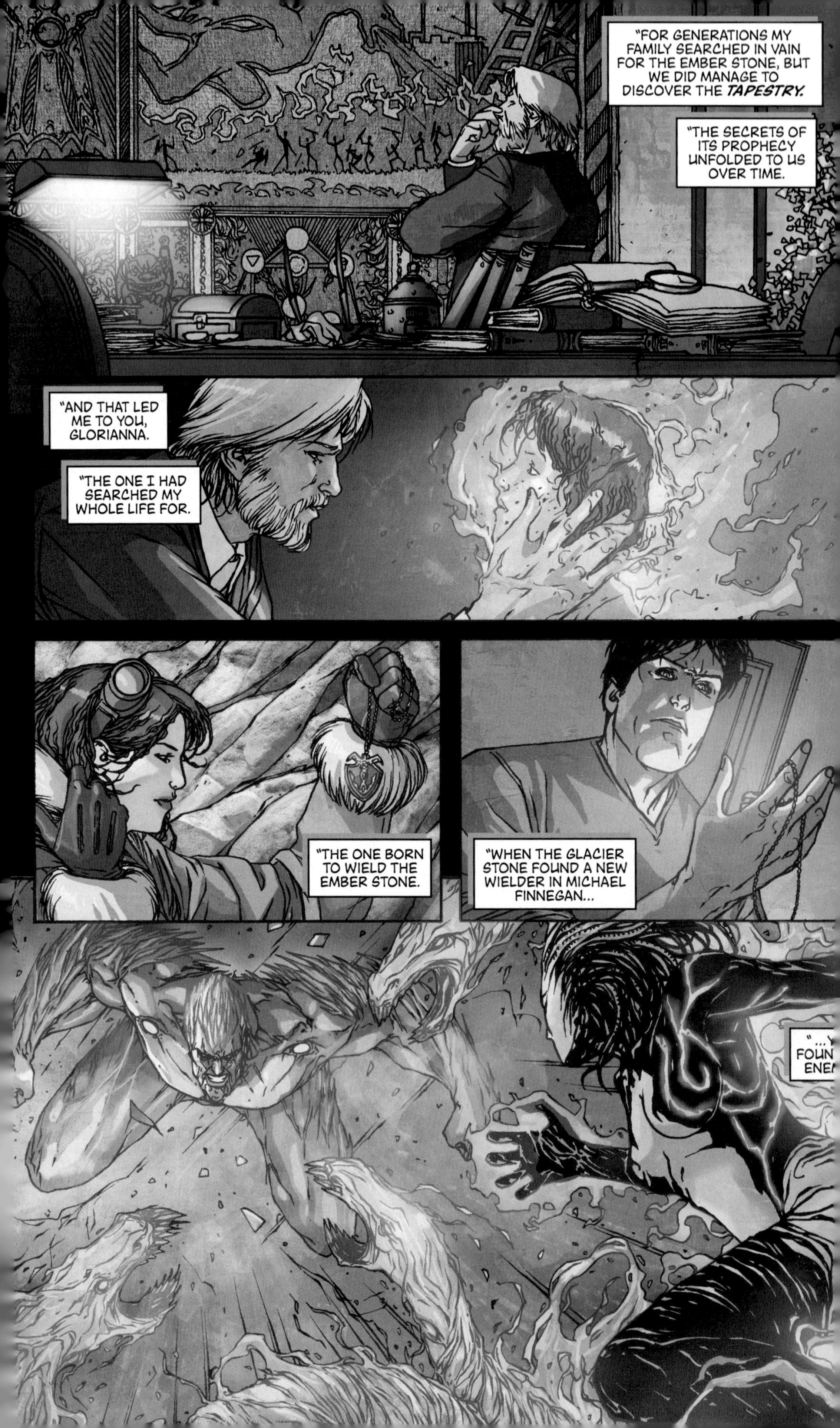
"FOR GENERATIONS MY FAMILY SEARCHED IN VAIN FOR THE EMBER STONE, BUT WE DID MANAGE TO DISCOVER THE *TAPESTRY.*
"THE SECRETS OF ITS PROPHECY UNFOLDED TO US OVER TIME.
"AND THAT LED ME TO YOU, GLORIANNA.
"THE ONE I HAD SEARCHED MY WHOLE LIFE FOR.
"THE ONE BORN TO WIELD THE EMBER STONE.
"WHEN THE GLACIER STONE FOUND A NEW WIELDER IN MICHAEL FINNEGAN...
"...Y
FOUN
ENE

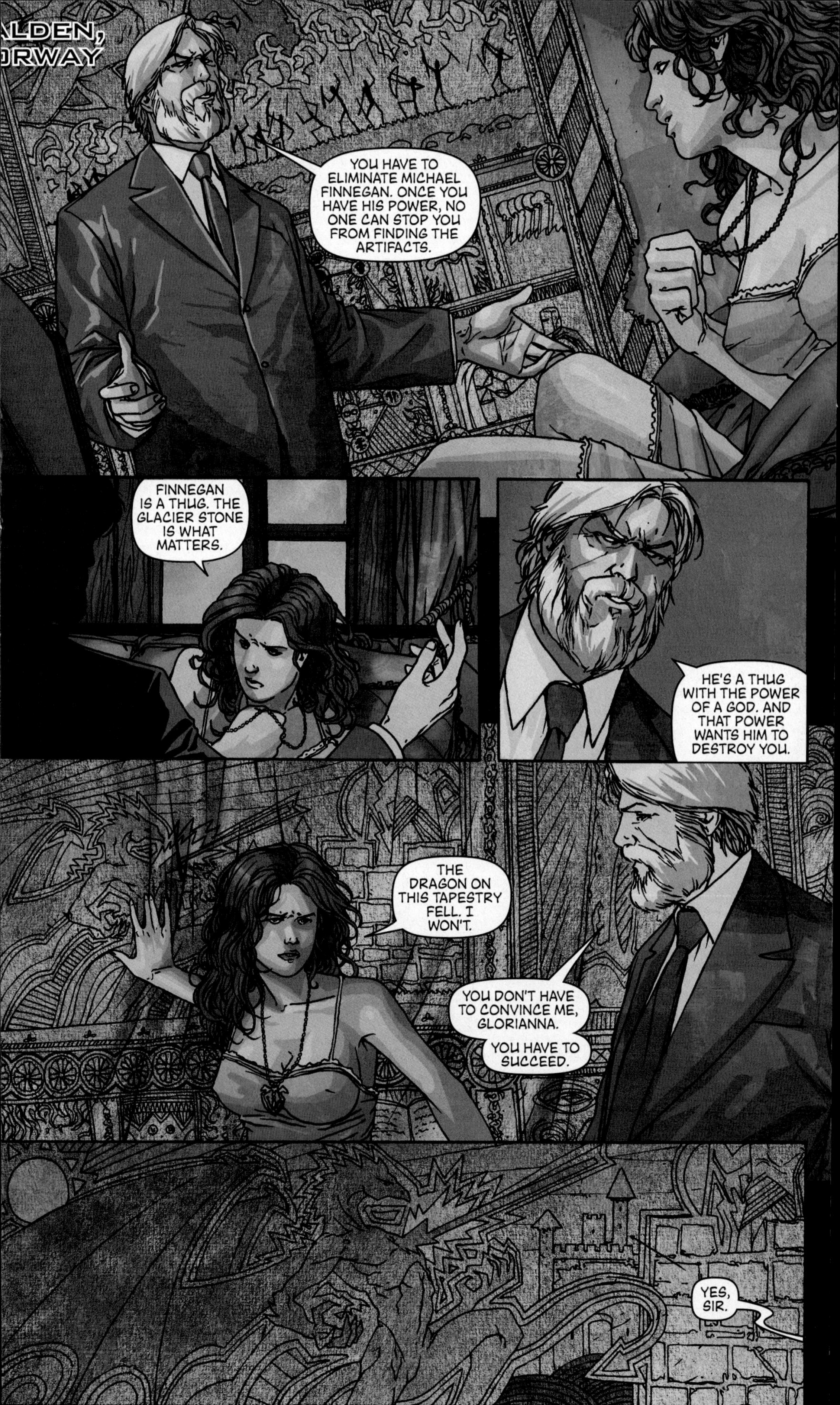
ALDEN,
ORWAY
YOU HAVE TO ELIMINATE MICHAEL FINNEGAN. ONCE YOU HAVE HIS POWER, NO ONE CAN STOP YOU FROM FINDING THE ARTIFACTS.
FINNEGAN IS A THUG. THE GLACIER STONE IS WHAT MATTERS.
HE'S A THUG WITH THE POWER OF A GOD. AND THAT POWER WANTS HIM TO DESTROY YOU.
THE DRAGON ON THIS TAPESTRY FELL. I WON'T.
YOU DON'T HAVE TO CONVINCE ME, GLORIANNA.
YOU HAVE TO SUCCEED.
YES, SIR.

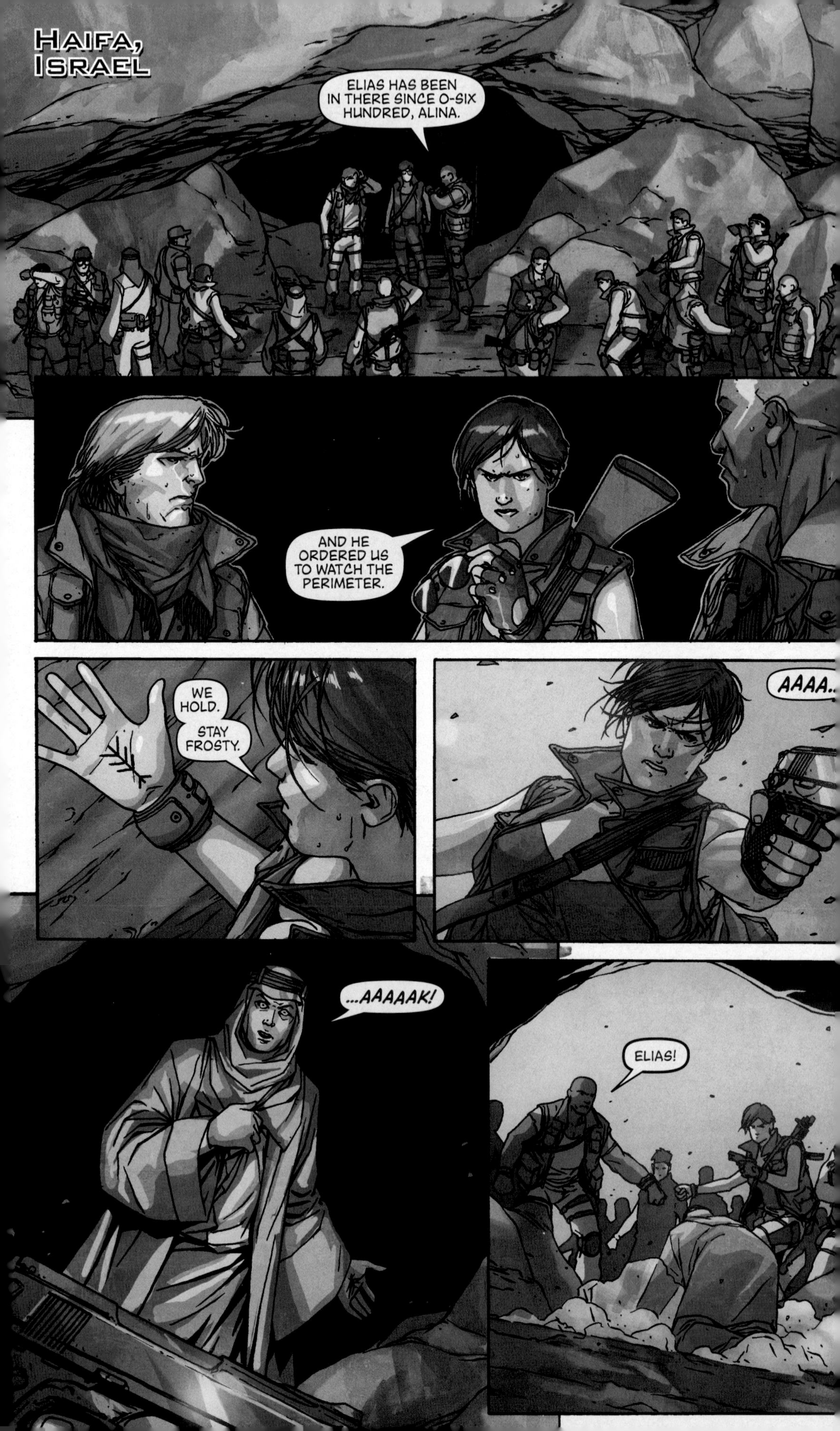
HAIFA, ISRAEL
ELIAS HAS BEEN IN THERE SINCE O-SIX HUNDRED, ALINA.
AND HE ORDERED US TO WATCH THE PERIMETER.
WE HOLD.
STAY FROSTY.
AAAA...
...AAAAAK!
ELIAS!

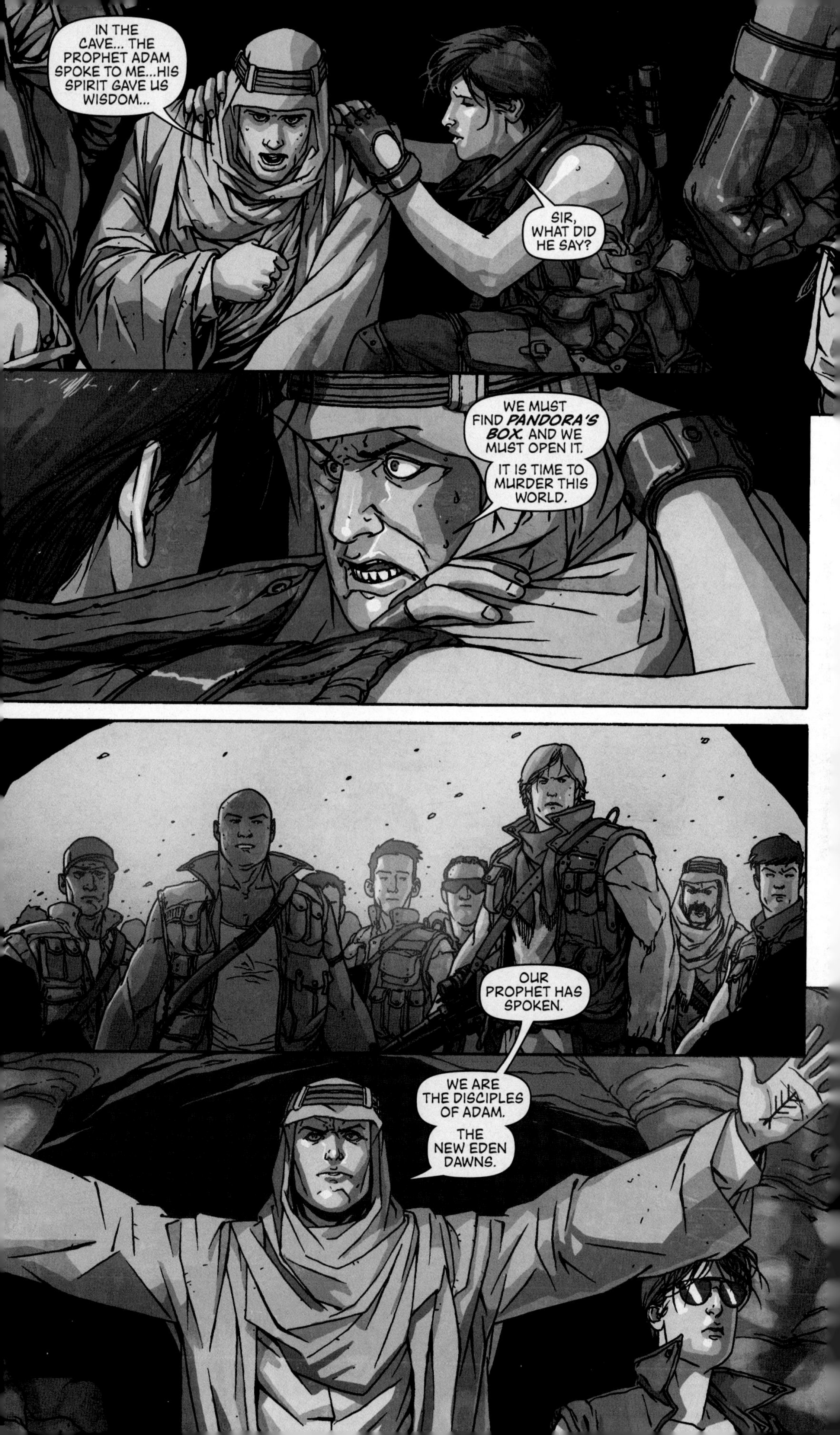
IN THE CAVE... THE PROPHET ADAM SPOKE TO ME...HIS SPIRIT GAVE US WISDOM...
SIR, WHAT DID HE SAY?
WE MUST FIND **PANDORA'S BOX.** AND WE MUST OPEN IT.
IT IS TIME TO MURDER THIS WORLD.
OUR PROPHET HAS SPOKEN.
WE ARE THE DISCIPLES OF ADAM.
THE NEW EDEN DAWNS.

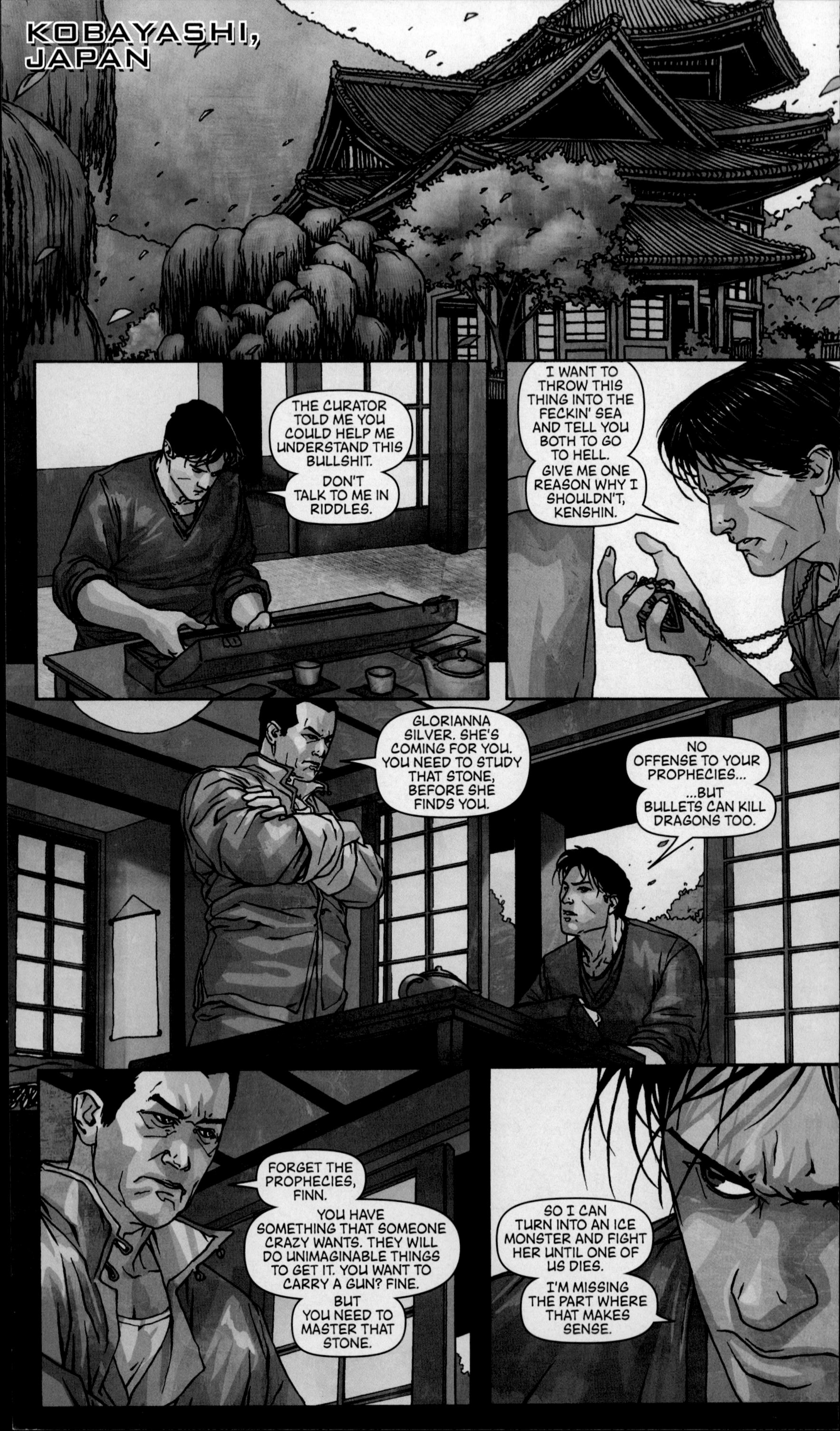
KOBAYASHI, JAPAN
THE CURATOR TOLD ME YOU COULD HELP ME UNDERSTAND THIS BULLSHIT.
DON'T TALK TO ME IN RIDDLES.
I WANT TO THROW THIS THING INTO THE FECKIN' SEA AND TELL YOU BOTH TO GO TO HELL.
GIVE ME ONE REASON WHY I SHOULDN'T, KENSHIN.
GLORIANNA SILVER. SHE'S COMING FOR YOU. YOU NEED TO STUDY THAT STONE, BEFORE SHE FINDS YOU.
NO OFFENSE TO YOUR PROPHECIES...
...BUT BULLETS CAN KILL DRAGONS TOO.
FORGET THE PROPHECIES, FINN.
YOU HAVE SOMETHING THAT SOMEONE CRAZY WANTS. THEY WILL DO UNIMAGINABLE THINGS TO GET IT. YOU WANT TO CARRY A GUN? FINE.
BUT YOU NEED TO MASTER THAT STONE.
SO I CAN TURN INTO AN ICE MONSTER AND FIGHT HER UNTIL ONE OF US DIES.
I'M MISSING THE PART WHERE THAT MAKES SENSE.

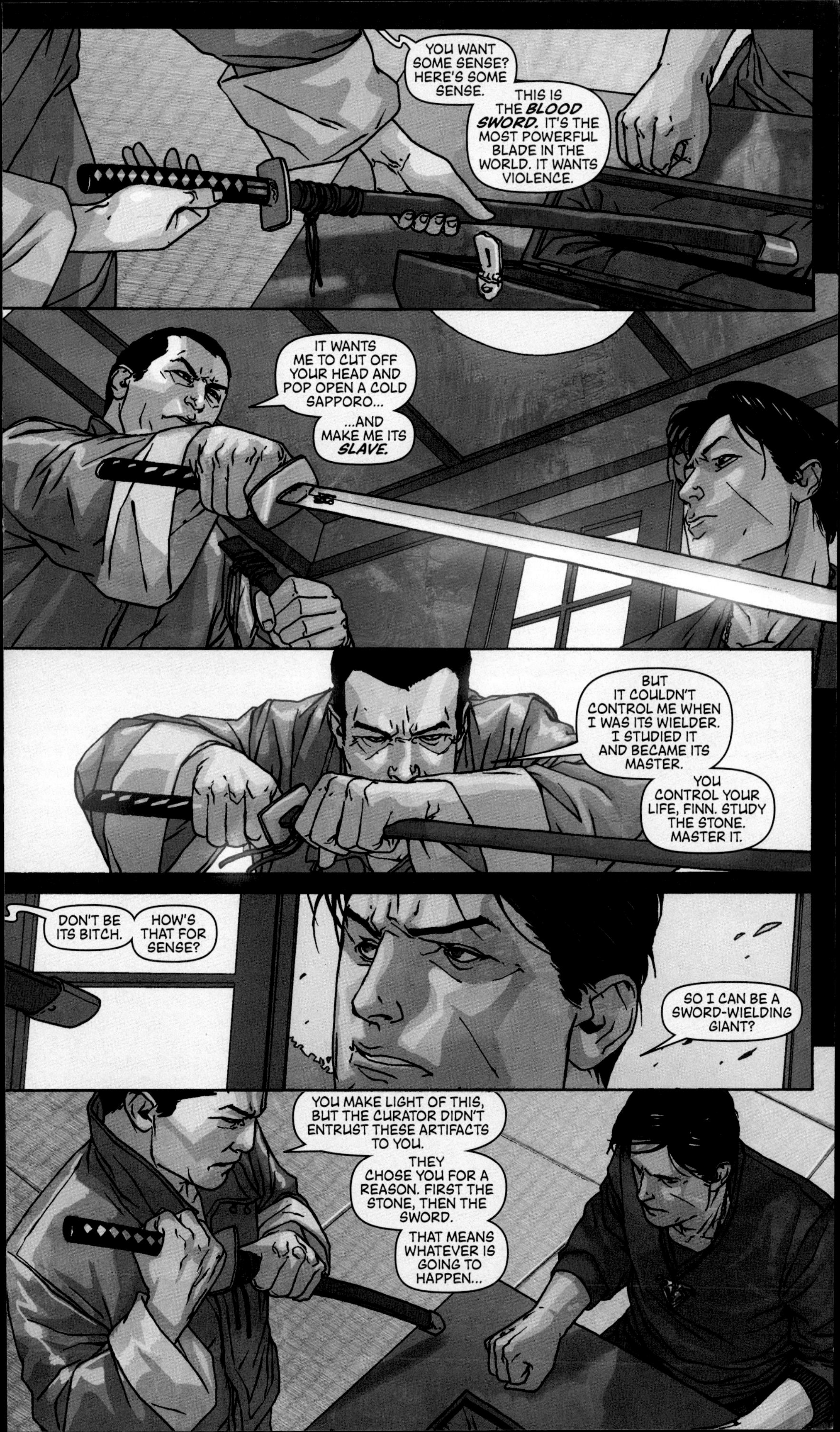
YOU WANT SOME SENSE? HERE'S SOME SENSE.
THIS IS THE BLOOD SWORD. IT'S THE MOST POWERFUL BLADE IN THE WORLD. IT WANTS VIOLENCE.
IT WANTS ME TO CUT OFF YOUR HEAD AND POP OPEN A COLD SAPPORO...
...AND MAKE ME ITS SLAVE.
BUT IT COULDN'T CONTROL ME WHEN I WAS ITS WIELDER. I STUDIED IT AND BECAME ITS MASTER.
YOU CONTROL YOUR LIFE, FINN. STUDY THE STONE. MASTER IT.
DON'T BE ITS BITCH.
HOW'S THAT FOR SENSE?
SO I CAN BE A SWORD-WIELDING GIANT?
YOU MAKE LIGHT OF THIS, BUT THE CURATOR DIDN'T ENTRUST THESE ARTIFACTS TO YOU.
THEY CHOSE YOU FOR A REASON. FIRST THE STONE, THEN THE SWORD.
THAT MEANS WHATEVER IS GOING TO HAPPEN...

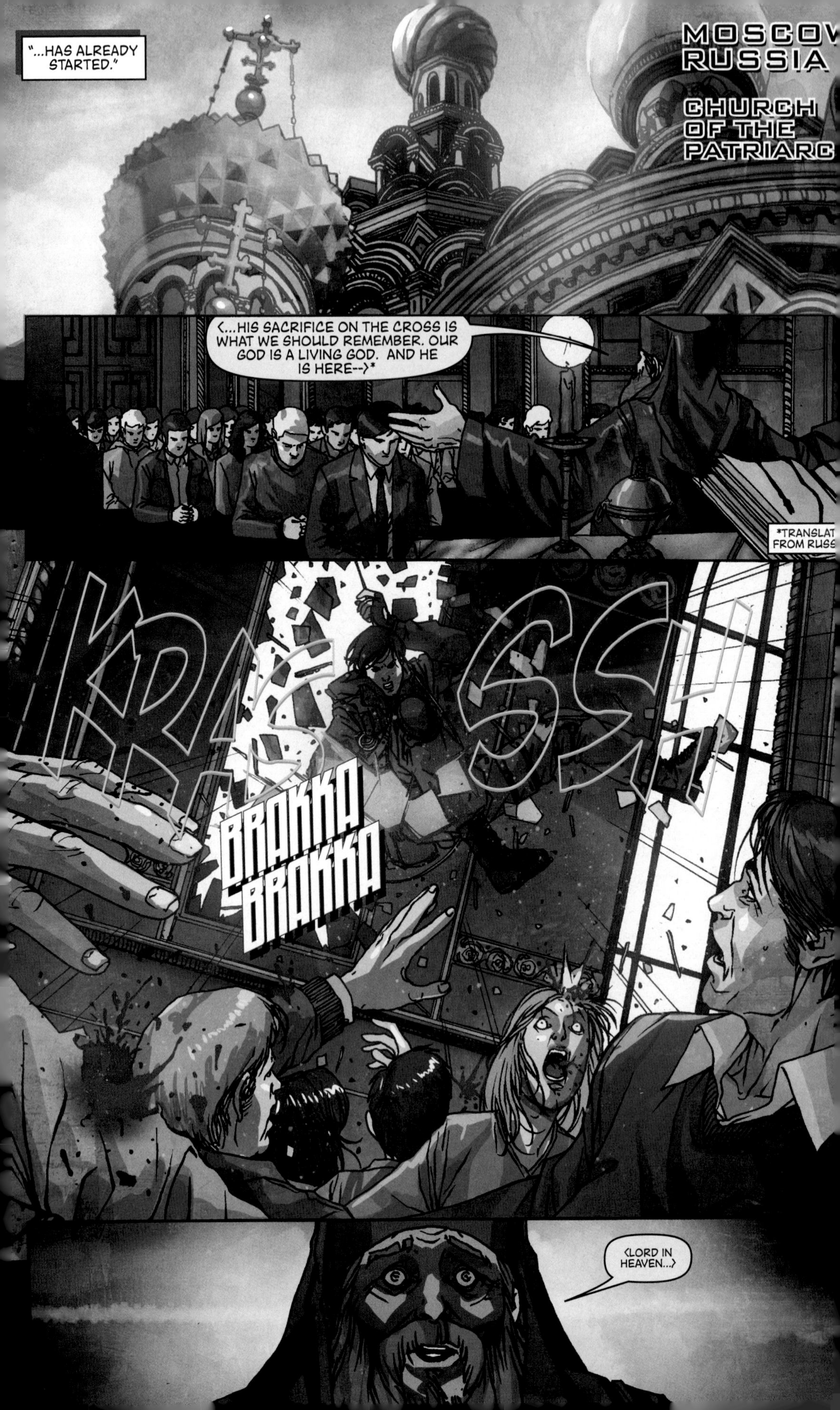
"...HAS ALREADY STARTED."
MOSCOW RUSSIA
CHURCH OF THE PATRIARC
<...HIS SACRIFICE ON THE CROSS IS WHAT WE SHOULD REMEMBER. OUR GOD IS A LIVING GOD. AND HE IS HERE-->*
*TRANSLAT FROM RUSS
KRASSH
BRAKKA BRAKKA
<LORD IN HEAVEN...>

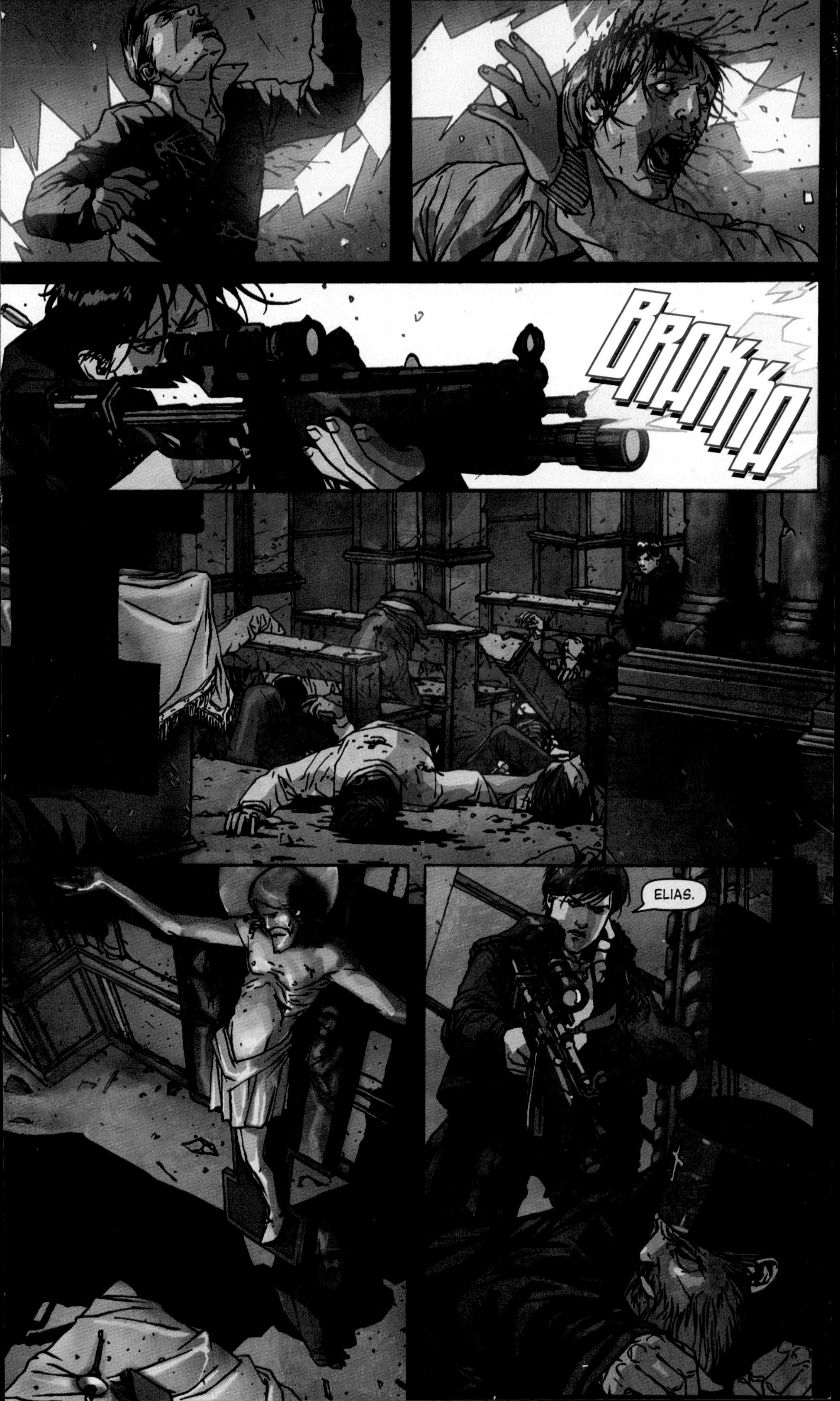
BRAKKA
ELIAS.

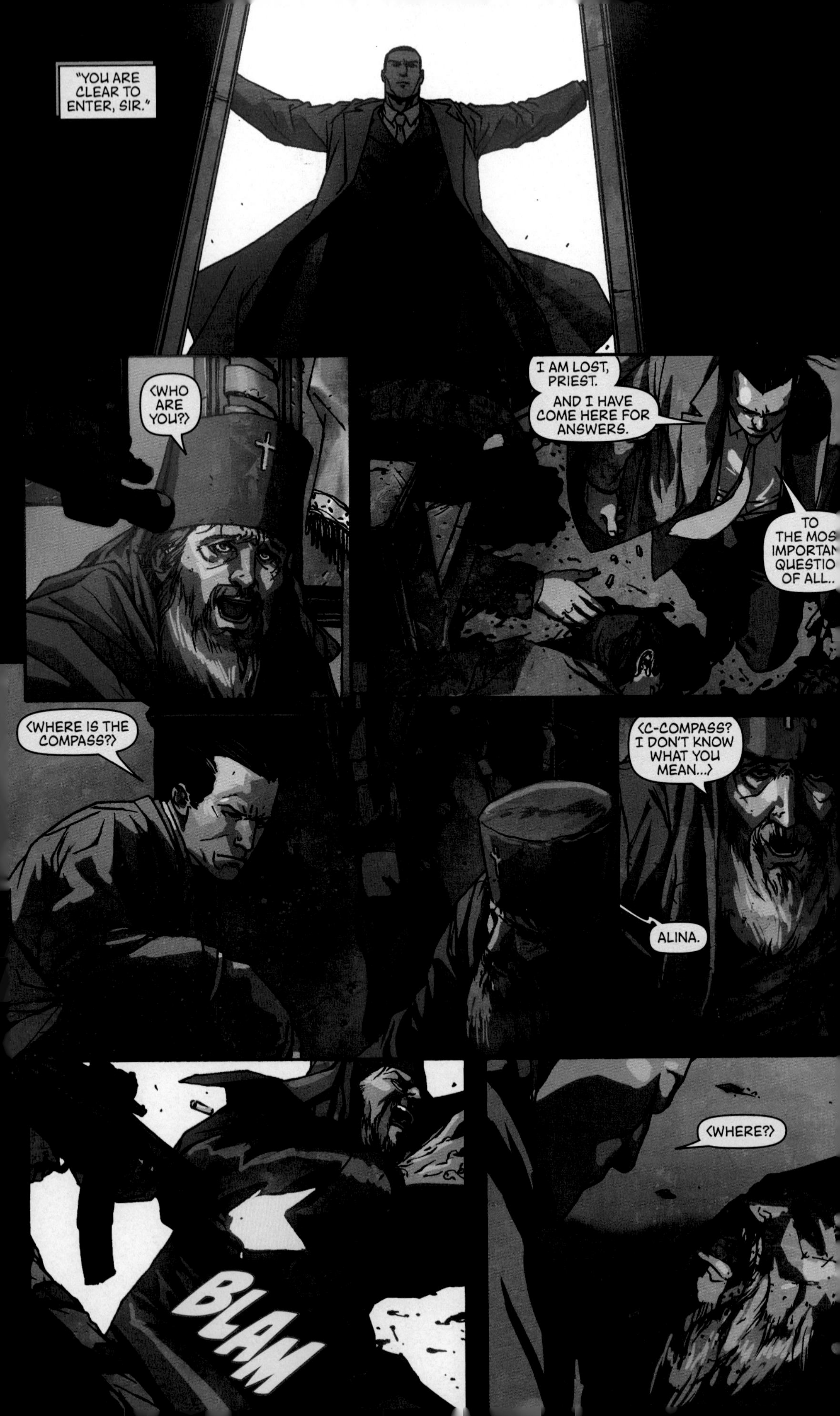
"YOU ARE CLEAR TO ENTER, SIR."
<WHO ARE YOU?>
I AM LOST, PRIEST.
AND I HAVE COME HERE FOR ANSWERS.
TO THE MOS IMPORTAN QUESTIO OF ALL..
<WHERE IS THE COMPASS?>
<C-COMPASS? I DON'T KNOW WHAT YOU MEAN...>
ALINA.
BLAM
<WHERE?>

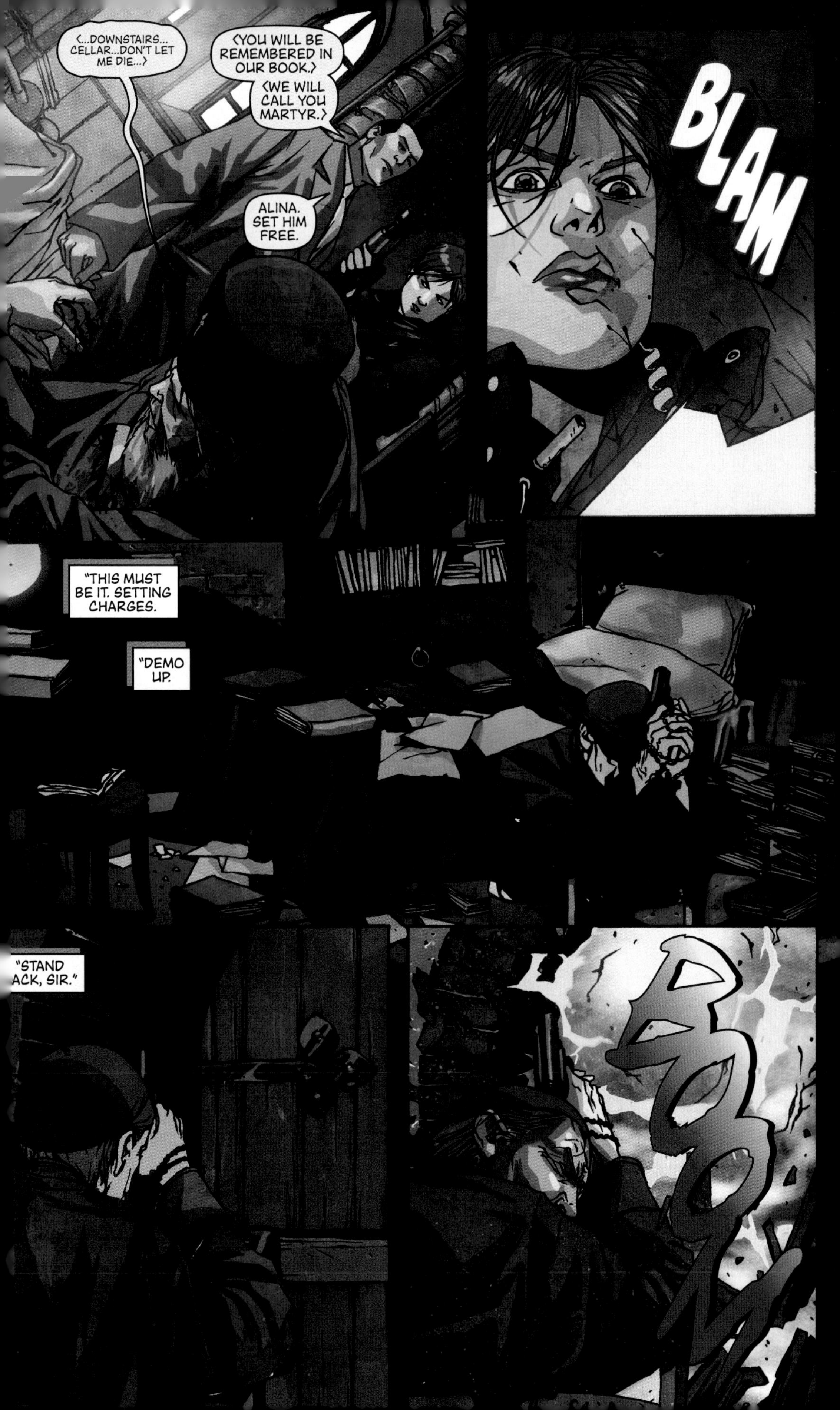
<...DOWNSTAIRS... CELLAR...DON'T LET ME DIE...>
<YOU WILL BE REMEMBERED IN OUR BOOK.>
<WE WILL CALL YOU MARTYR.>
ALINA. SET HIM FREE.
BLAM
"THIS MUST BE IT. SETTING CHARGES.
"DEMO UP.
"STAND ACK, SIR."
BOOM

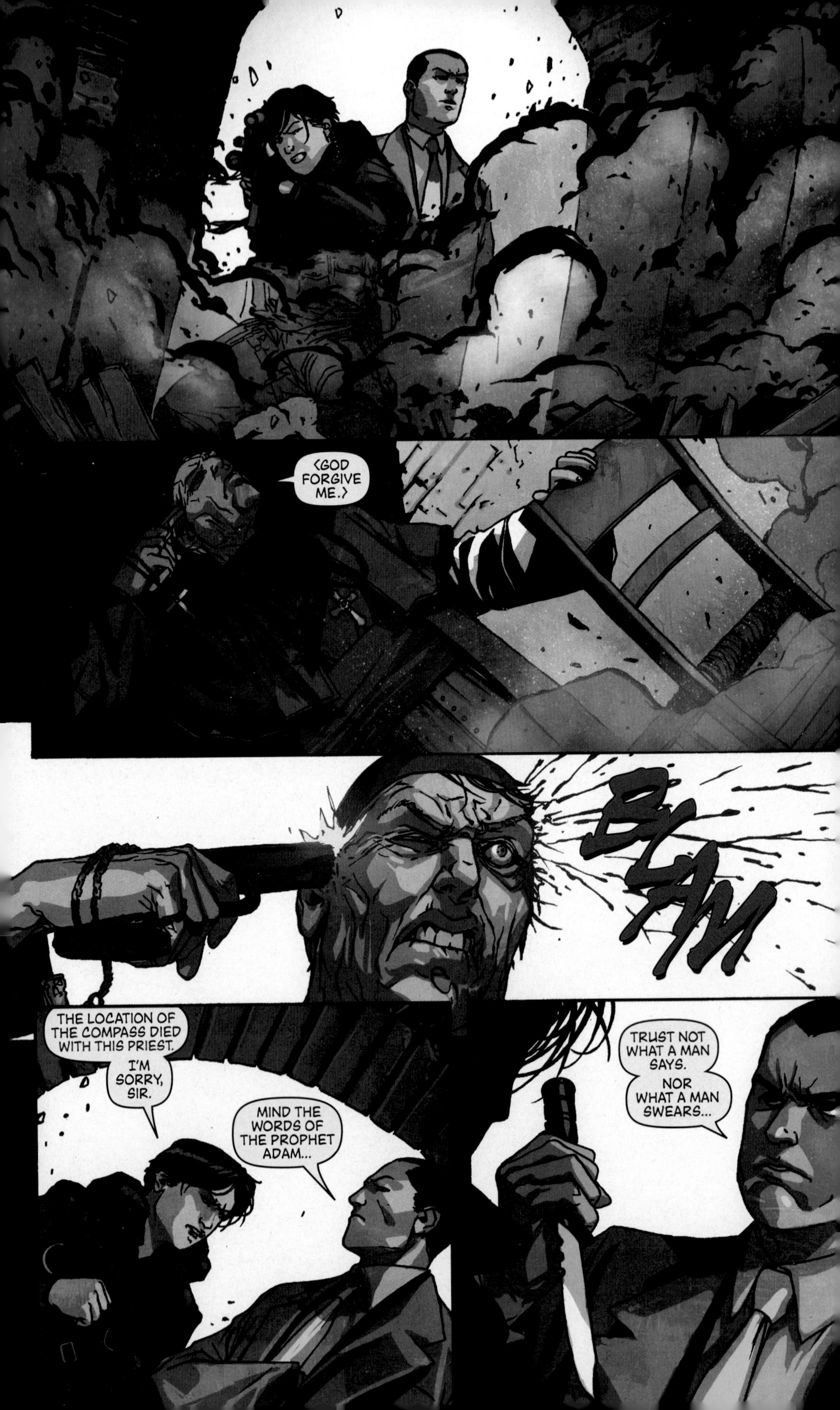
<GOD FORGIVE ME.>
BLAM
THE LOCATION OF THE COMPASS DIED WITH THIS PRIEST.
I'M SORRY, SIR.
MIND THE WORDS OF THE PROPHET ADAM...
TRUST NOT WHAT A MAN SAYS.
NOR WHAT A MAN SWEARS...

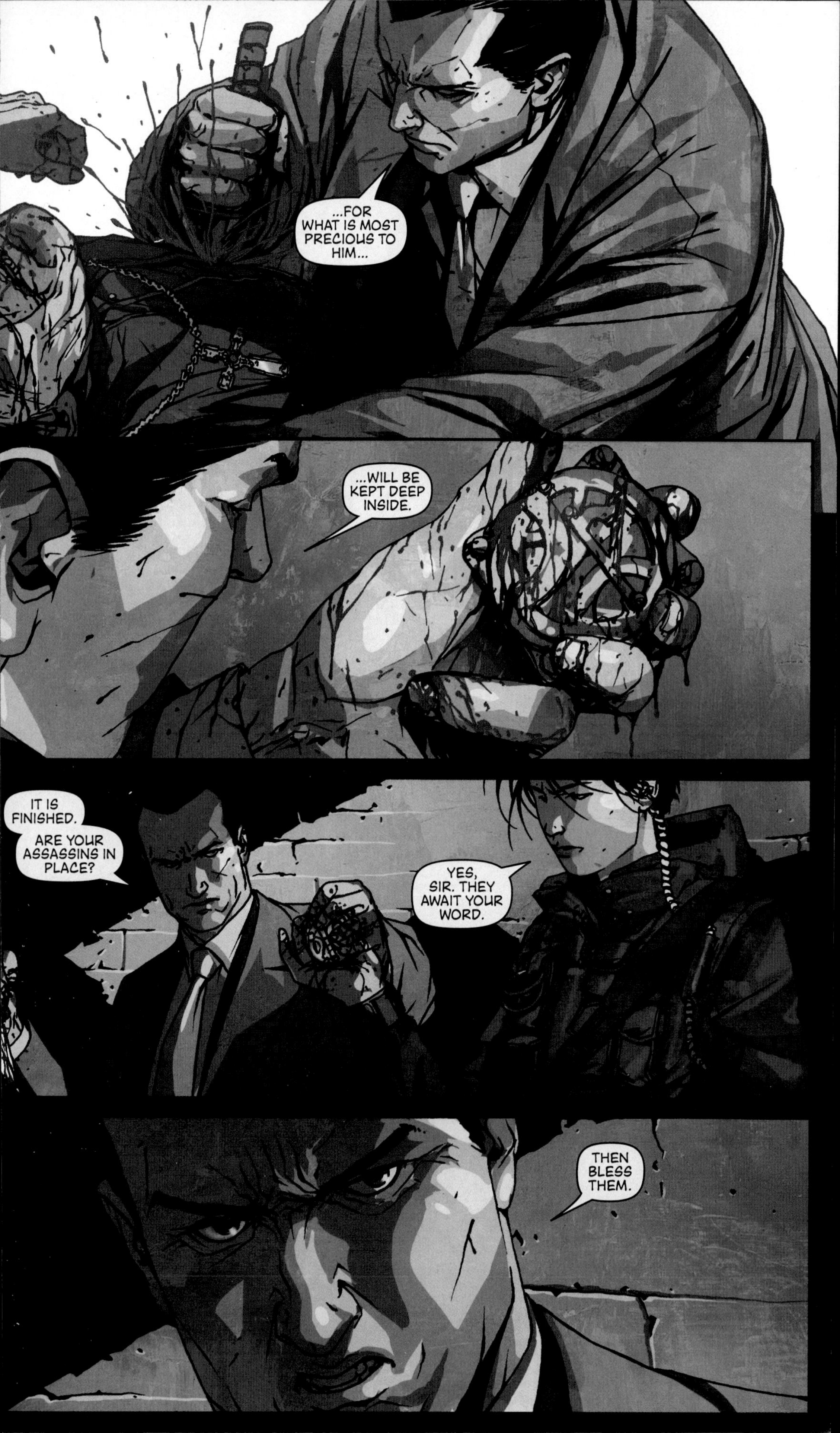
...FOR WHAT IS MOST PRECIOUS TO HIM...
...WILL BE KEPT DEEP INSIDE.
IT IS FINISHED.
ARE YOUR ASSASSINS IN PLACE?
YES, SIR. THEY AWAIT YOUR WORD.
THEN BLESS THEM.

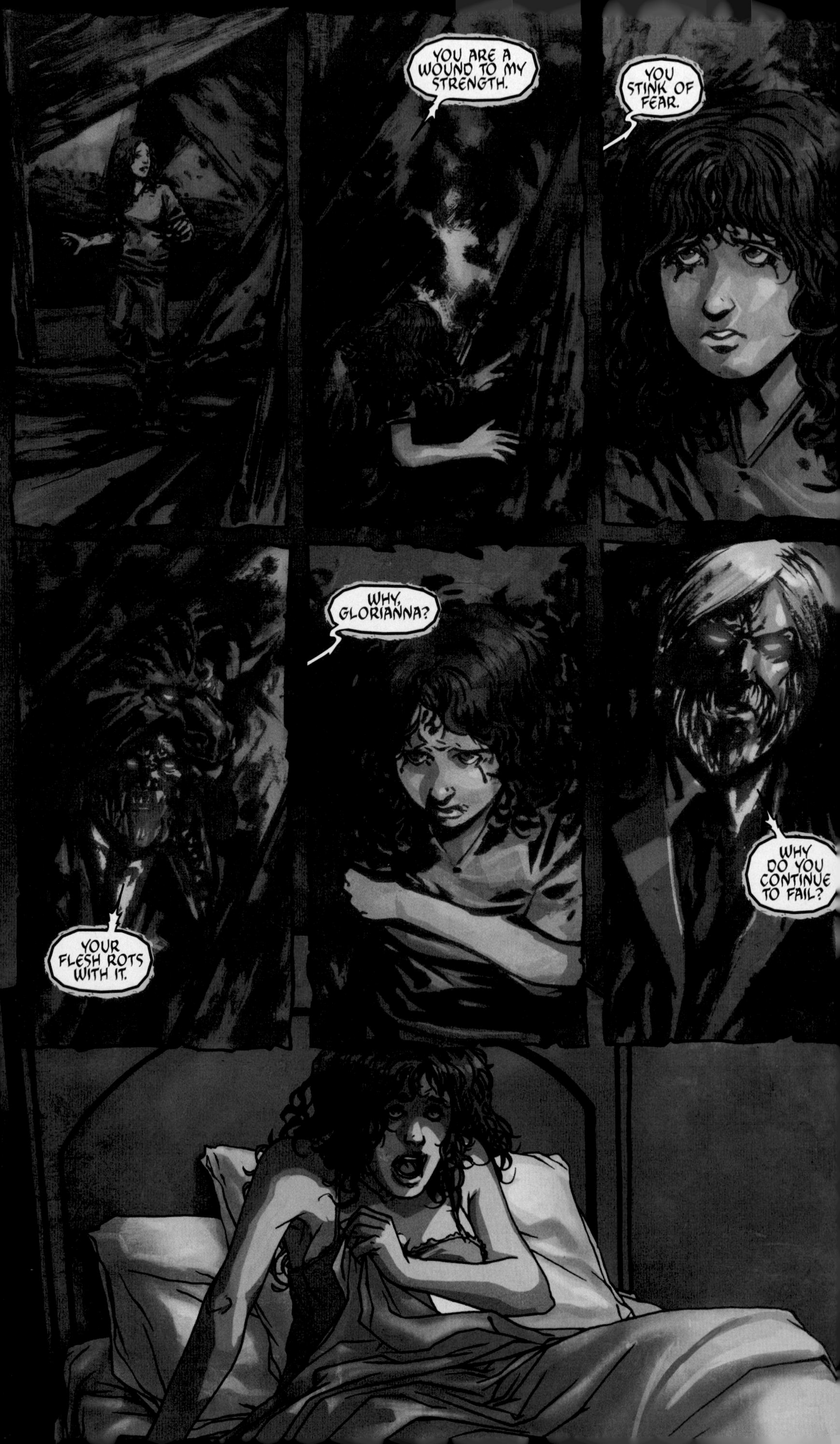
YOU ARE A WOUND TO MY STRENGTH.
YOU STINK OF FEAR.
YOUR FLESH ROTS WITH IT.
WHY, GLORIANNA?
WHY DO YOU CONTINUE TO FAIL?

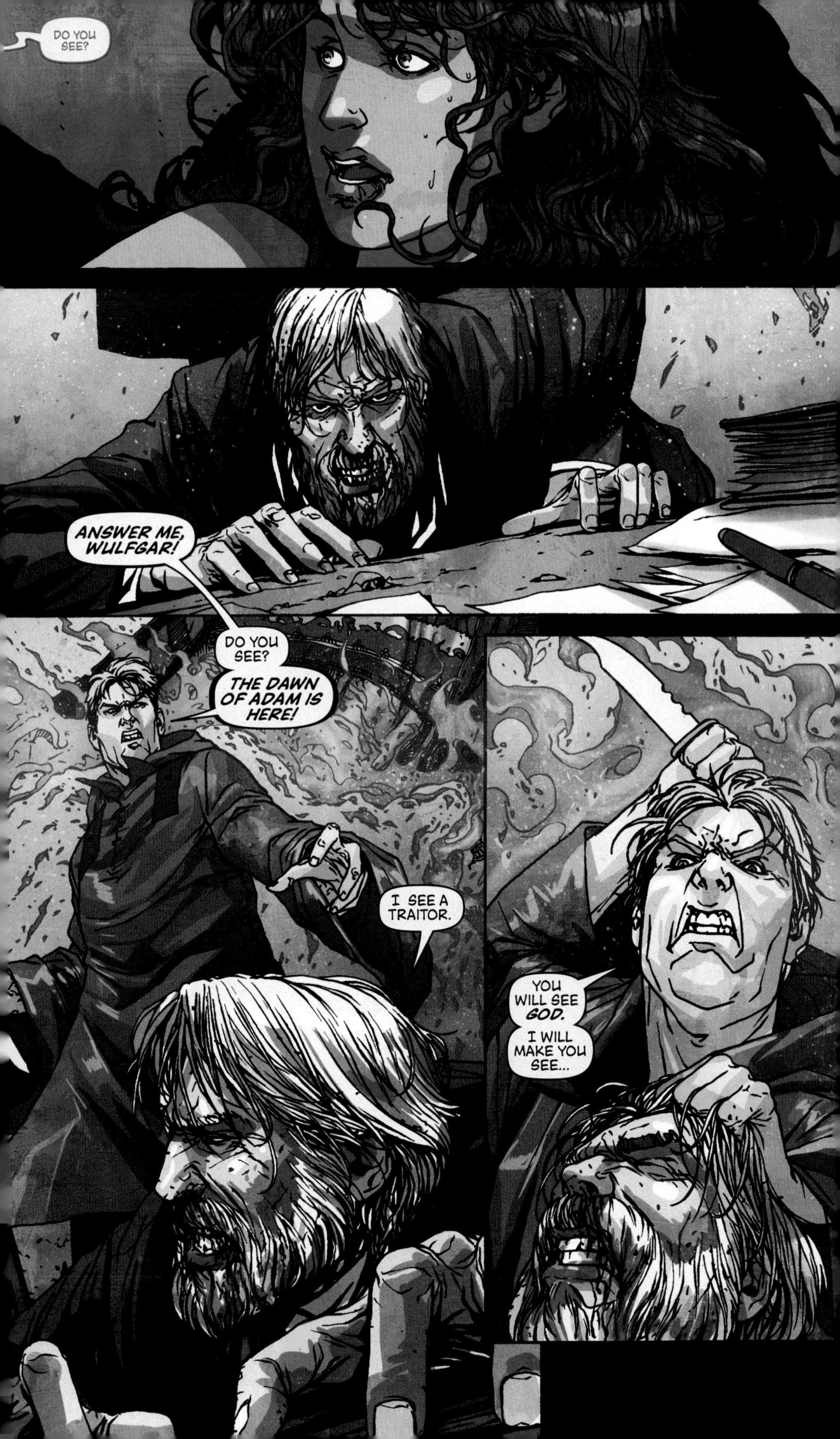
DO YOU SEE?
ANSWER ME, WULFGAR!
DO YOU SEE?
THE DAWN OF ADAM IS HERE!
I SEE A TRAITOR.
YOU WILL SEE GOD.
I WILL MAKE YOU SEE...

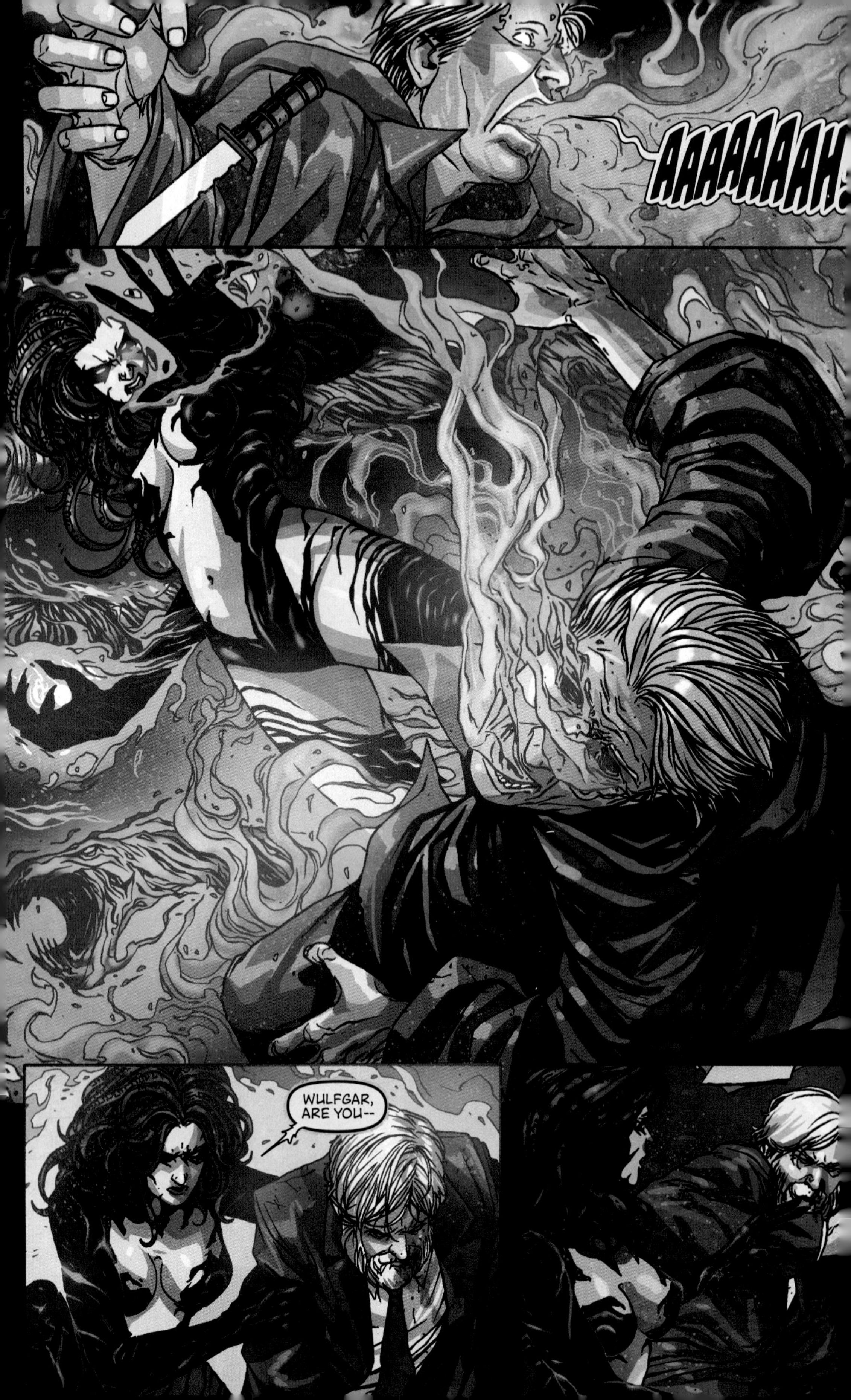
AAAAAAAH!
WULFGAR, ARE YOU--

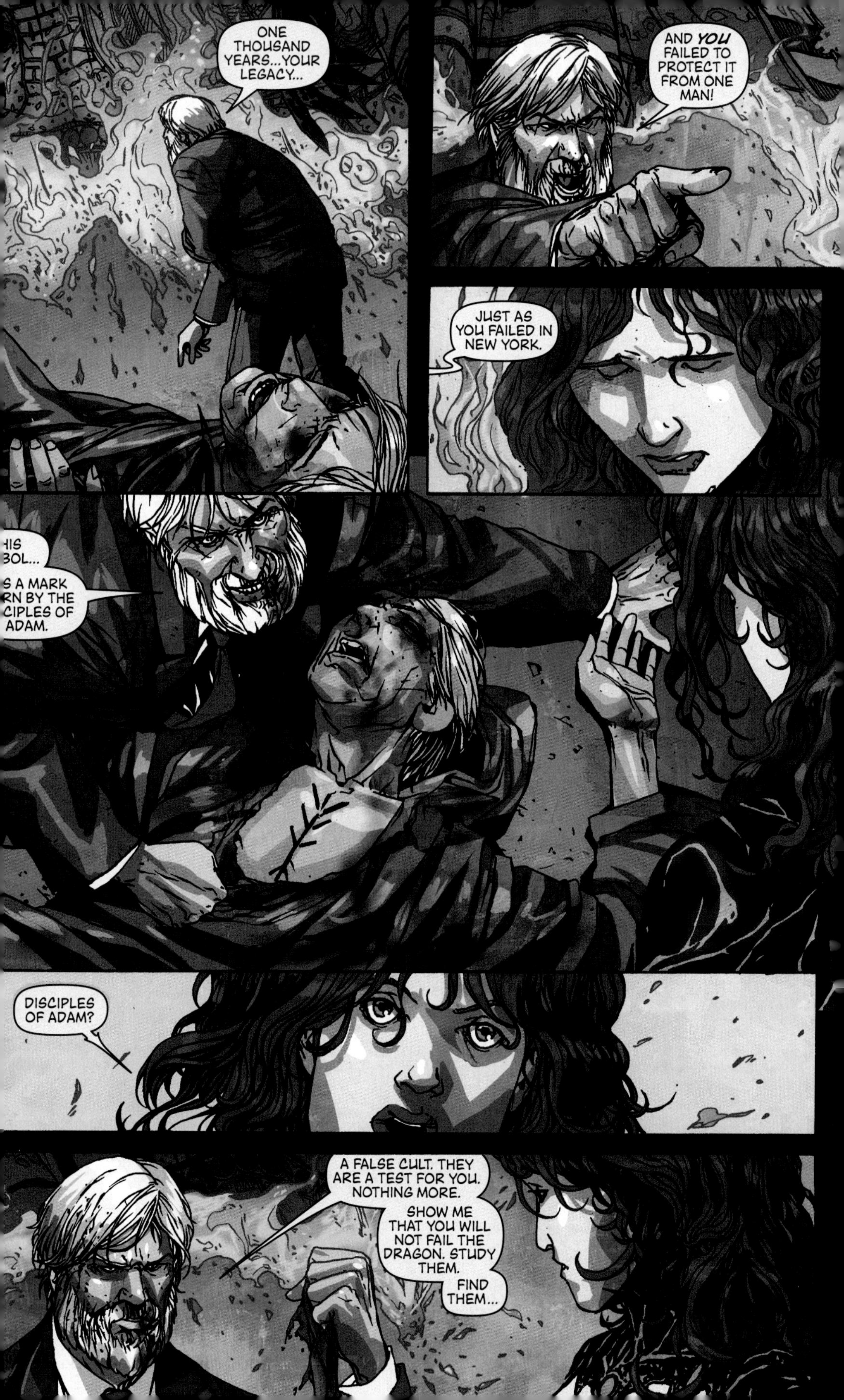
ONE THOUSAND YEARS...YOUR LEGACY...
AND YOU FAILED TO PROTECT IT FROM ONE MAN!
JUST AS YOU FAILED IN NEW YORK.
HIS BOL...
S A MARK RN BY THE CIPLES OF ADAM.
DISCIPLES OF ADAM?
A FALSE CULT. THEY ARE A TEST FOR YOU. NOTHING MORE.
SHOW ME THAT YOU WILL NOT FAIL THE DRAGON. STUDY THEM.
FIND THEM...

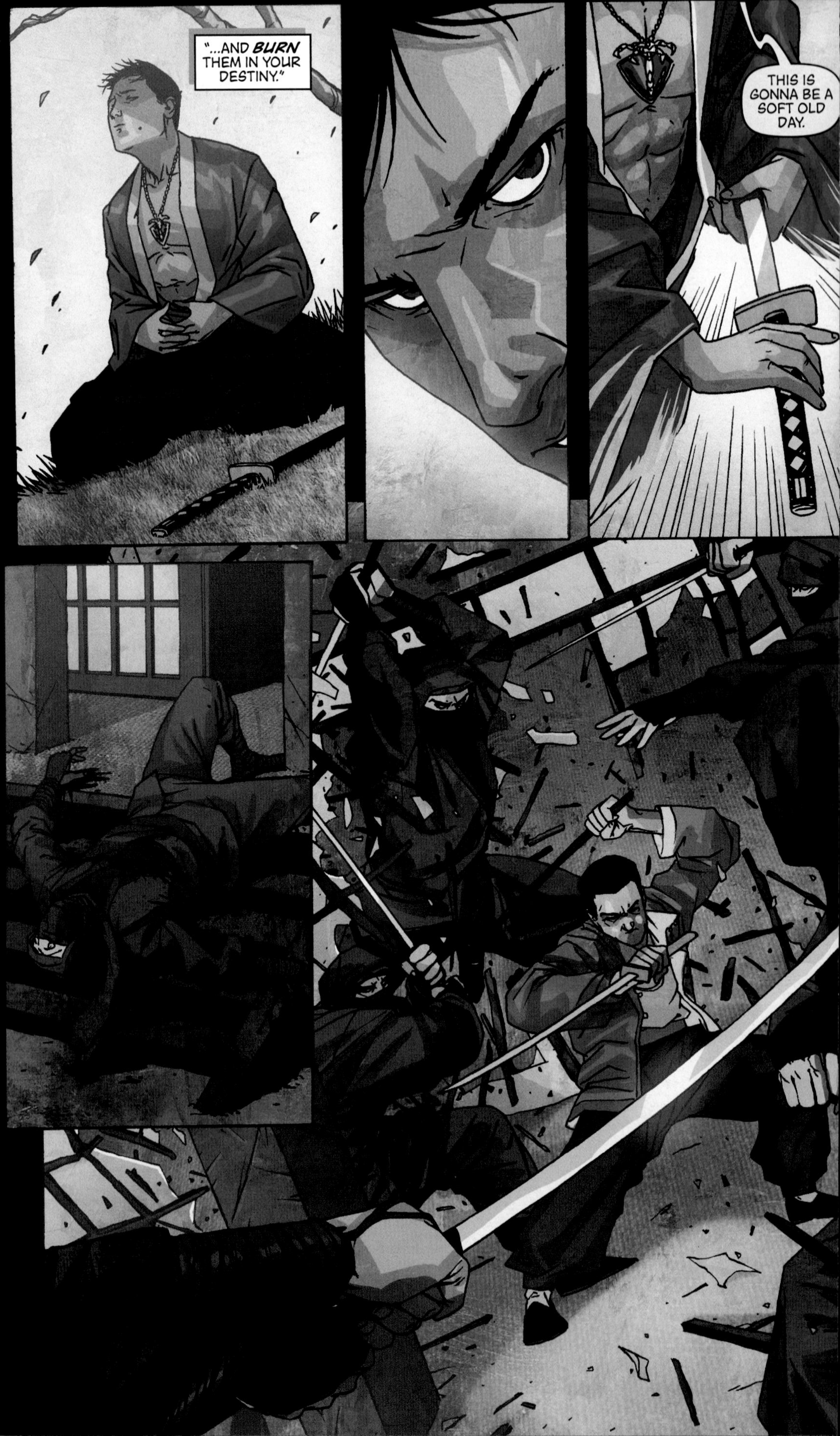
"...AND BURN THEM IN YOUR DESTINY."
THIS IS GONNA BE A SOFT OLD DAY.

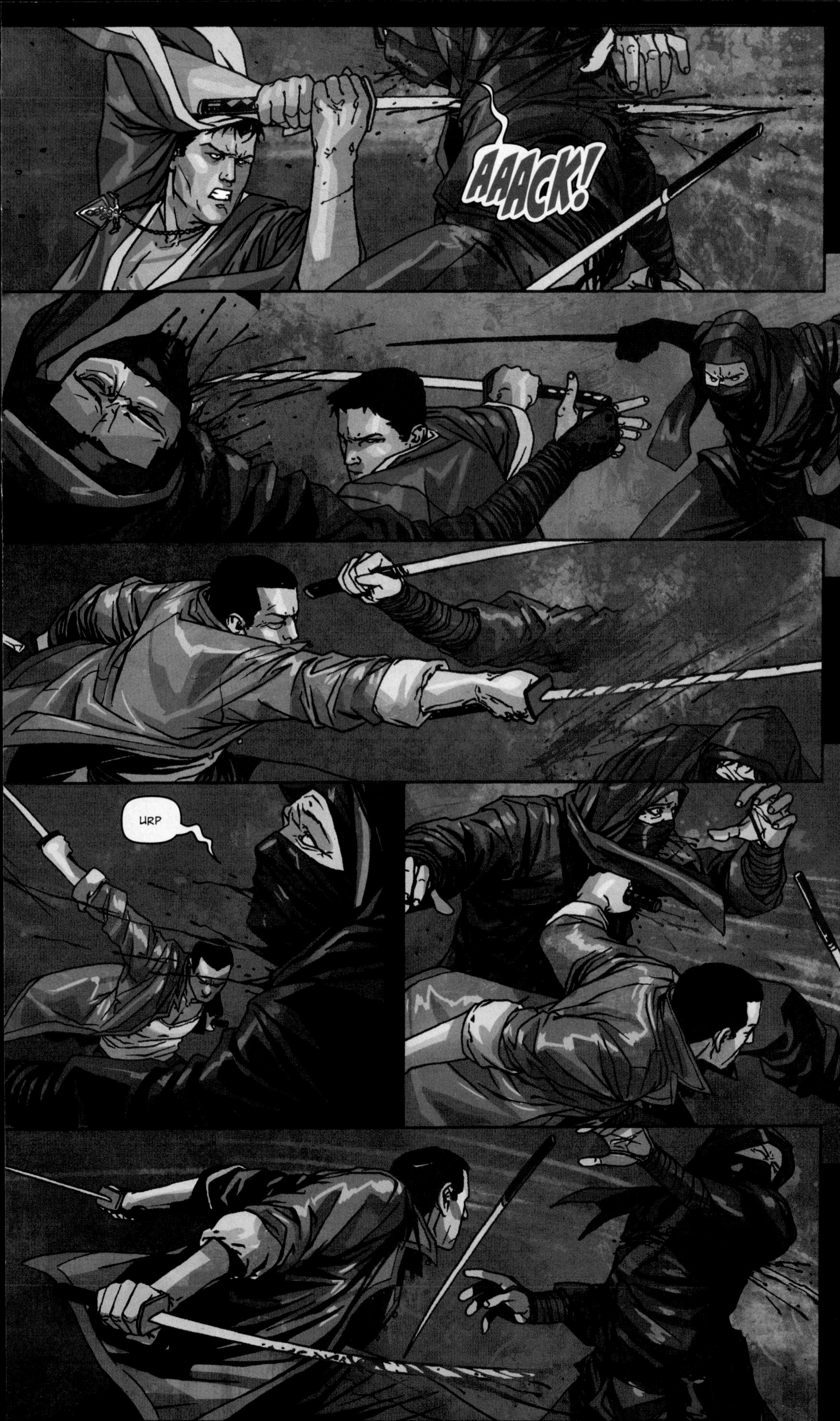
AAACK!
URP

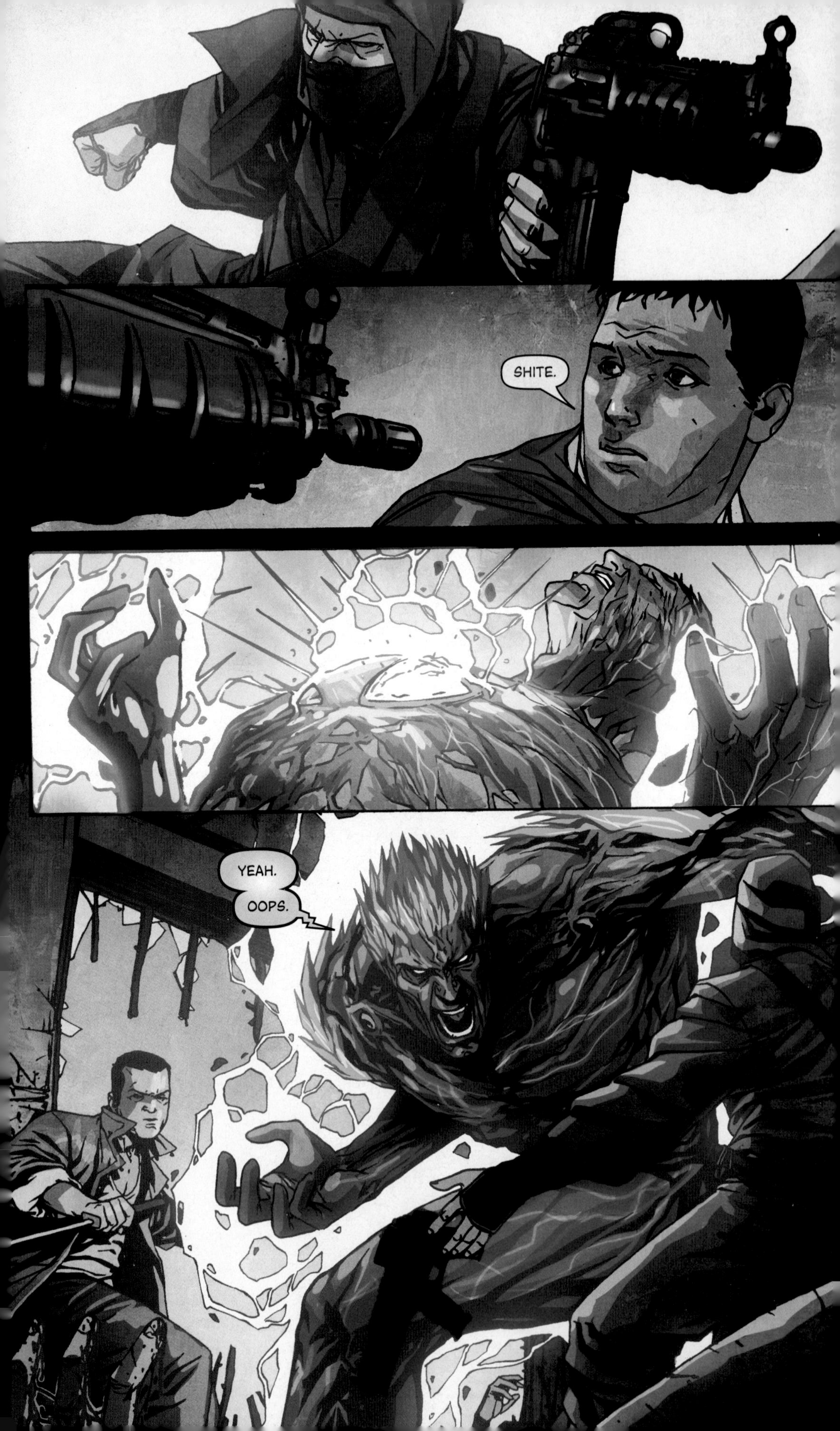
SHITE.
YEAH.
OOPS.

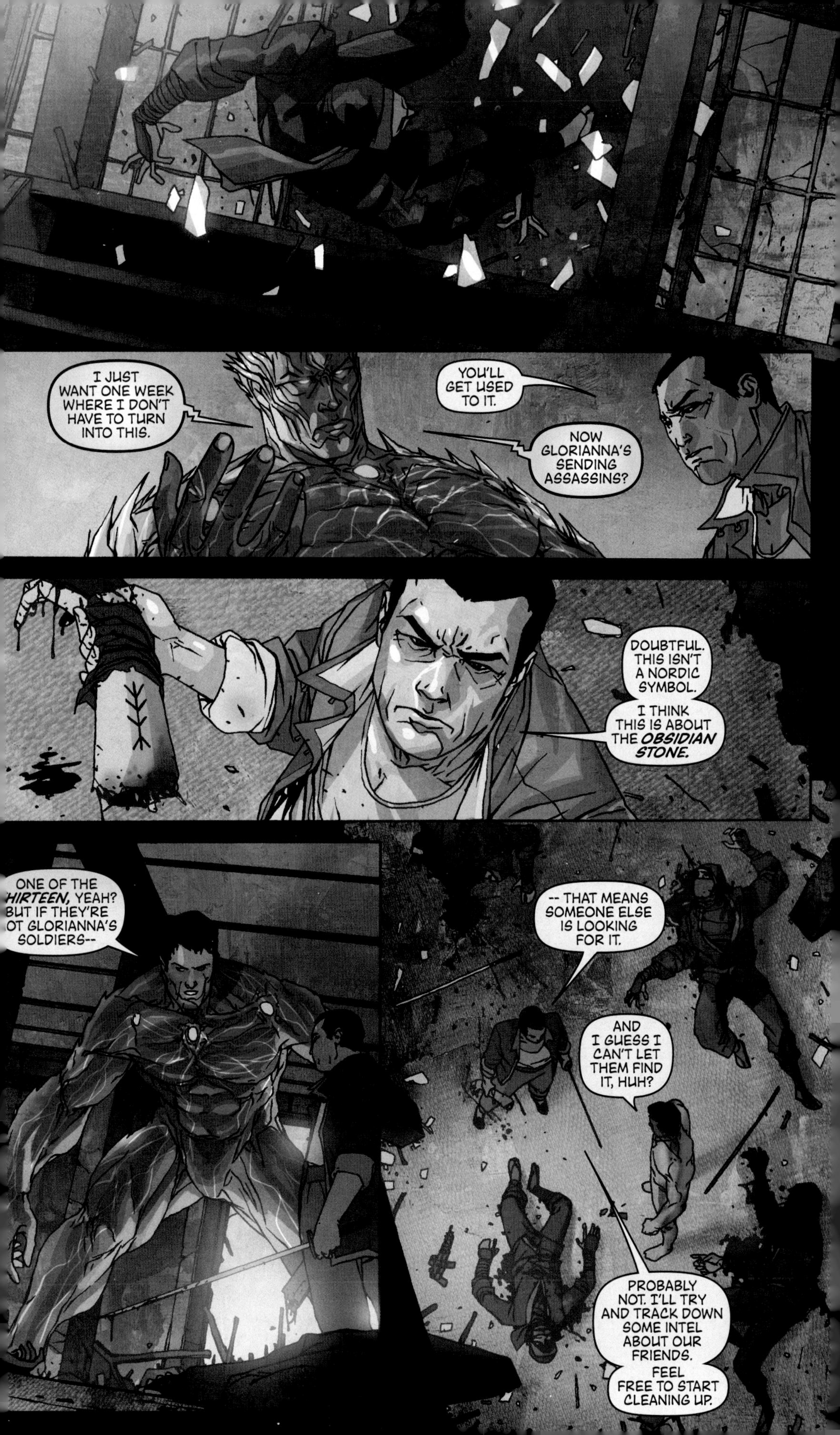
I JUST WANT ONE WEEK WHERE I DON'T HAVE TO TURN INTO THIS.
YOU'LL GET USED TO IT.
NOW GLORIANNA'S SENDING ASSASSINS?
DOUBTFUL. THIS ISN'T A NORDIC SYMBOL.
I THINK THIS IS ABOUT THE OBSIDIAN STONE.
ONE OF THE HIRTEEN, YEAH? BUT IF THEY'RE OT GLORIANNA'S SOLDIERS--
-- THAT MEANS SOMEONE ELSE IS LOOKING FOR IT.
AND I GUESS I CAN'T LET THEM FIND IT, HUH?
PROBABLY NOT. I'LL TRY AND TRACK DOWN SOME INTEL ABOUT OUR FRIENDS.
FEEL FREE TO START CLEANING UP.

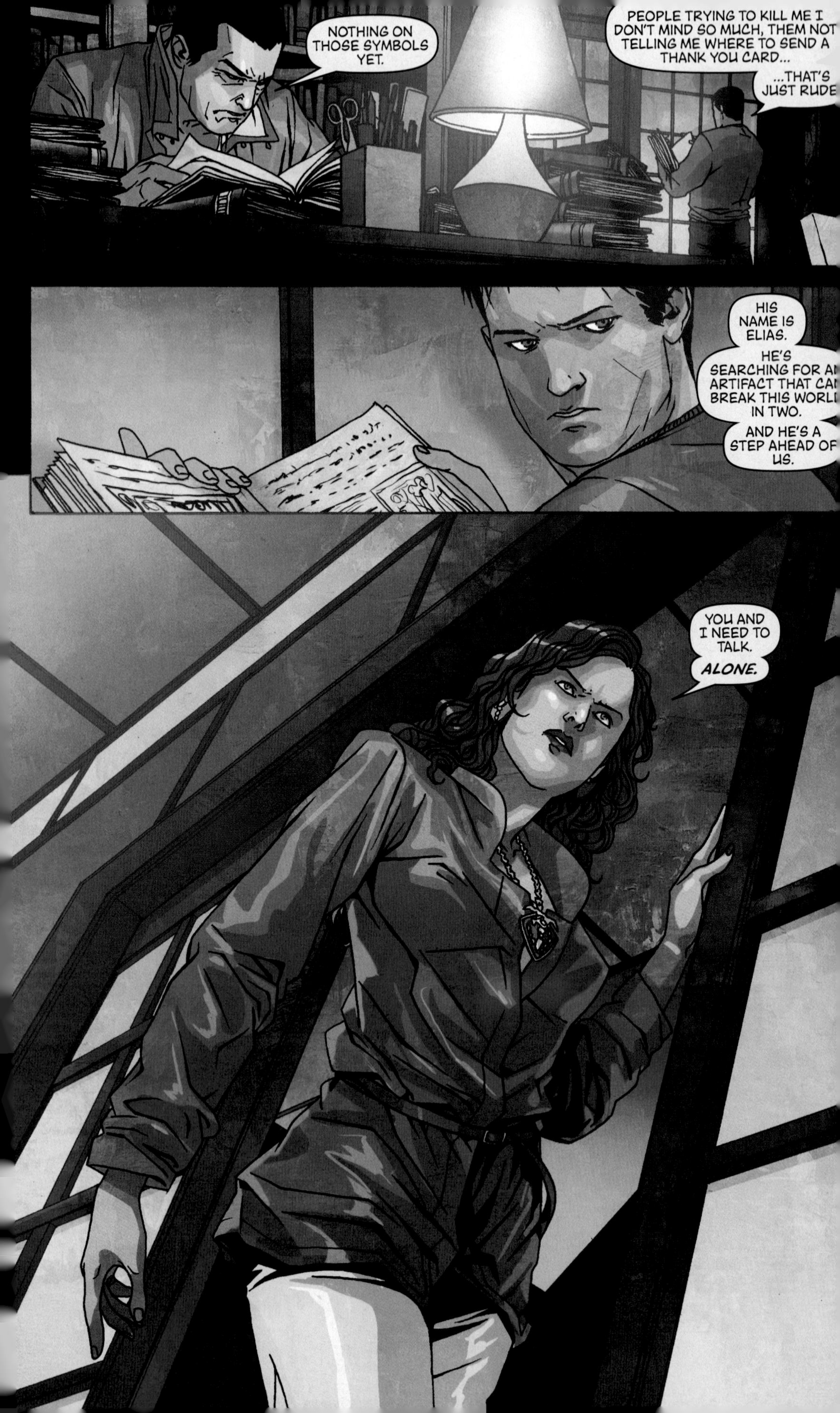
NOTHING ON THOSE SYMBOLS YET.
PEOPLE TRYING TO KILL ME I DON'T MIND SO MUCH, THEM NOT TELLING ME WHERE TO SEND A THANK YOU CARD...
...THAT'S JUST RUDE
HIS NAME IS ELIAS.
HE'S SEARCHING FOR A ARTIFACT THAT CA BREAK THIS WORL IN TWO.
AND HE'S A STEP AHEAD OF US.
YOU AND I NEED TO TALK. *ALONE.*

BROKEN TRINITY

"PANDORA'S BOX" Part 2

{
written by: **Bryan Edward Hill & Rob Levin**
art by: **Alessandro Vitti**
colors by: **Sunny Gho of IFS**
letters by: **Troy Peteri**
}

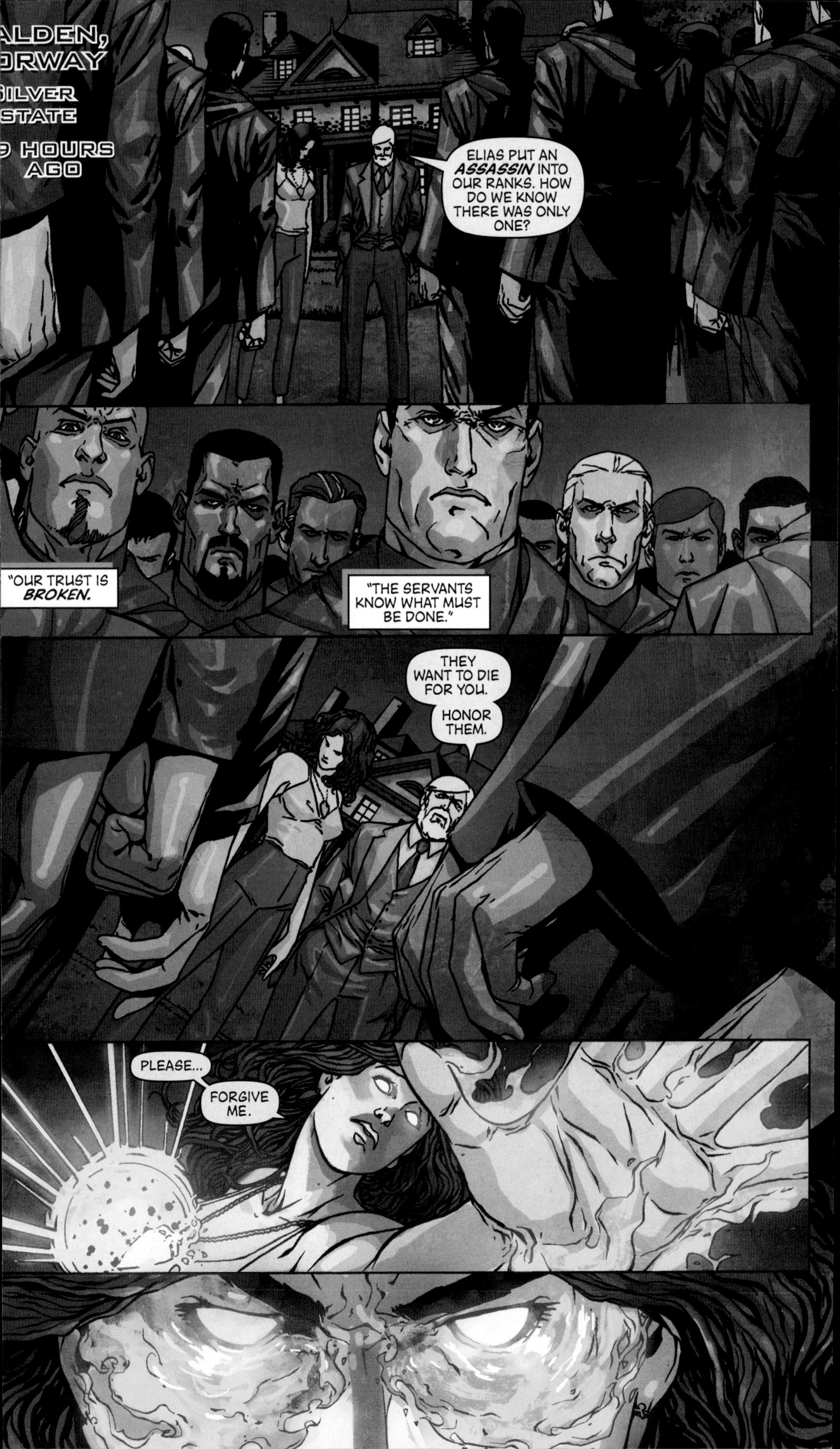
ALDEN,
ORWAY
SILVER
STATE
9 HOURS
AGO
ELIAS PUT AN ASSASSIN INTO OUR RANKS. HOW DO WE KNOW THERE WAS ONLY ONE?
"OUR TRUST IS BROKEN.
"THE SERVANTS KNOW WHAT MUST BE DONE."
THEY WANT TO DIE FOR YOU.
HONOR THEM.
PLEASE...
FORGIVE ME.

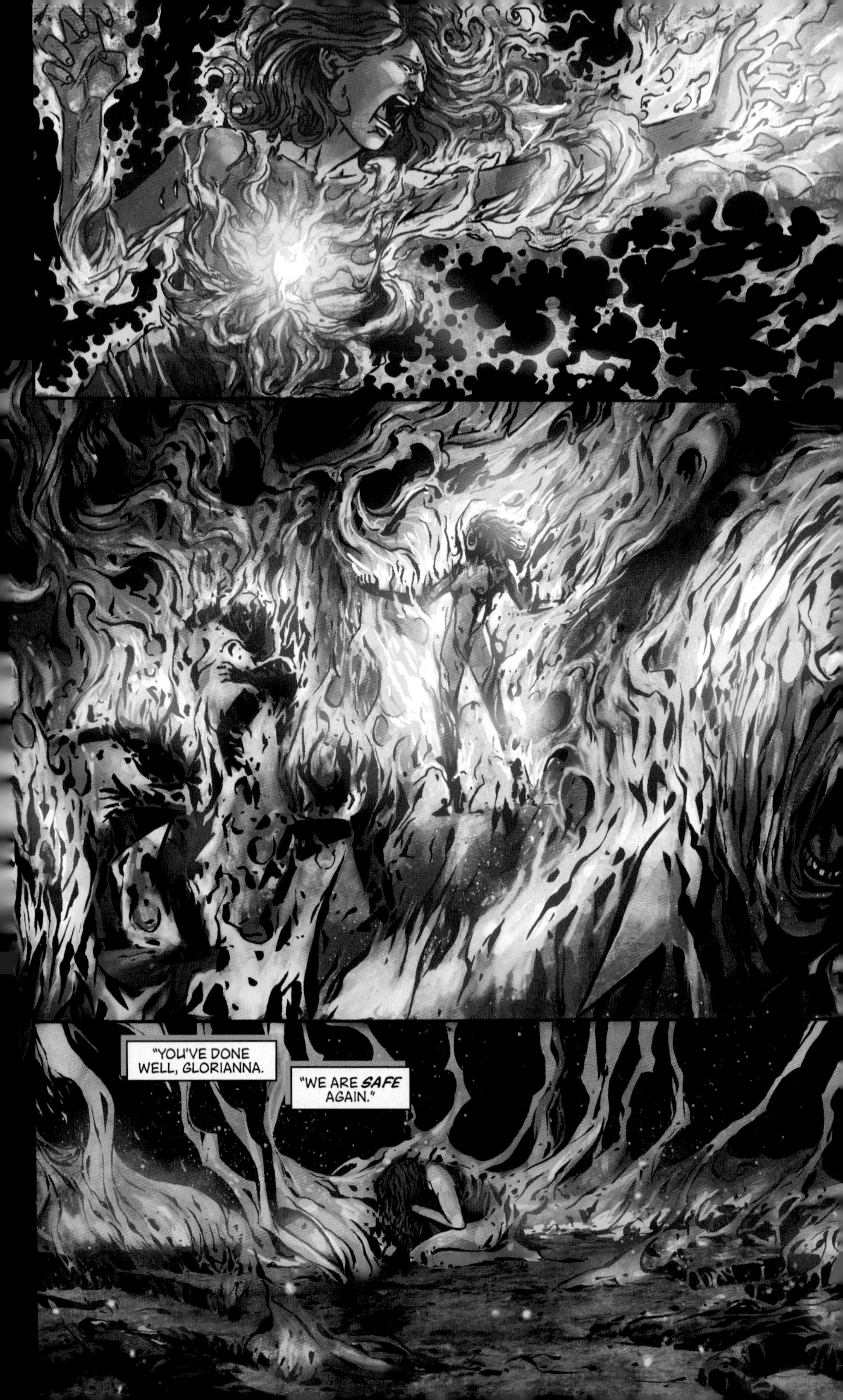
"YOU'VE DONE WELL, GLORIANNA.
"WE ARE *SAFE* AGAIN."

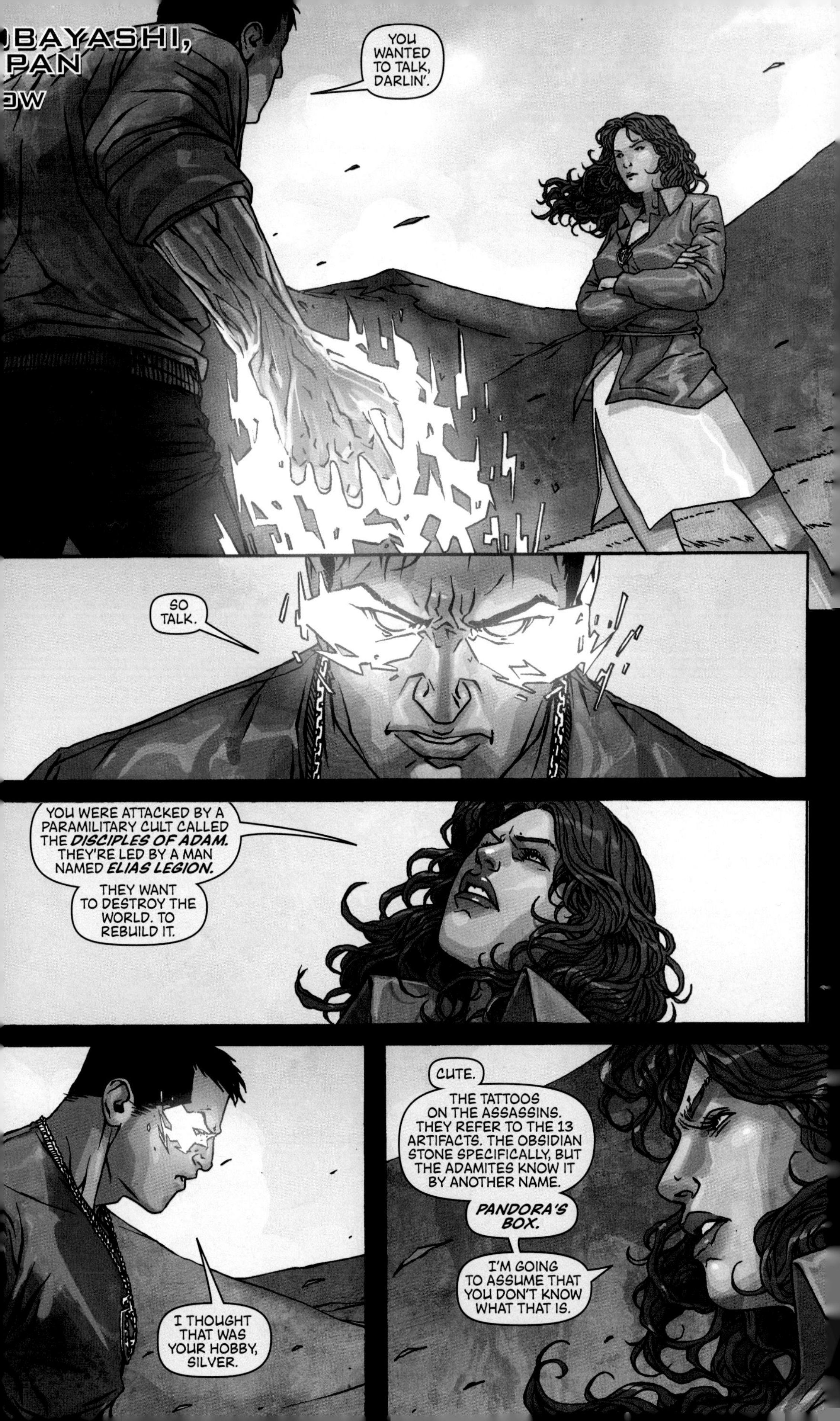
BAYASHI,
PAN
OW
YOU WANTED TO TALK, DARLIN'.
SO TALK.
YOU WERE ATTACKED BY A PARAMILITARY CULT CALLED THE DISCIPLES OF ADAM. THEY'RE LED BY A MAN NAMED ELIAS LEGION.
THEY WANT TO DESTROY THE WORLD. TO REBUILD IT.
I THOUGHT THAT WAS YOUR HOBBY, SILVER.
CUTE.
THE TATTOOS ON THE ASSASSINS. THEY REFER TO THE 13 ARTIFACTS. THE OBSIDIAN STONE SPECIFICALLY, BUT THE ADAMITES KNOW IT BY ANOTHER NAME.
PANDORA'S BOX.
I'M GOING TO ASSUME THAT YOU DON'T KNOW WHAT THAT IS.

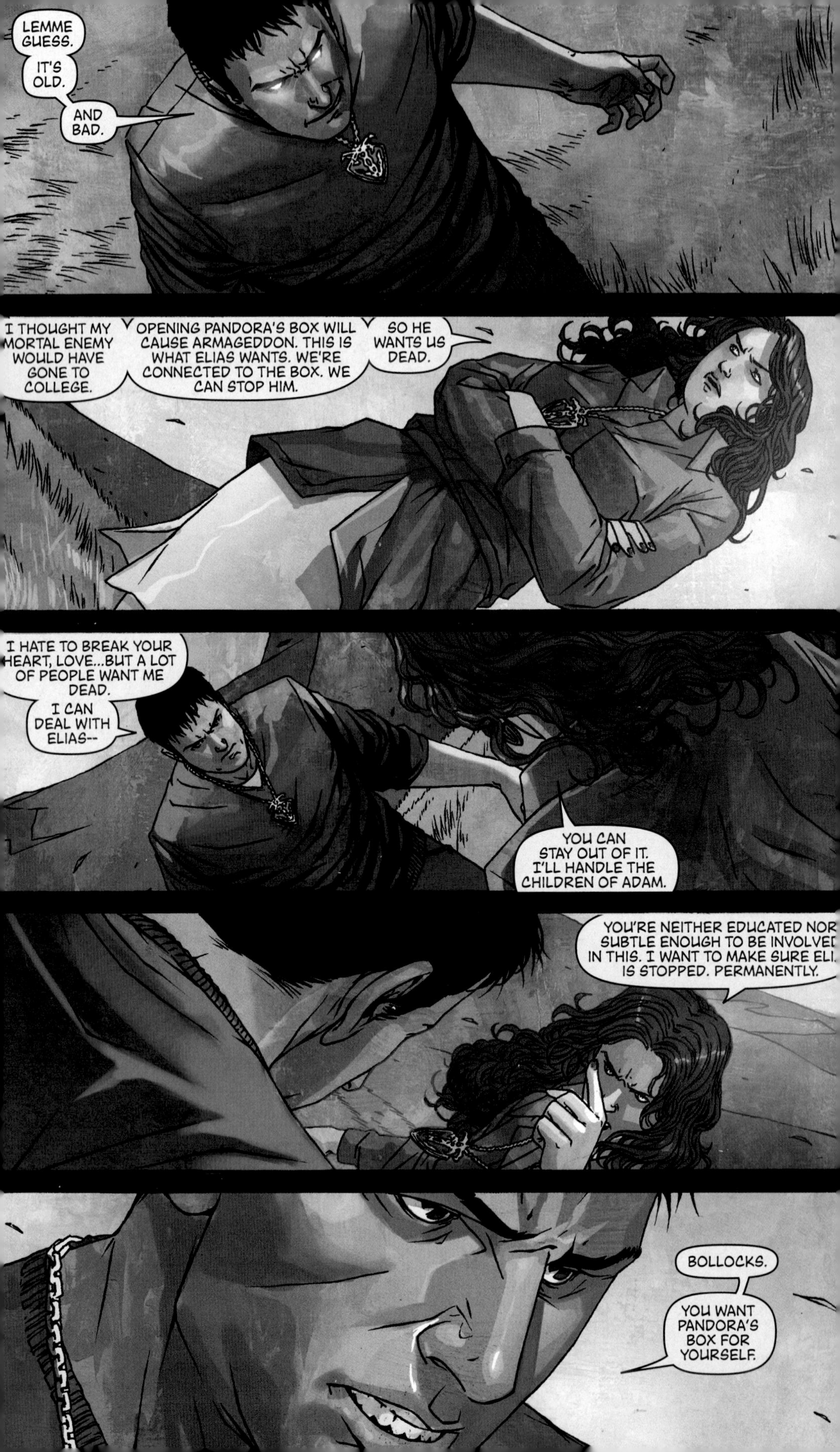
LEMME GUESS.
IT'S OLD.
AND BAD.
I THOUGHT MY MORTAL ENEMY WOULD HAVE GONE TO COLLEGE.
OPENING PANDORA'S BOX WILL CAUSE ARMAGEDDON. THIS IS WHAT ELIAS WANTS. WE'RE CONNECTED TO THE BOX. WE CAN STOP HIM.
SO HE WANTS US DEAD.
I HATE TO BREAK YOUR HEART, LOVE...BUT A LOT OF PEOPLE WANT ME DEAD.
I CAN DEAL WITH ELIAS--
YOU CAN STAY OUT OF IT. I'LL HANDLE THE CHILDREN OF ADAM.
YOU'RE NEITHER EDUCATED NOR SUBTLE ENOUGH TO BE INVOLVED IN THIS. I WANT TO MAKE SURE ELIAS IS STOPPED. PERMANENTLY.
BOLLOCKS.
YOU WANT PANDORA'S BOX FOR YOURSELF.

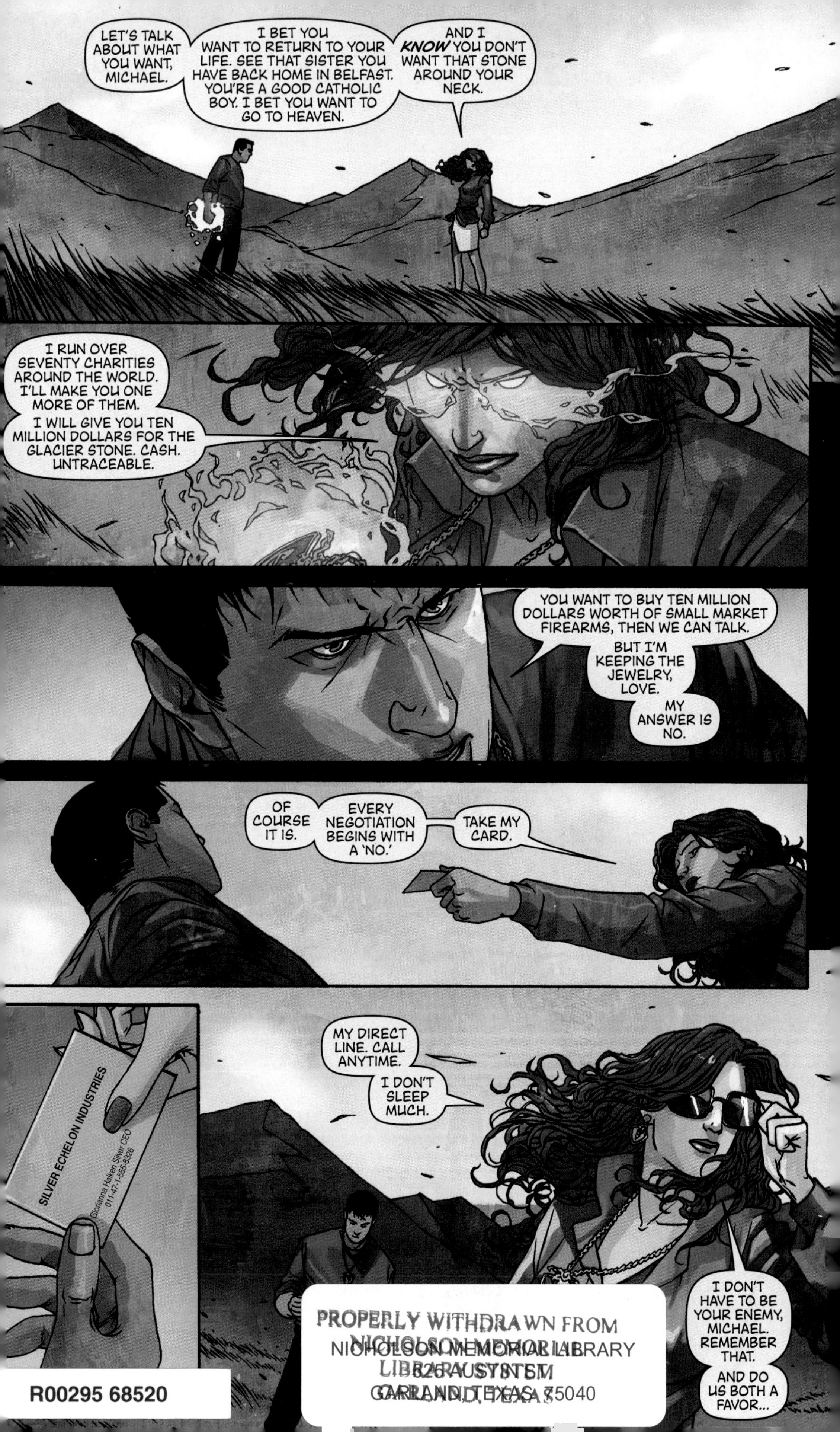
LET'S TALK ABOUT WHAT YOU WANT, MICHAEL.
I BET YOU WANT TO RETURN TO YOUR LIFE. SEE THAT SISTER YOU HAVE BACK HOME IN BELFAST. YOU'RE A GOOD CATHOLIC BOY. I BET YOU WANT TO GO TO HEAVEN.
AND I *KNOW* YOU DON'T WANT THAT STONE AROUND YOUR NECK.
I RUN OVER SEVENTY CHARITIES AROUND THE WORLD. I'LL MAKE YOU ONE MORE OF THEM.
I WILL GIVE YOU TEN MILLION DOLLARS FOR THE GLACIER STONE. CASH. UNTRACEABLE.
YOU WANT TO BUY TEN MILLION DOLLARS WORTH OF SMALL MARKET FIREARMS, THEN WE CAN TALK.
BUT I'M KEEPING THE JEWELRY, LOVE.
MY ANSWER IS NO.
OF COURSE IT IS.
EVERY NEGOTIATION BEGINS WITH A 'NO.'
TAKE MY CARD.
SILVER ECHELON INDUSTRIES
Glorianna Halken Silver CEO
011-47-1-555-8326
MY DIRECT LINE. CALL ANYTIME.
I DON'T SLEEP MUCH.
I DON'T HAVE TO BE YOUR ENEMY, MICHAEL. REMEMBER THAT.
AND DO US BOTH A FAVOR...

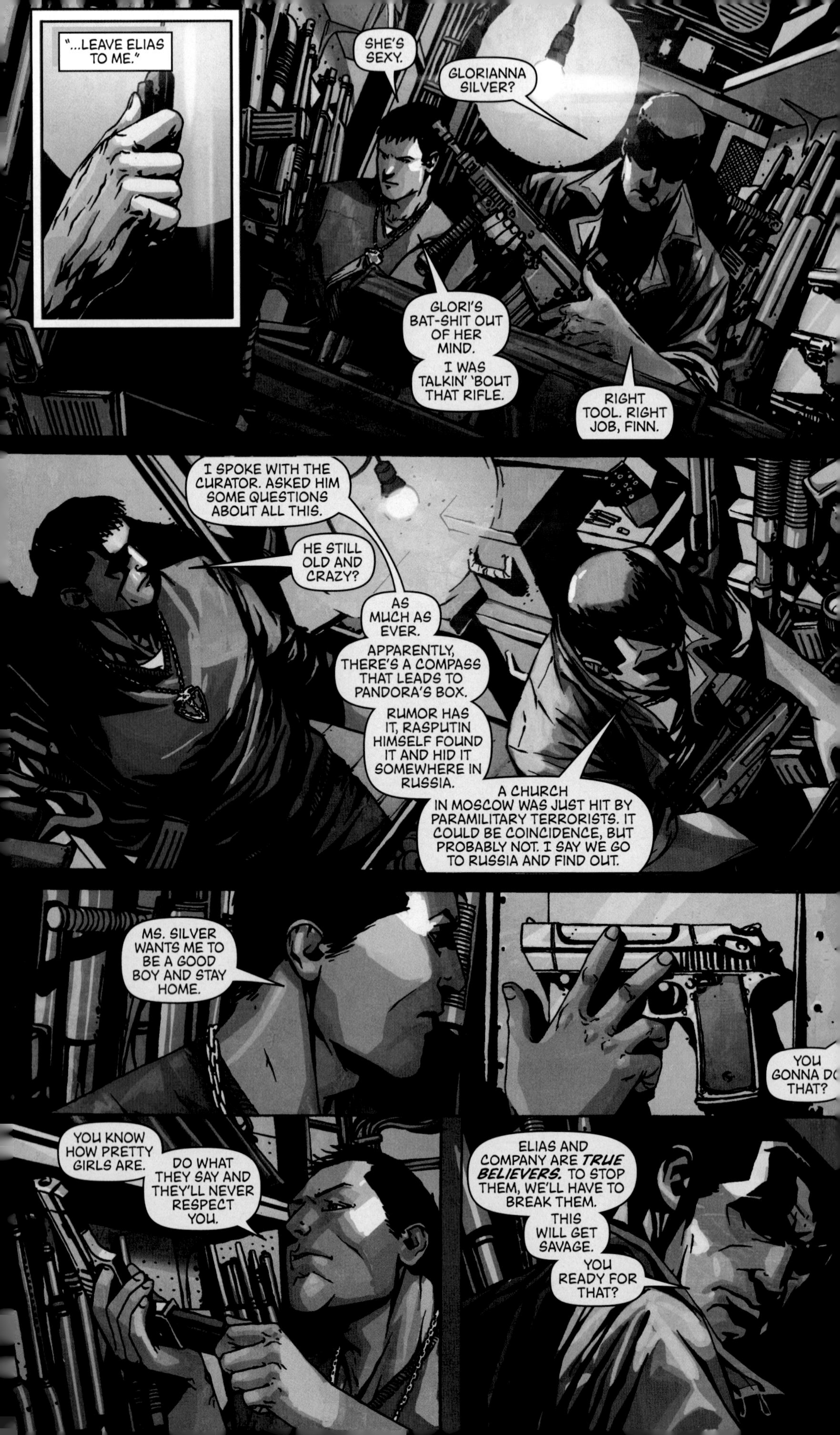
"...LEAVE ELIAS TO ME."
SHE'S SEXY.
GLORIANNA SILVER?
GLORI'S BAT-SHIT OUT OF HER MIND.
I WAS TALKIN' 'BOUT THAT RIFLE.
RIGHT TOOL. RIGHT JOB, FINN.
I SPOKE WITH THE CURATOR. ASKED HIM SOME QUESTIONS ABOUT ALL THIS.
HE STILL OLD AND CRAZY?
AS MUCH AS EVER.
APPARENTLY, THERE'S A COMPASS THAT LEADS TO PANDORA'S BOX.
RUMOR HAS IT, RASPUTIN HIMSELF FOUND IT AND HID IT SOMEWHERE IN RUSSIA.
A CHURCH IN MOSCOW WAS JUST HIT BY PARAMILITARY TERRORISTS. IT COULD BE COINCIDENCE, BUT PROBABLY NOT. I SAY WE GO TO RUSSIA AND FIND OUT.
MS. SILVER WANTS ME TO BE A GOOD BOY AND STAY HOME.
YOU GONNA DO THAT?
YOU KNOW HOW PRETTY GIRLS ARE.
DO WHAT THEY SAY AND THEY'LL NEVER RESPECT YOU.
ELIAS AND COMPANY ARE *TRUE BELIEVERS.* TO STOP THEM, WE'LL HAVE TO BREAK THEM.
THIS WILL GET SAVAGE.
YOU READY FOR THAT?

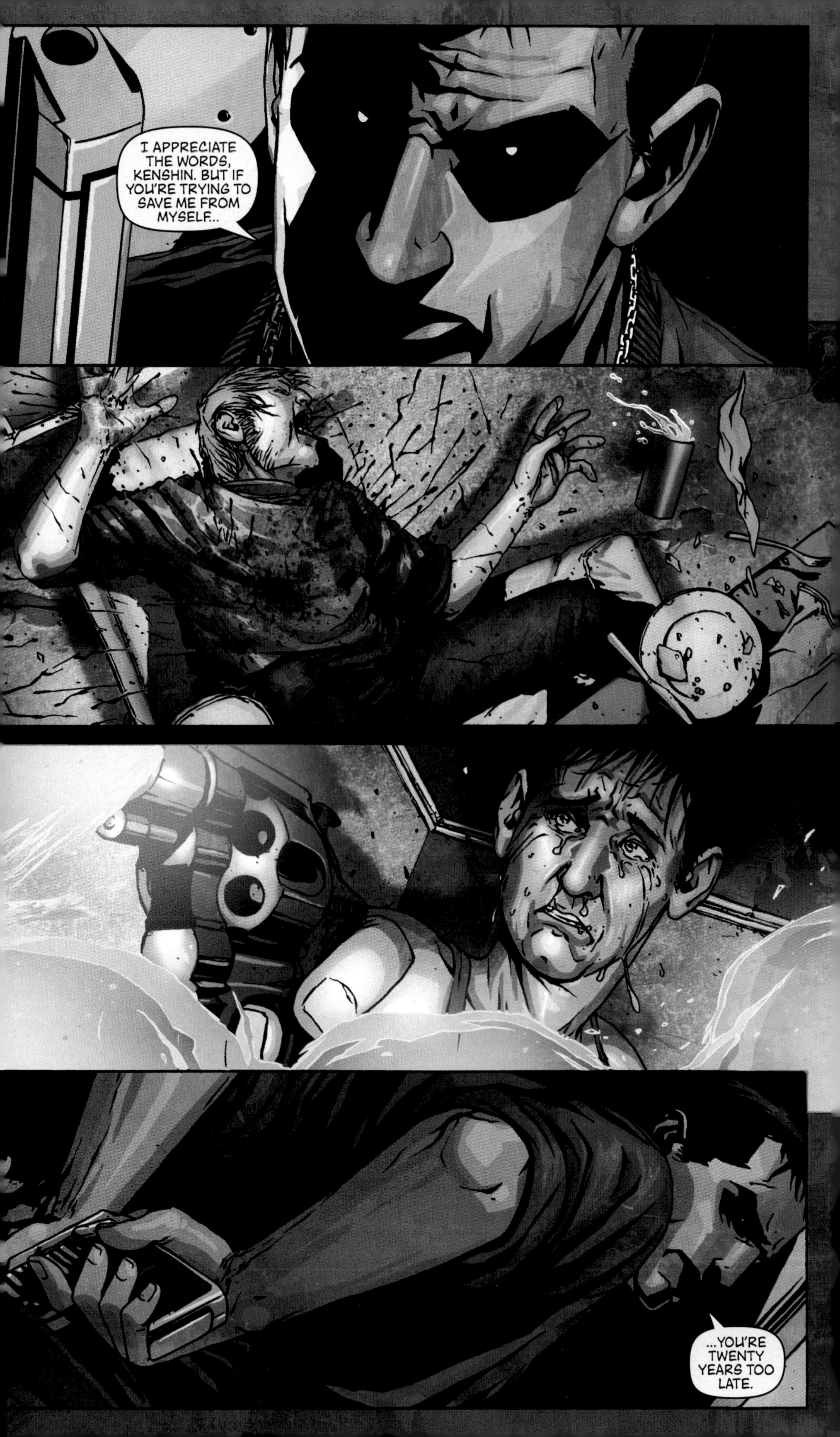
I APPRECIATE THE WORDS, KENSHIN. BUT IF YOU'RE TRYING TO SAVE ME FROM MYSELF...
...YOU'RE TWENTY YEARS TOO LATE.

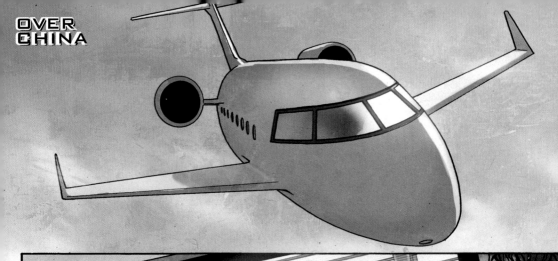

WHEN YOU GET TO MOSCOW, SEE A MAN NAMED NIKO ROMANOV. DESCENDENT OF THE MONARCHY TURNED DRUG DEALER.

HE HAS A WEAKNESS FOR BEAUTIFUL WOMEN.

IF ELIAS FOUND ANYTHING IN RUSSIA, ROMANOV WILL KNOW.

MAKE HIM TELL YOU.

SIR.

REMEMBER GLORIANNA, YOU ARE THE DRAGON.

AND THE DRAGON IS A GOD.

A GOD IS NOT GOVERNED BY MORALITY. A GOD DEFINES IT.

EVERYTHING YOU DO IS JUSTIFIED.

SIR.

I AM THE WILL OF THE DRAGON.

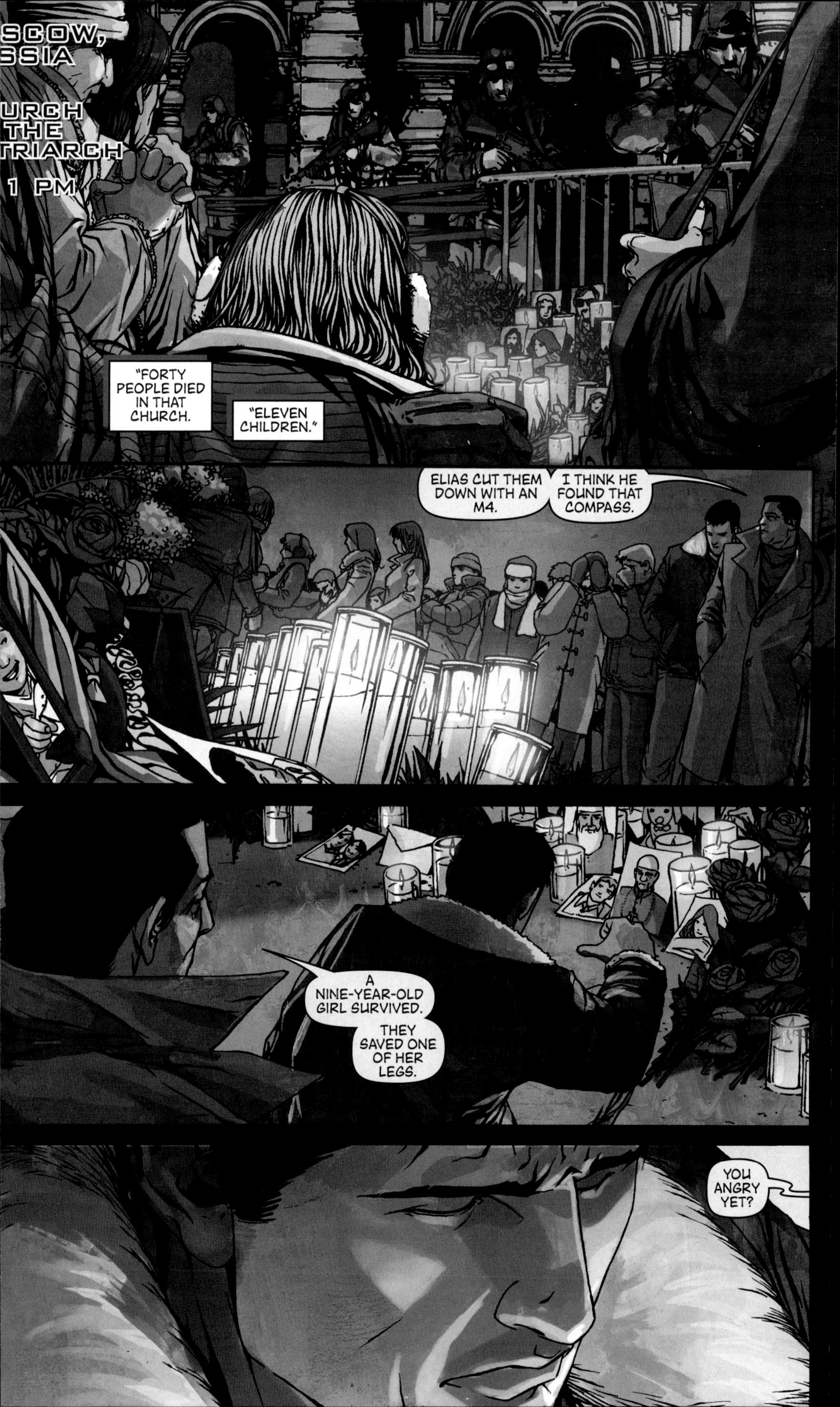
SCOW,
SSIA
URCH
THE
TRIARCH
1 PM
"FORTY PEOPLE DIED IN THAT CHURCH.
"ELEVEN CHILDREN."
ELIAS CUT THEM DOWN WITH AN M4.
I THINK HE FOUND THAT COMPASS.
A NINE-YEAR-OLD GIRL SURVIVED.
THEY SAVED ONE OF HER LEGS.
YOU ANGRY YET?

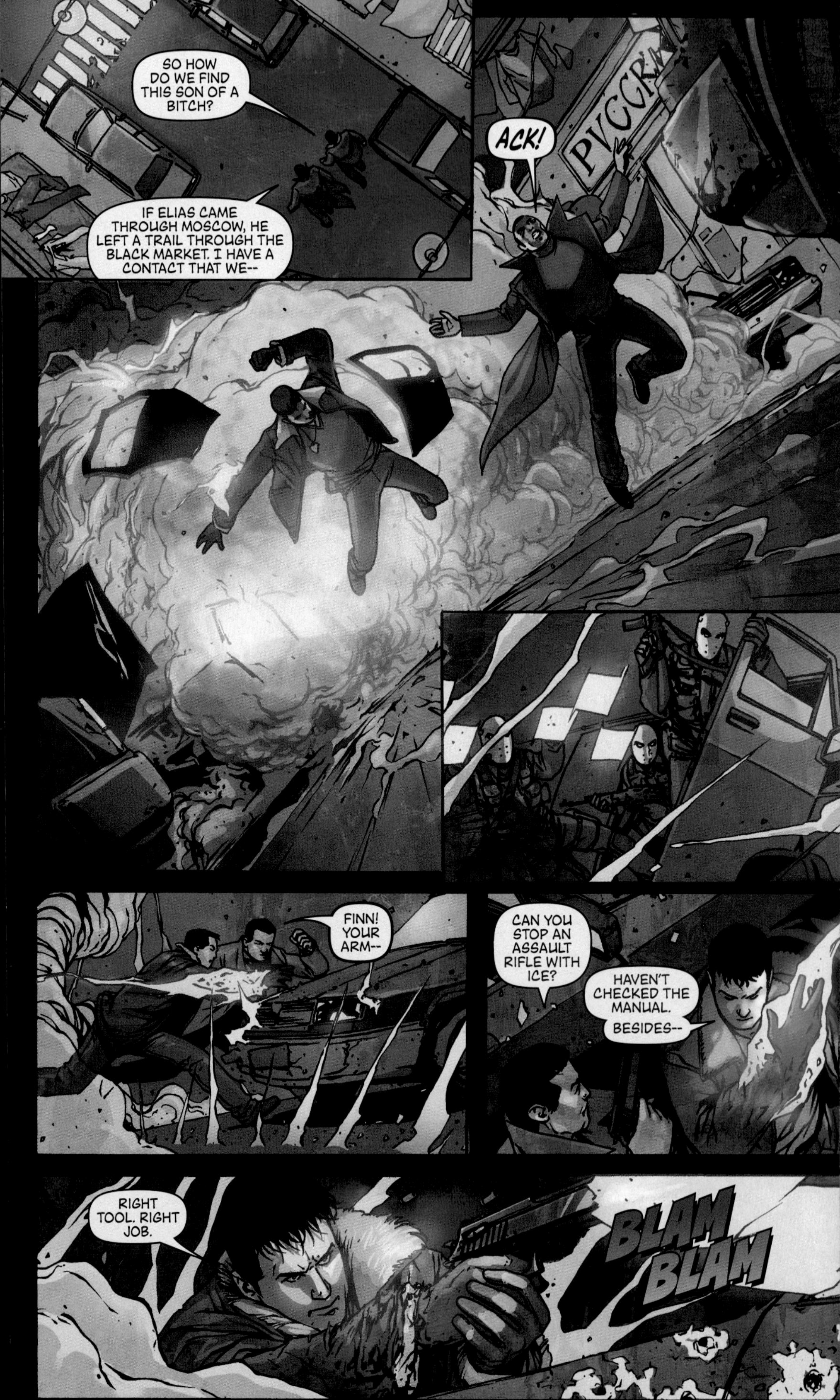
SO HOW DO WE FIND THIS SON OF A BITCH?
IF ELIAS CAME THROUGH MOSCOW, HE LEFT A TRAIL THROUGH THE BLACK MARKET. I HAVE A CONTACT THAT WE--
ACK!
PVCCK
FINN! YOUR ARM--
CAN YOU STOP AN ASSAULT RIFLE WITH ICE?
HAVEN'T CHECKED THE MANUAL.
BESIDES--
RIGHT TOOL. RIGHT JOB.
BLAM BLAM

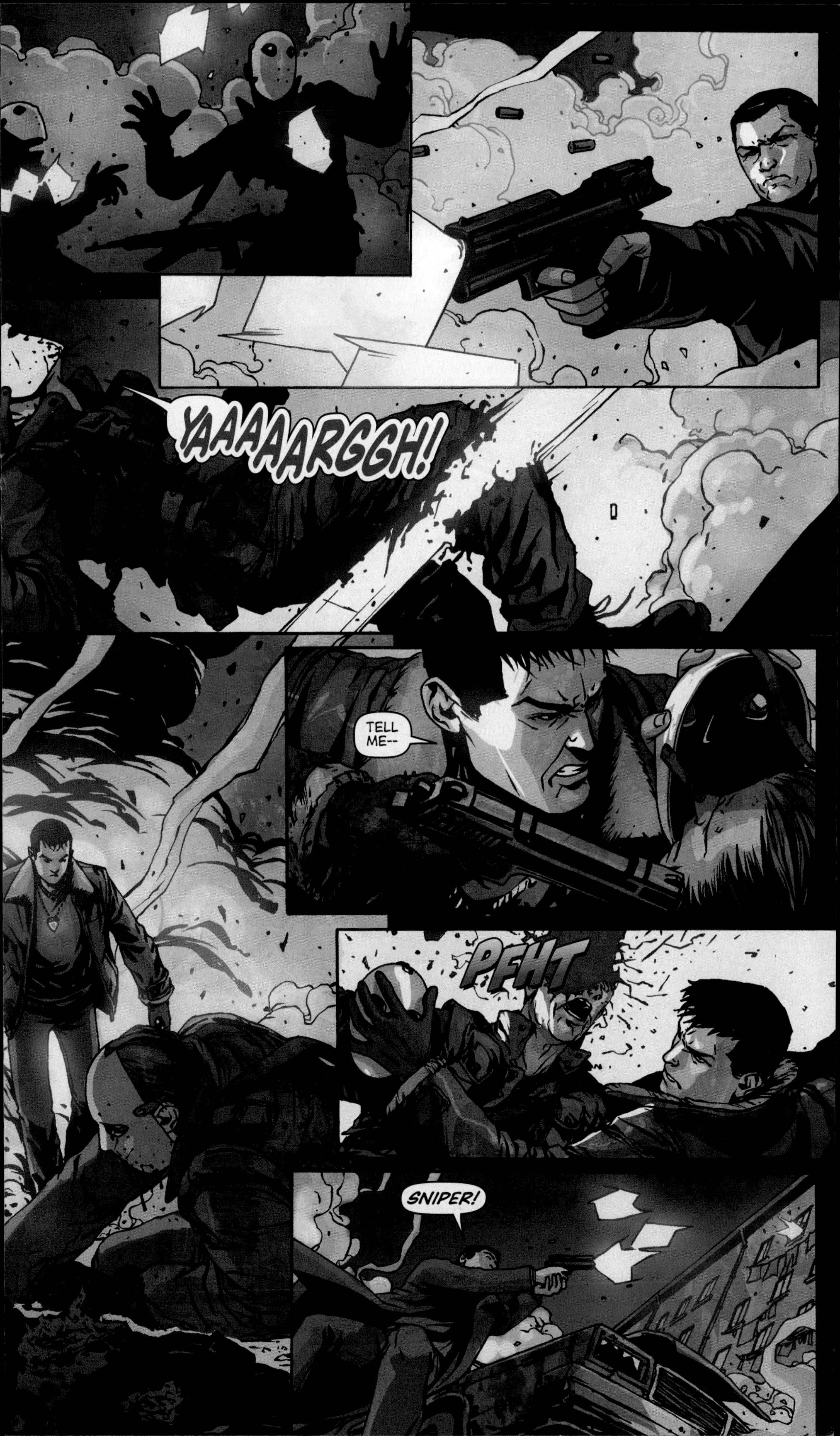
YAAAAARGGH!
TELL ME--
PFHT
SNIPER!

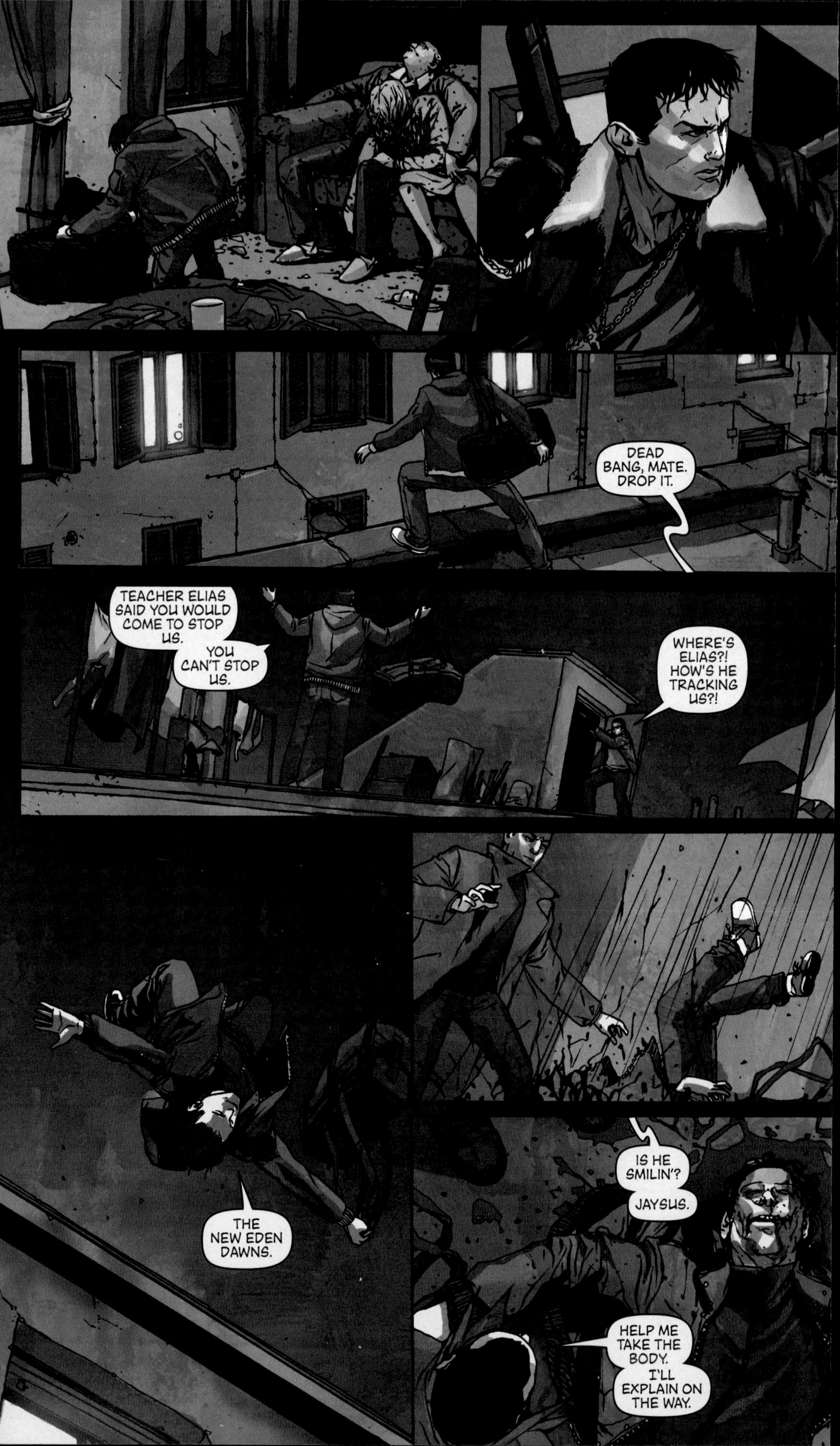
DEAD BANG, MATE. DROP IT.
TEACHER ELIAS SAID YOU WOULD COME TO STOP US.
YOU CAN'T STOP US.
WHERE'S ELIAS?! HOW'S HE TRACKING US?!
THE NEW EDEN DAWNS.
IS HE SMILIN'?
JAYSUS.
HELP ME TAKE THE BODY.
I'LL EXPLAIN ON THE WAY.

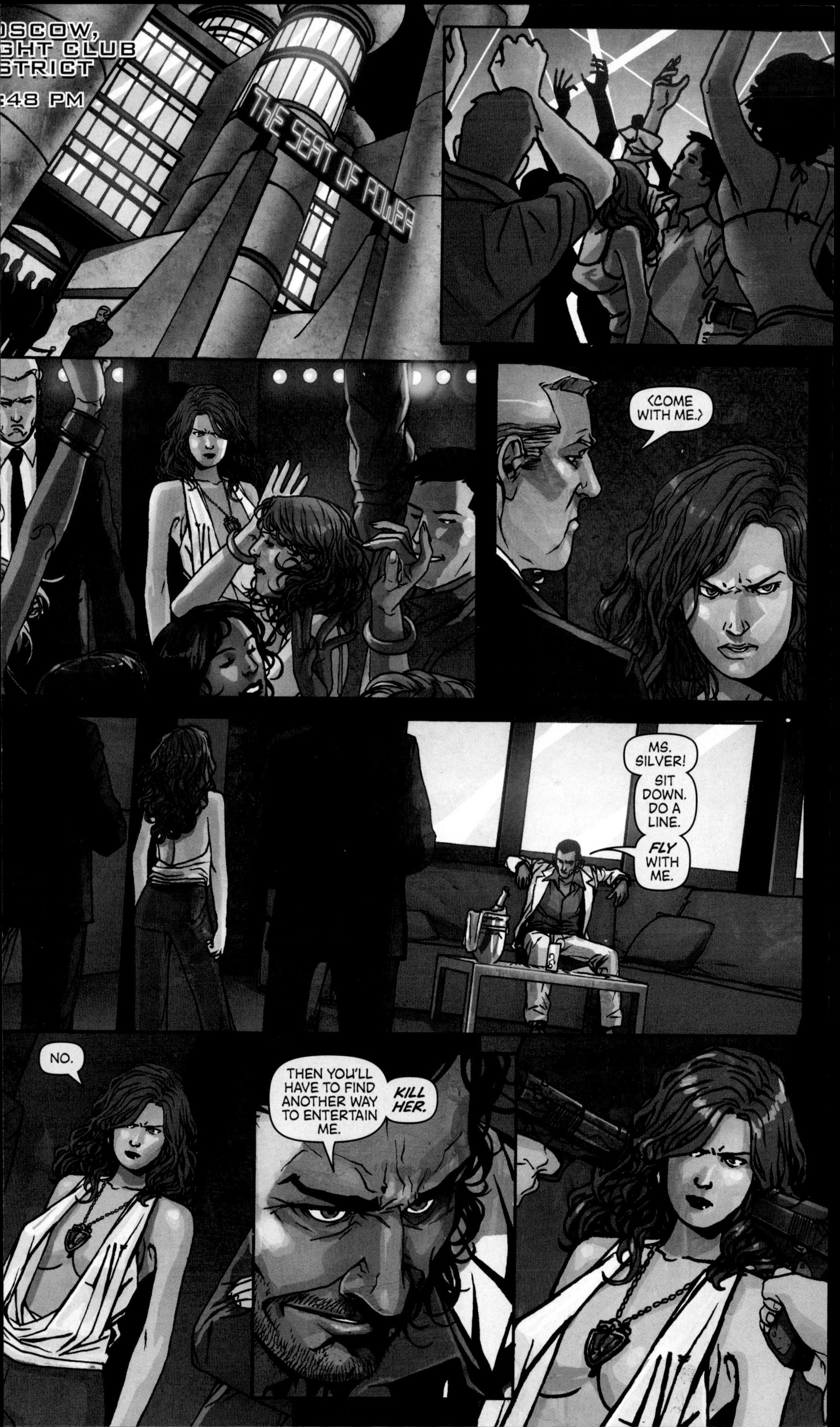
OSCOW,
GHT CLUB
STRICT
:48 PM
THE SEAT OF POWER
<COME WITH ME.>
MS. SILVER!
SIT DOWN. DO A LINE.
FLY WITH ME.
NO.
THEN YOU'LL HAVE TO FIND ANOTHER WAY TO ENTERTAIN ME.
KILL HER.

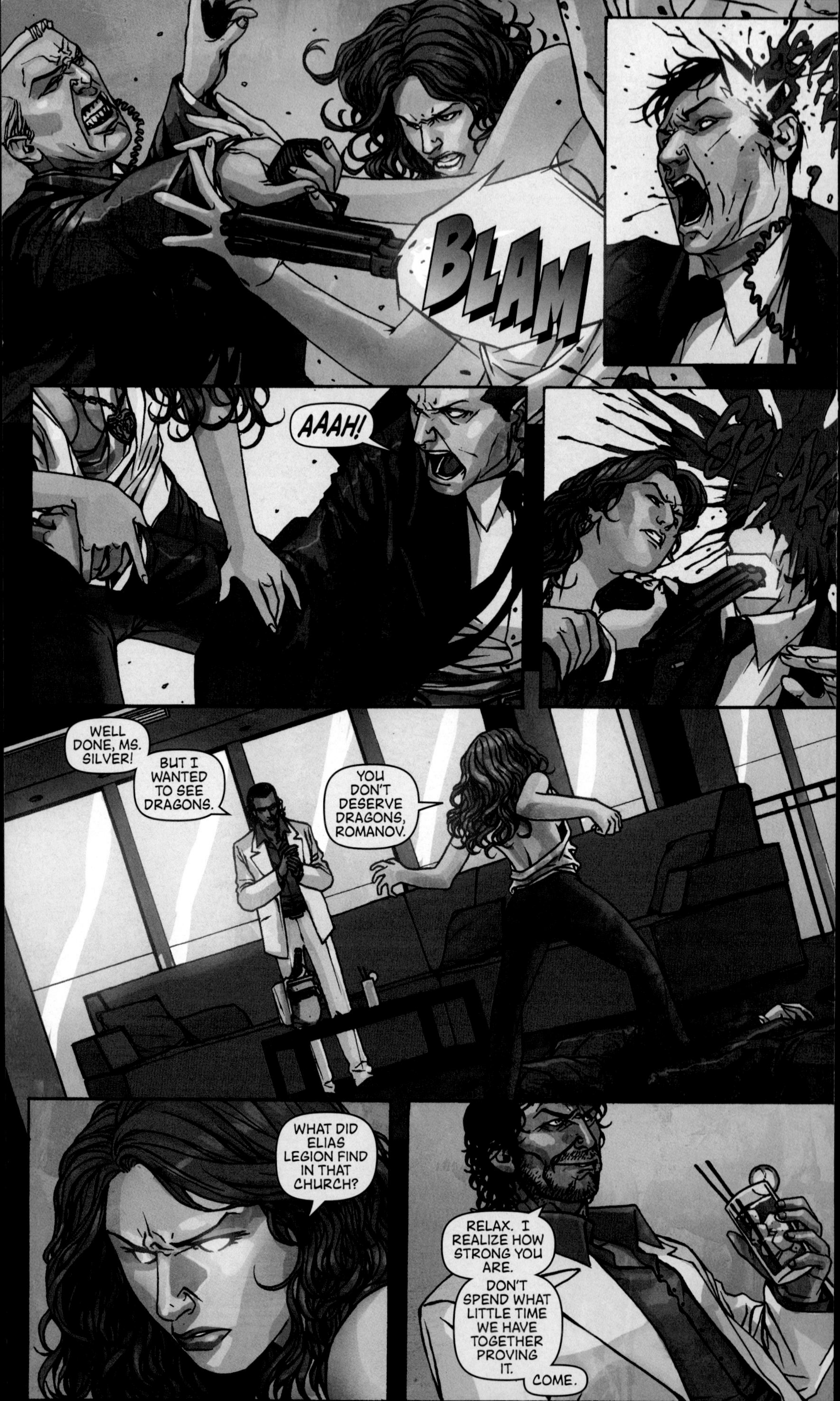
BLAM
AAAH!
WELL DONE, MS. SILVER!
BUT I WANTED TO SEE DRAGONS.
YOU DON'T DESERVE DRAGONS, ROMANOV.
WHAT DID ELIAS LEGION FIND IN THAT CHURCH?
RELAX. I REALIZE HOW STRONG YOU ARE.
DON'T SPEND WHAT LITTLE TIME WE HAVE TOGETHER PROVING IT.
COME.

RASPUTIN DREW SO MANY THINGS...CRAZY BASTARD... WHERE...

...AH. HERE WE ARE.

IT'S CALLED THE COMPASS OF THE ANCIENTS.

THESE THINGS ALWAYS HAVE RIDICULOUS NAMES, DA?

RASPUTIN BELIEVED THE OBSIDIAN STONE WAS SOMEWHERE IN TUNISIA AND THIS COMPASS WOULD TELL HIM WHERE.

IF IT EVEN EXISTS.

I THOUGHT YOU BELIEVED, ROMANOV.

ONLY IN NINETY PERCENT HEROIN AND BLACK MARKET FIREARMS.

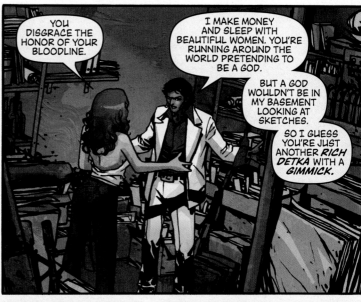

YOU DISGRACE THE HONOR OF YOUR BLOODLINE.

I MAKE MONEY AND SLEEP WITH BEAUTIFUL WOMEN. YOU'RE RUNNING AROUND THE WORLD PRETENDING TO BE A GOD.

BUT A GOD WOULDN'T BE IN MY BASEMENT LOOKING AT SKETCHES.

SO I GUESS YOU'RE JUST ANOTHER RICH DETKA WITH A GIMMICK.

OH.

DID WULFGAR TELL YOU THAT YOU WERE IMPORTANT?

NONE OF US ARE IMPORTANT. THIS WORLD WILL END WHEN IT WANTS.

NO MAN CAN CAUSE IT.

NO MAN CAN SAVE IT.

I'M NOT A MAN.

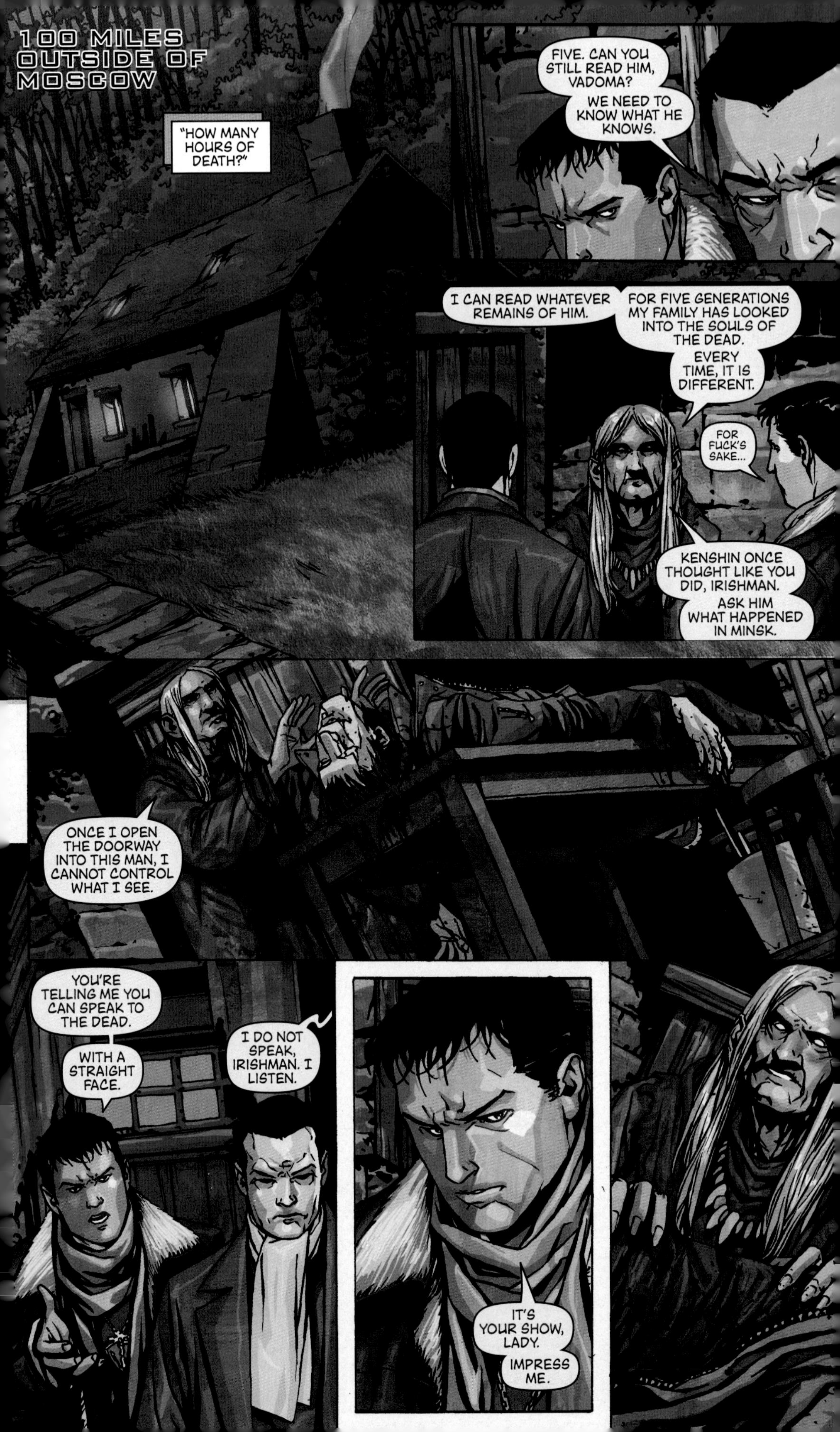
100 MILES OUTSIDE OF MOSCOW
"HOW MANY HOURS OF DEATH?"
FIVE. CAN YOU STILL READ HIM, VADOMA?
WE NEED TO KNOW WHAT HE KNOWS.
I CAN READ WHATEVER REMAINS OF HIM.
FOR FIVE GENERATIONS MY FAMILY HAS LOOKED INTO THE SOULS OF THE DEAD.
EVERY TIME, IT IS DIFFERENT.
FOR FUCK'S SAKE...
KENSHIN ONCE THOUGHT LIKE YOU DID, IRISHMAN.
ASK HIM WHAT HAPPENED IN MINSK.
ONCE I OPEN THE DOORWAY INTO THIS MAN, I CANNOT CONTROL WHAT I SEE.
YOU'RE TELLING ME YOU CAN SPEAK TO THE DEAD.
WITH A STRAIGHT FACE.
I DO NOT SPEAK, IRISHMAN. I LISTEN.
IT'S YOUR SHOW, LADY.
IMPRESS ME.

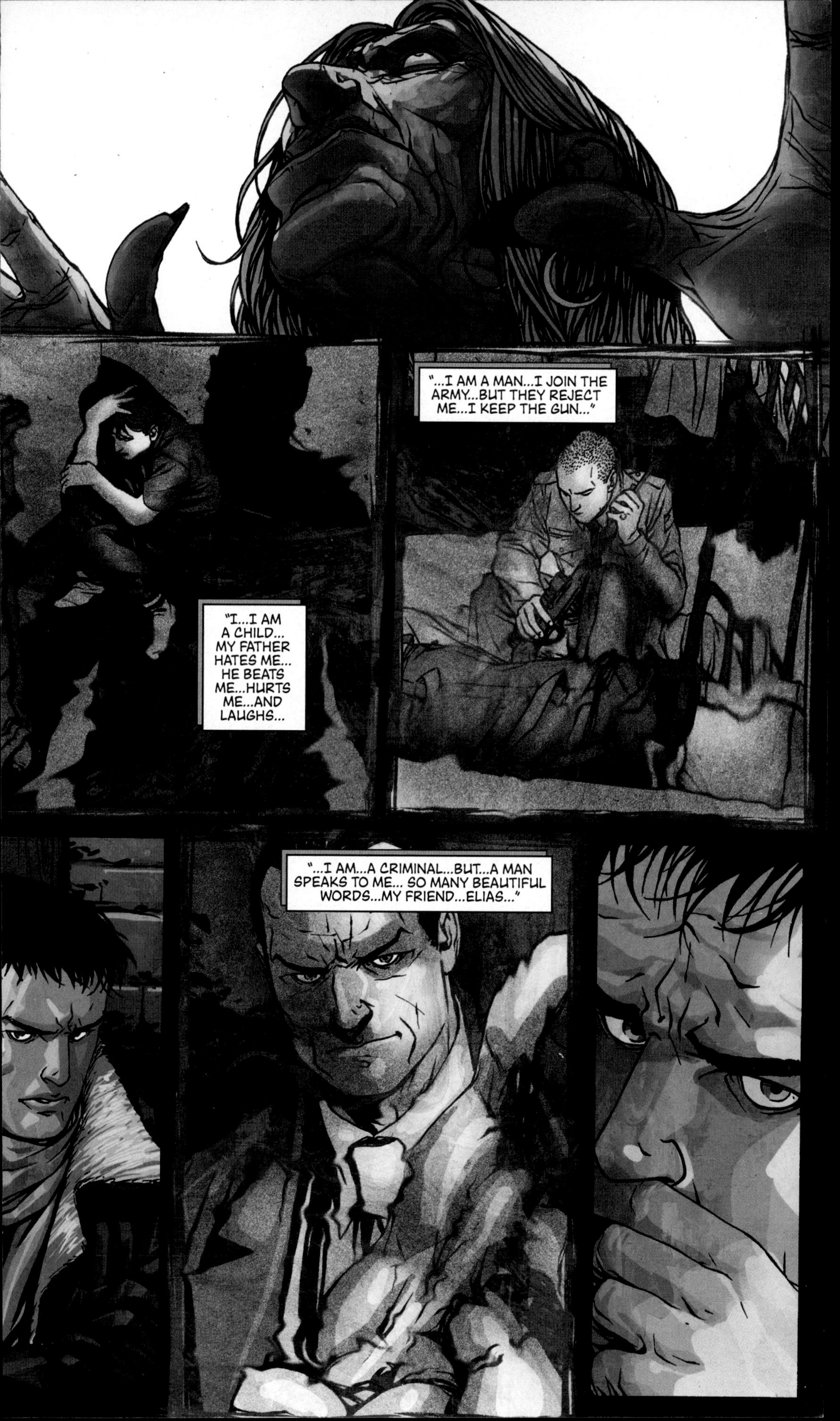
"I...I AM A CHILD... MY FATHER HATES ME... HE BEATS ME...HURTS ME...AND LAUGHS...
"...I AM A MAN...I JOIN THE ARMY...BUT THEY REJECT ME...I KEEP THE GUN..."
"...I AM...A CRIMINAL...BUT...A MAN SPEAKS TO ME... SO MANY BEAUTIFUL WORDS...MY FRIEND...ELIAS..."

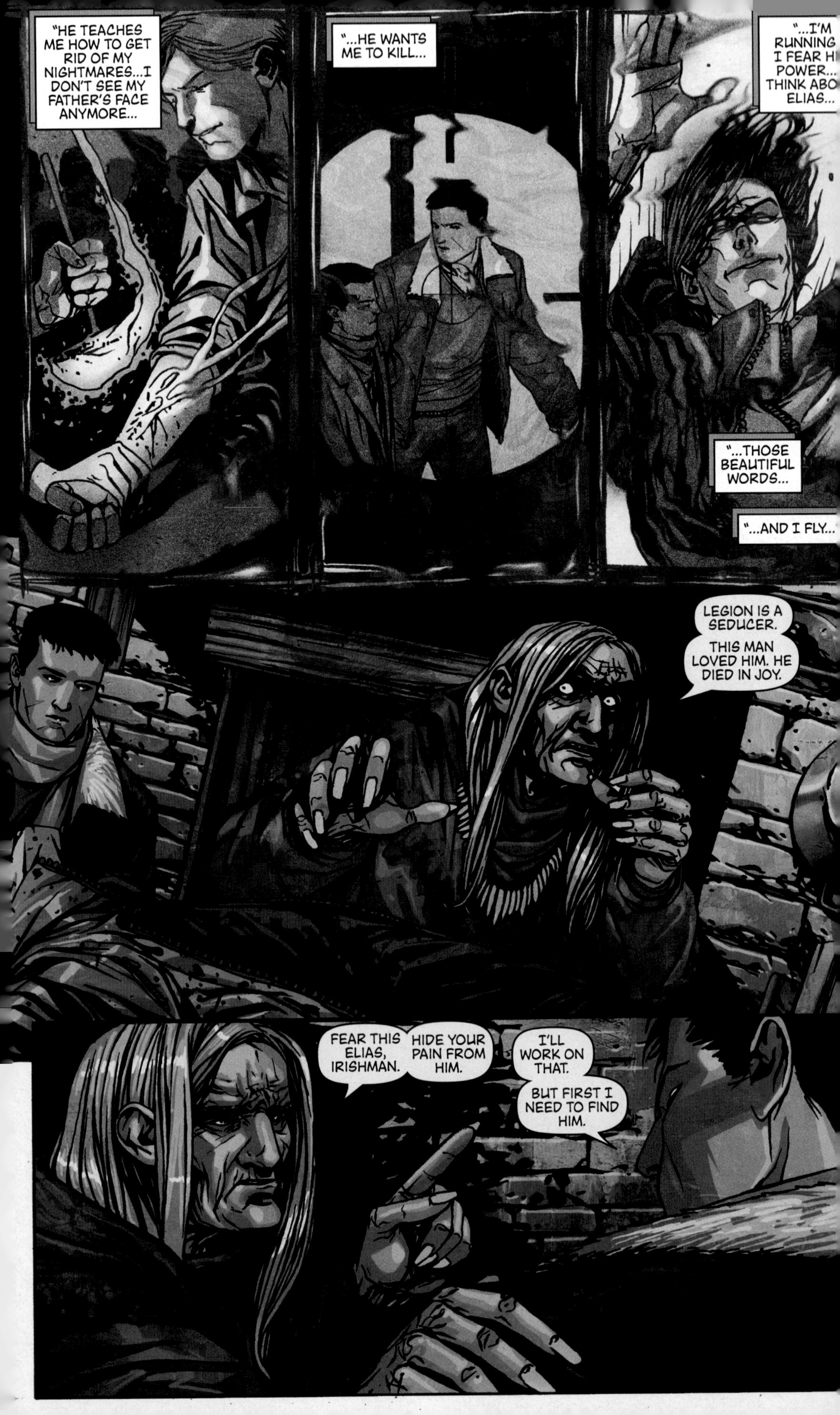
"HE TEACHES ME HOW TO GET RID OF MY NIGHTMARES...I DON'T SEE MY FATHER'S FACE ANYMORE...
"...HE WANTS ME TO KILL...
"...I'M RUNNING I FEAR H POWER... THINK ABO ELIAS...
"...THOSE BEAUTIFUL WORDS...
"...AND I FLY...
LEGION IS A SEDUCER.
THIS MAN LOVED HIM. HE DIED IN JOY.
FEAR THIS ELIAS, IRISHMAN.
HIDE YOUR PAIN FROM HIM.
I'LL WORK ON THAT.
BUT FIRST I NEED TO FIND HIM.

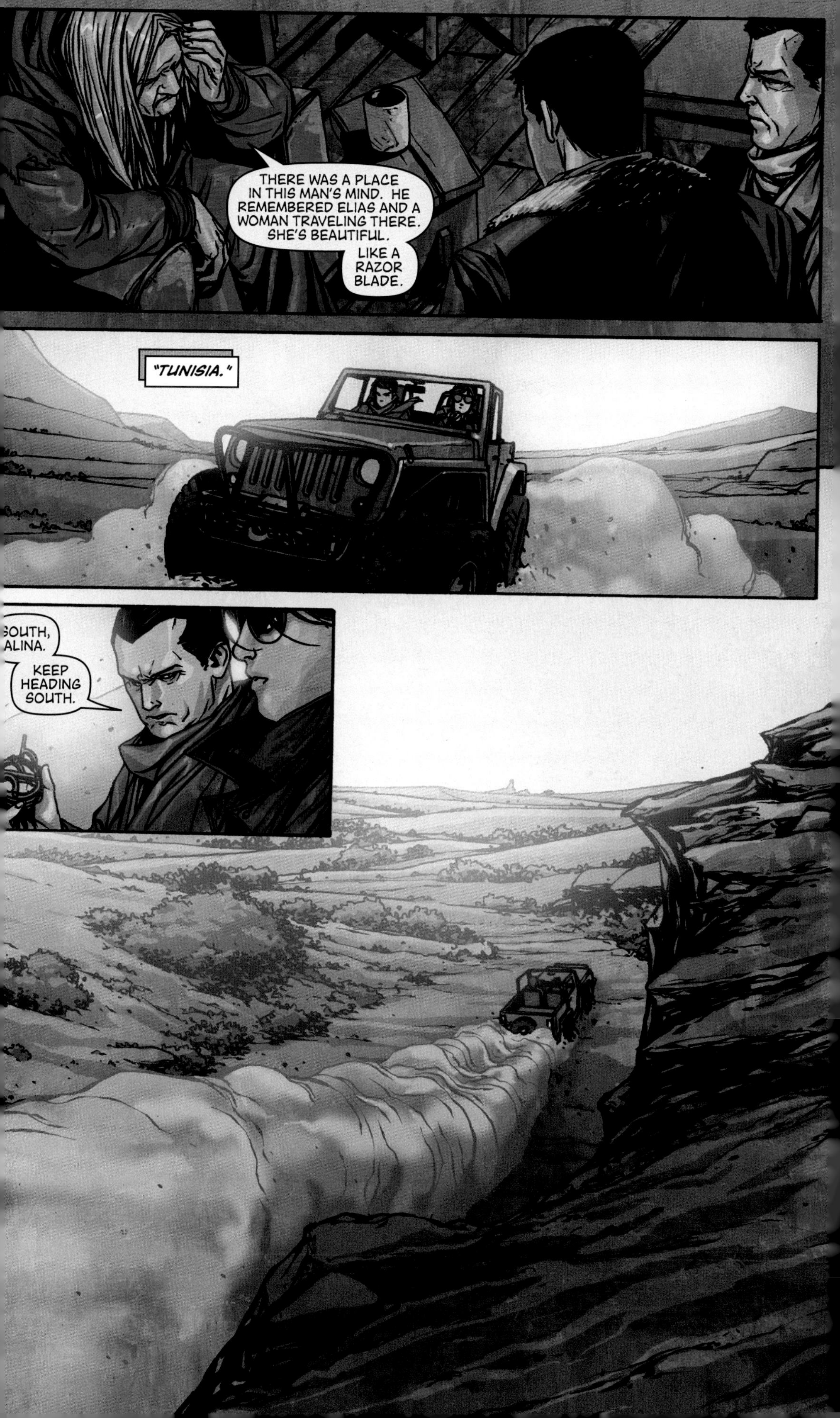

THERE WAS A PLACE IN THIS MAN'S MIND. HE REMEMBERED ELIAS AND A WOMAN TRAVELING THERE. SHE'S BEAUTIFUL.
LIKE A RAZOR BLADE.
"TUNISIA."
SOUTH, ALINA.
KEEP HEADING SOUTH.

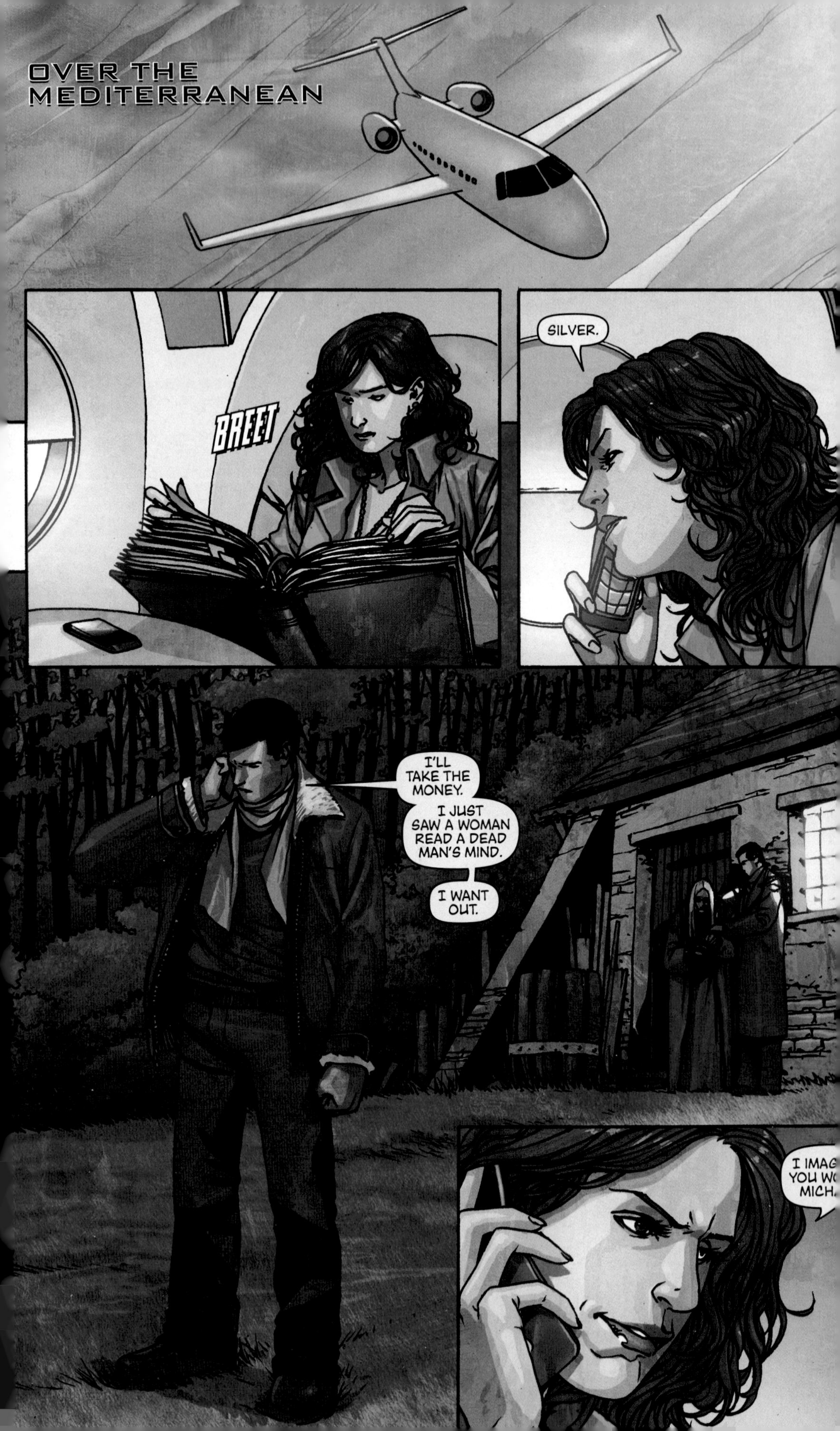
OVER THE MEDITERRANEAN
BREET
SILVER.
I'LL TAKE THE MONEY.
I JUST SAW A WOMAN READ A DEAD MAN'S MIND.
I WANT OUT.
I IMAG
YOU W
MICH

BROKEN TRINITY

"PANDORA'S BOX" Part 3

written by: **Bryan Edward Hill & Rob Levin**
art by: **Alessandro Vitti & Facundo Percio**
colors by: **Sunny Gho of IFS**
letters by: **Troy Peteri**

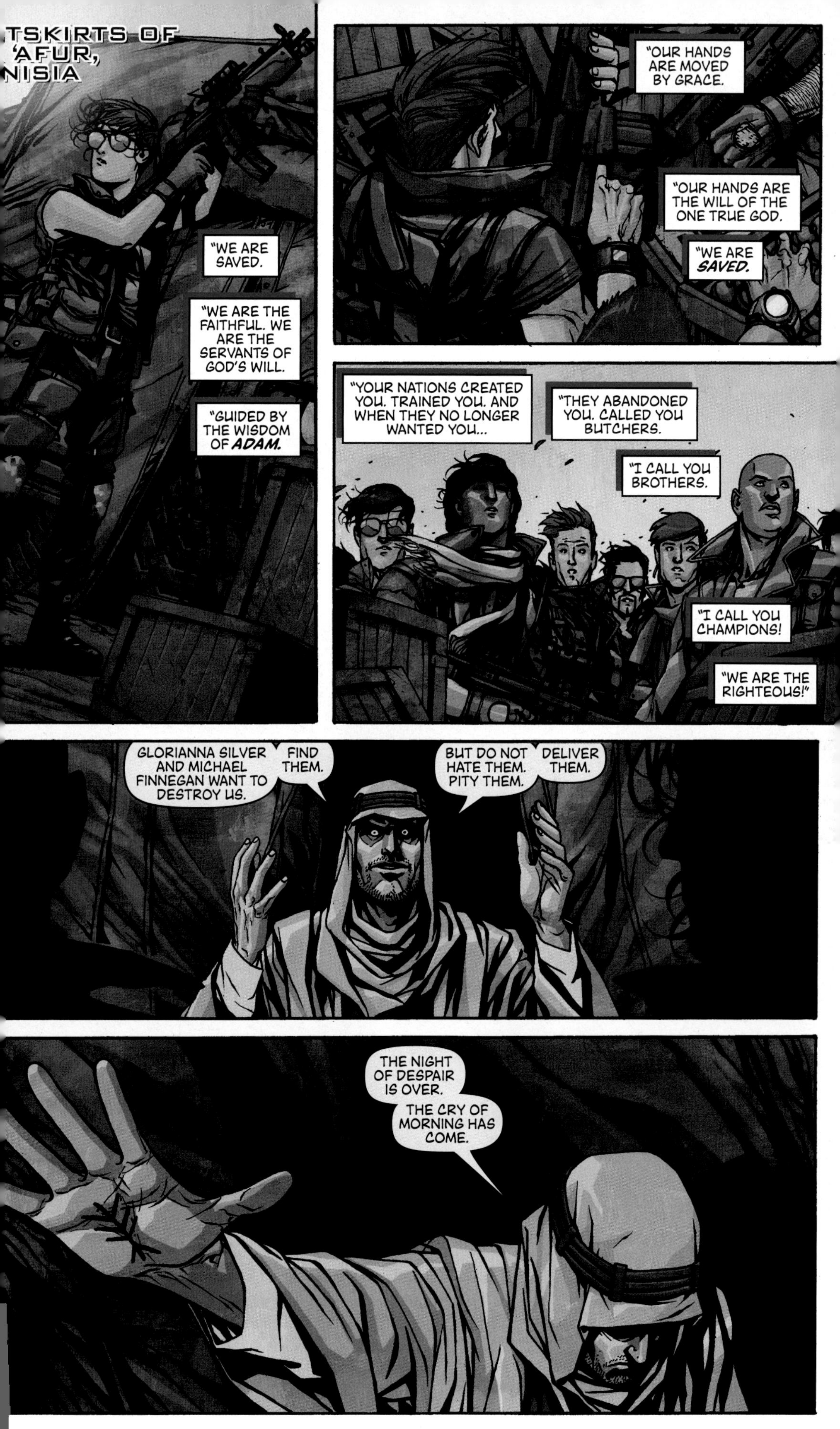
TSKIRTS OF
'AFUR,
NISIA
"WE ARE SAVED.
"WE ARE THE FAITHFUL. WE ARE THE SERVANTS OF GOD'S WILL.
"GUIDED BY THE WISDOM OF ADAM.
"OUR HANDS ARE MOVED BY GRACE.
"OUR HANDS ARE THE WILL OF THE ONE TRUE GOD.
"WE ARE SAVED.
"YOUR NATIONS CREATED YOU. TRAINED YOU. AND WHEN THEY NO LONGER WANTED YOU...
"THEY ABANDONED YOU. CALLED YOU BUTCHERS.
"I CALL YOU BROTHERS.
"I CALL YOU CHAMPIONS!
"WE ARE THE RIGHTEOUS!"
GLORIANNA SILVER AND MICHAEL FINNEGAN WANT TO DESTROY US.
FIND THEM.
BUT DO NOT HATE THEM. PITY THEM.
DELIVER THEM.
THE NIGHT OF DESPAIR IS OVER.
THE CRY OF MORNING HAS COME.

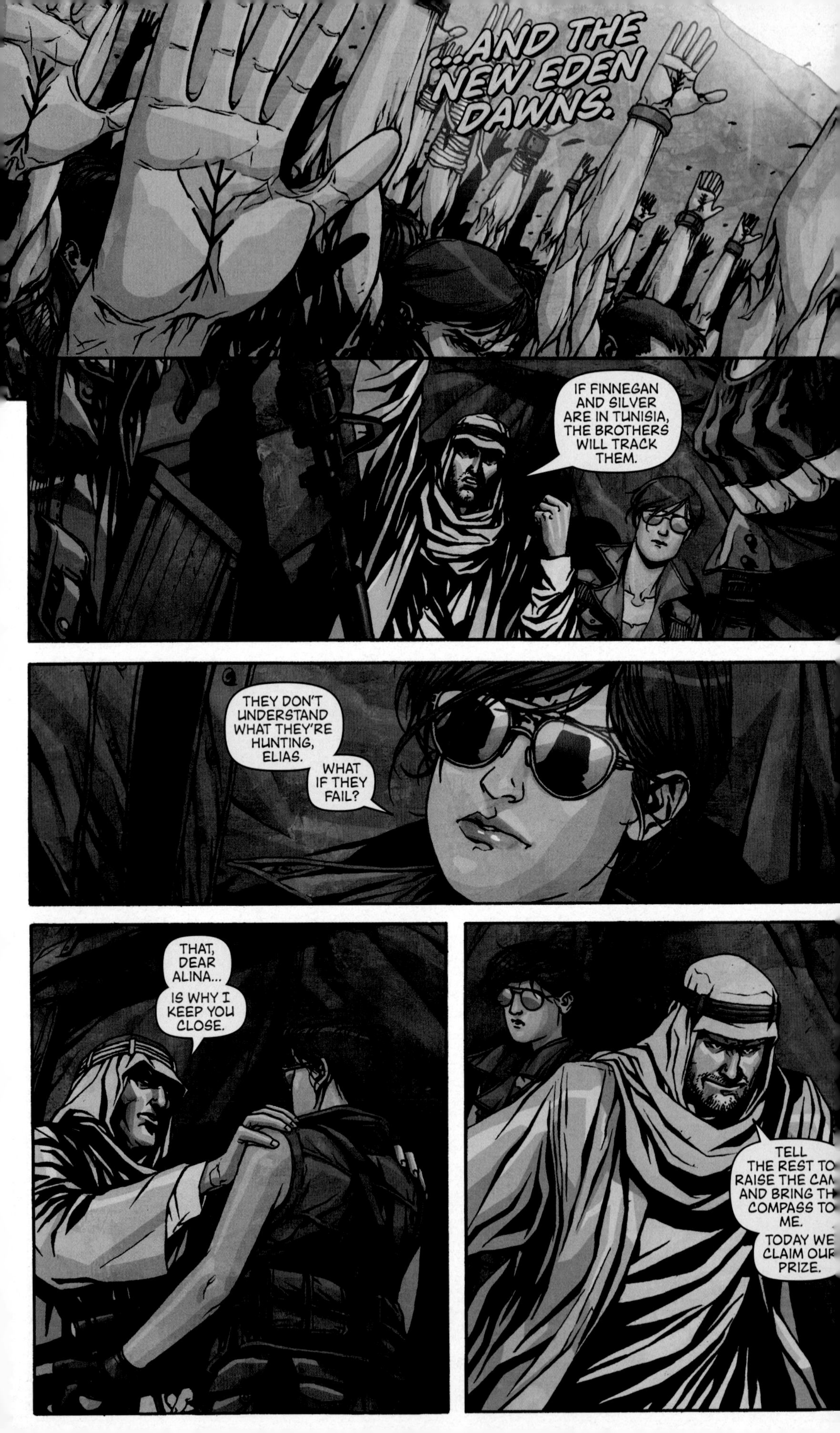
...AND THE NEW EDEN DAWNS.
IF FINNEGAN AND SILVER ARE IN TUNISIA, THE BROTHERS WILL TRACK THEM.
THEY DON'T UNDERSTAND WHAT THEY'RE HUNTING, ELIAS.
WHAT IF THEY FAIL?
THAT, DEAR ALINA...
IS WHY I KEEP YOU CLOSE.
TELL THE REST TO RAISE THE CAM AND BRING TH COMPASS TO ME.
TODAY WE CLAIM OUR PRIZE.

BARKA
LITARY
RPORT
TABARKA,
TUNISIA

SO HOW DO YOU WANT TO DO THIS, SILVER? THE TRADE.

YOU'RE NOT GETTING THE GLACIER STONE UNTIL I SEE THE TEN MILLION.

CORRECTION.

UNTIL I *HAVE* THE TEN MILLION.

THAT'S THE FUNNY THING ABOUT THE POOR.

TSIDE OF ESALA, NISIA

THEY NEVER TRUST ANYONE. EVEN THE PEOPLE WHO WANT TO HELP THEM MOST.

I'LL SEND YOU A LOCATION FOR THE MEET.

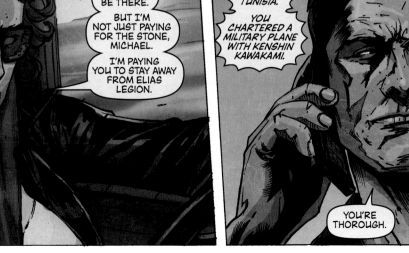

THE MONEY WILL BE THERE.

BUT I'M NOT JUST PAYING FOR THE STONE, MICHAEL.

I'M PAYING YOU TO STAY AWAY FROM ELIAS LEGION.

YOU'RE IN TUNISIA.

YOU CHARTERED A MILITARY PLANE WITH KENSHIN KAWAKAMI.

YOU'RE THOROUGH.

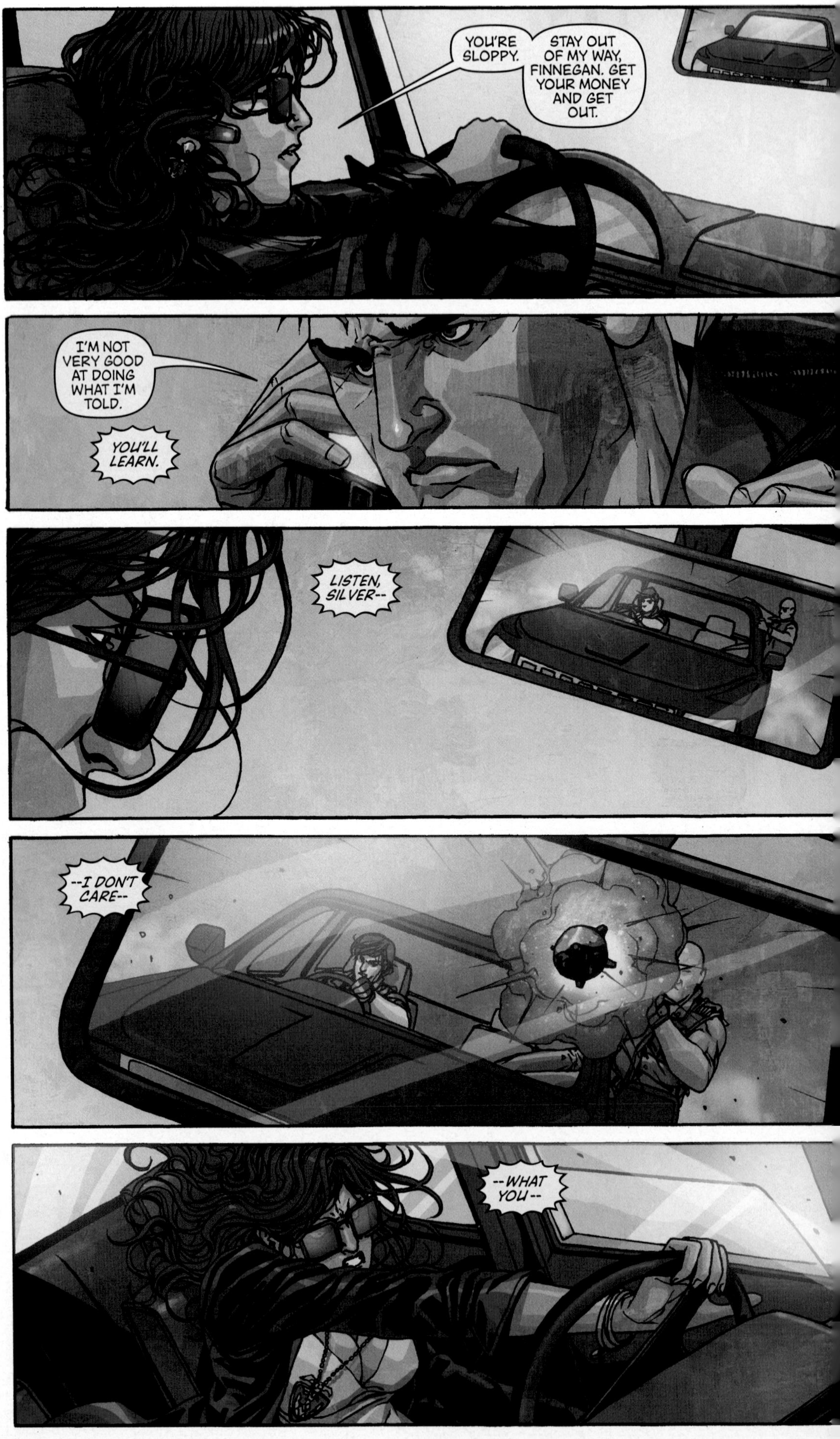
YOU'RE SLOPPY.
STAY OUT OF MY WAY, FINNEGAN. GET YOUR MONEY AND GET OUT.
I'M NOT VERY GOOD AT DOING WHAT I'M TOLD.
YOU'LL LEARN.
LISTEN, SILVER--
--I DON'T CARE--
--WHAT YOU--

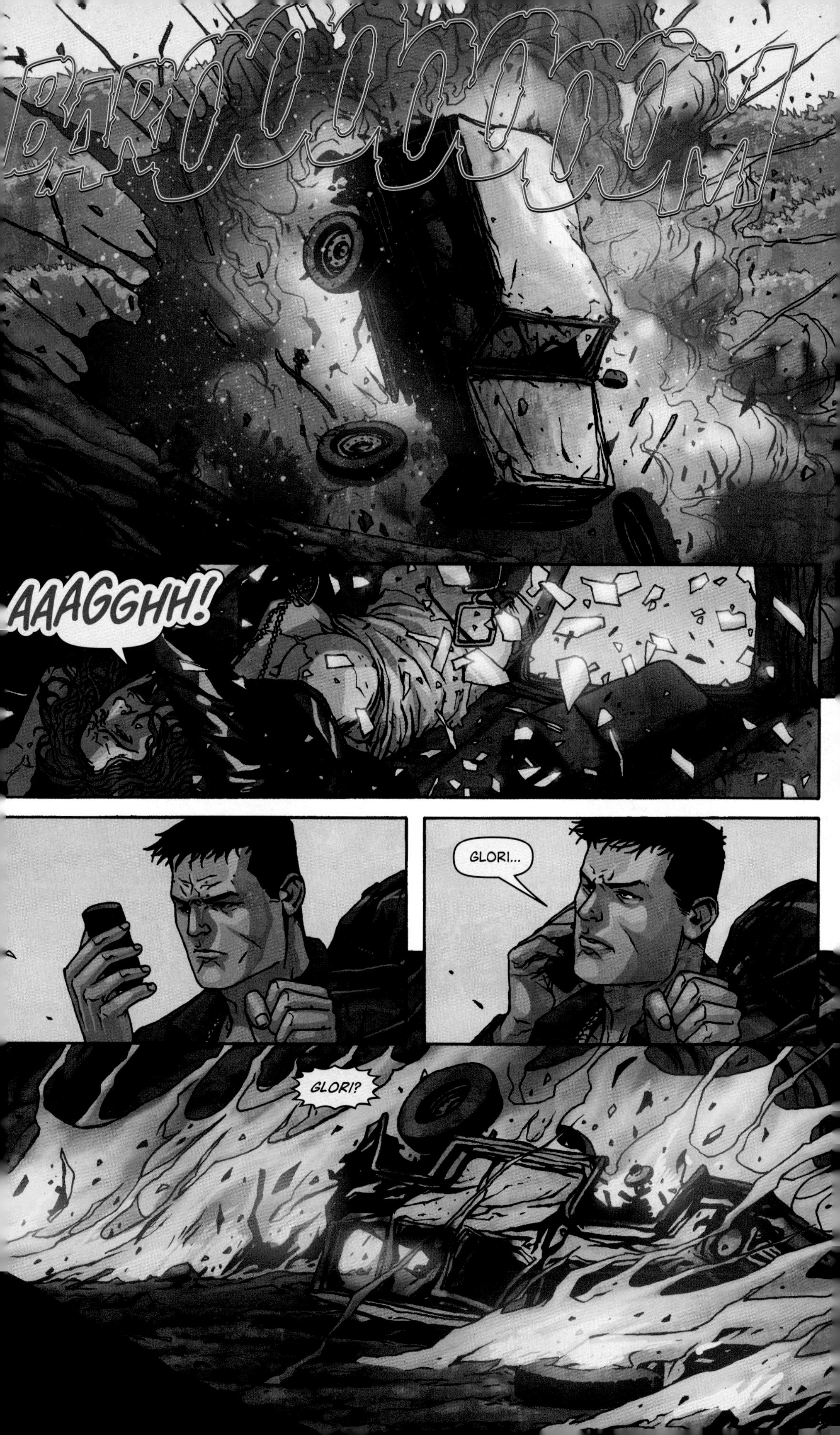
BRROOOOOOOM
AAAGGHH!
GLORI...
GLORI?

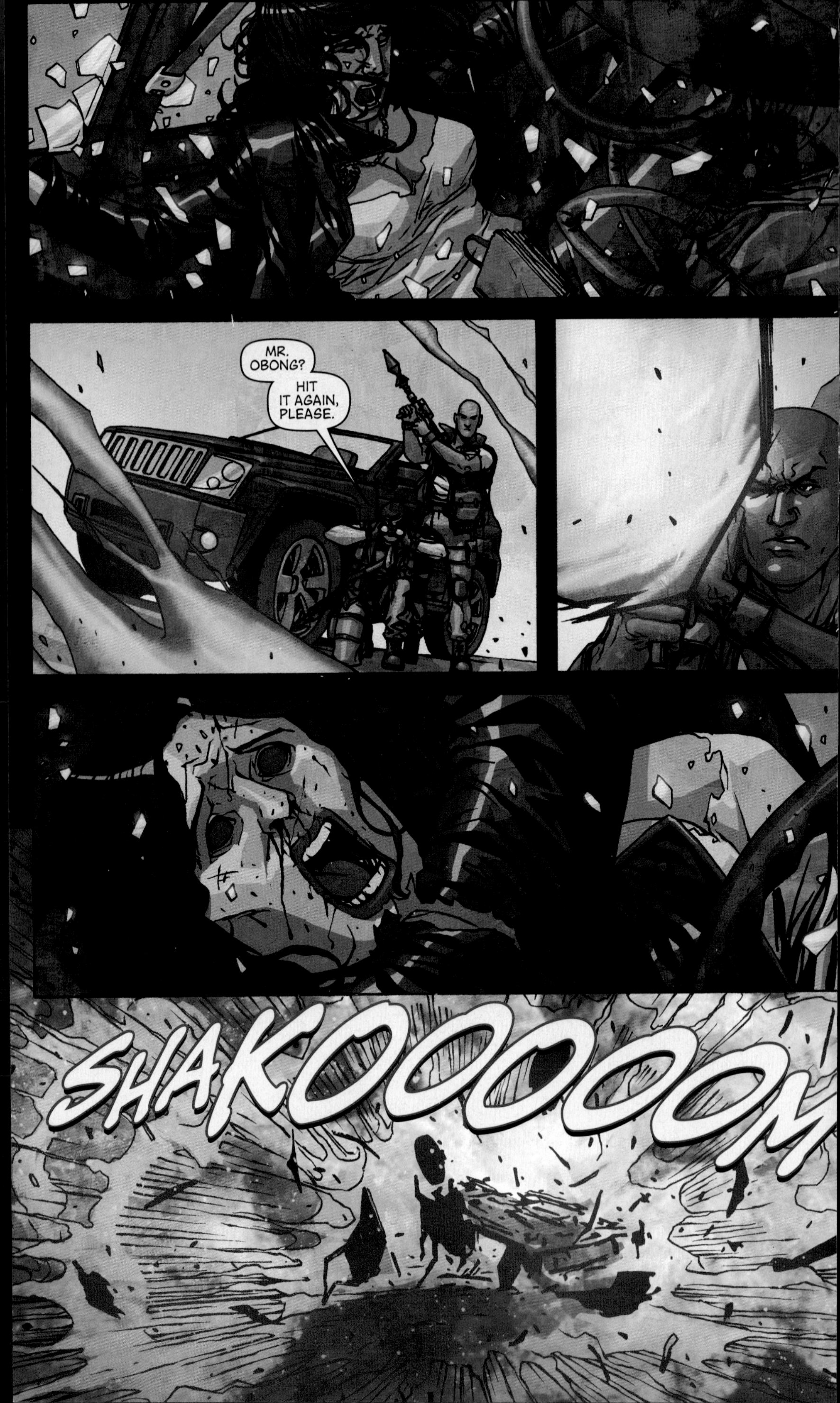
MR. OBONG? HIT IT AGAIN, PLEASE.
SHAKOOOOOOM

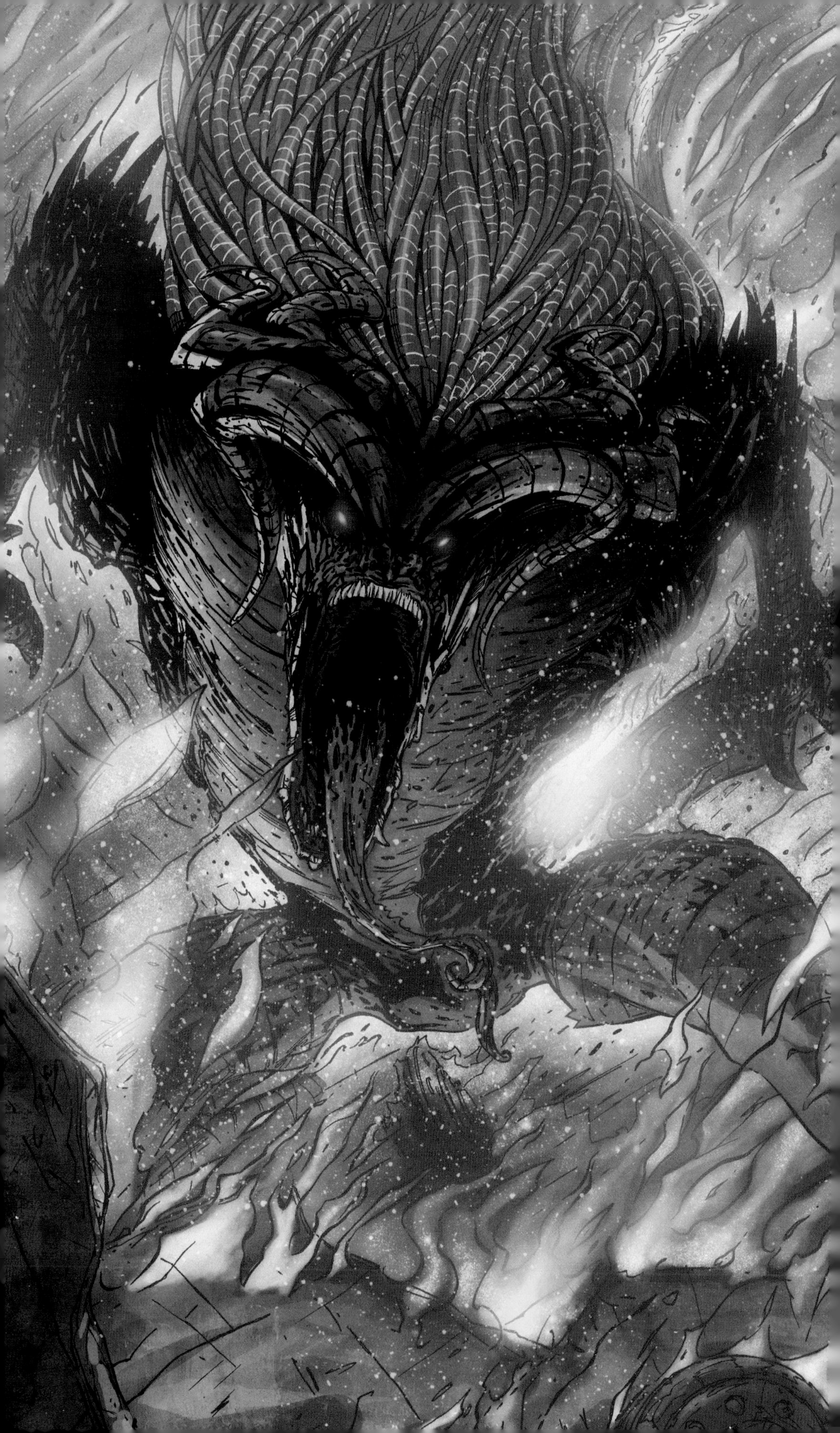

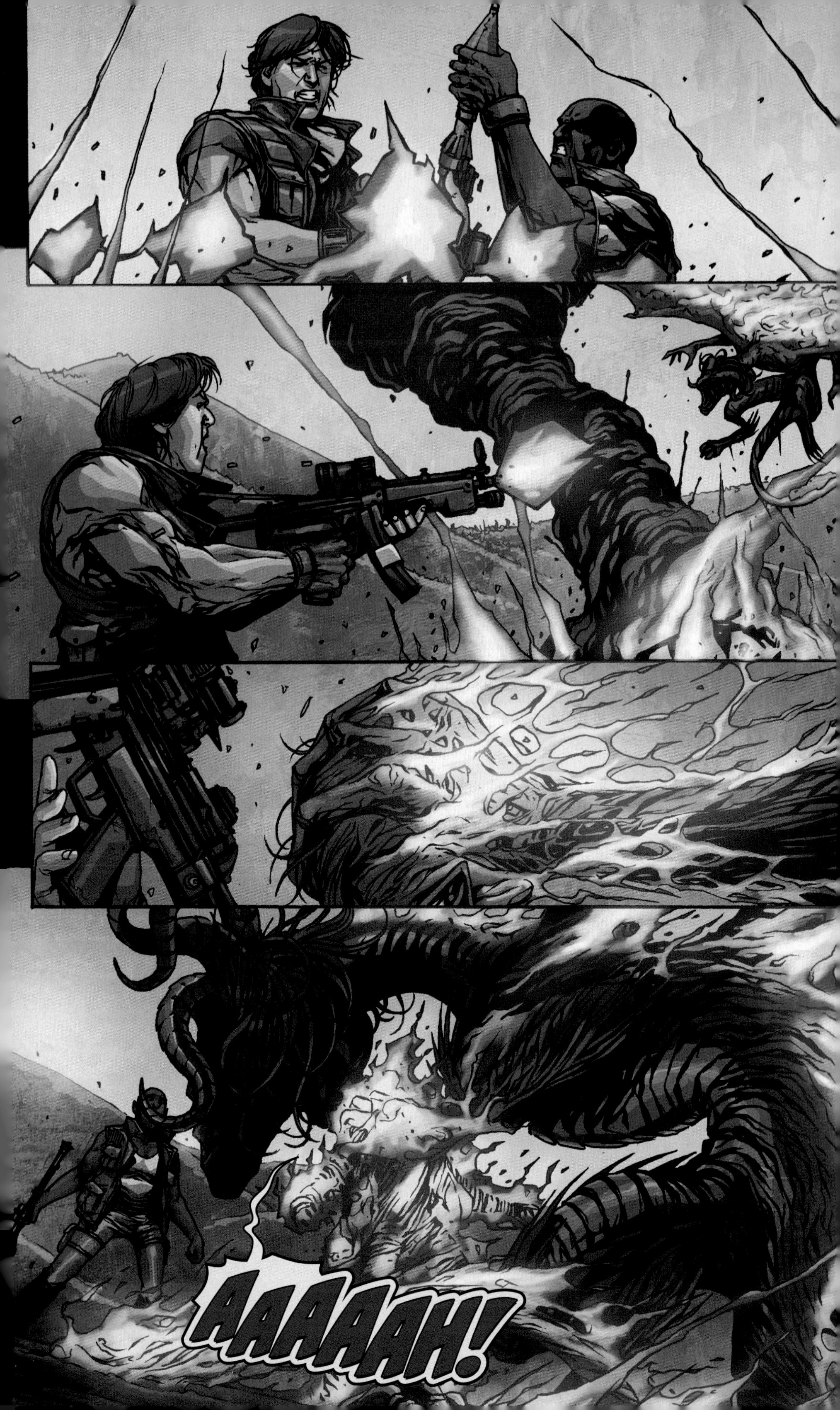
AAAAAH!

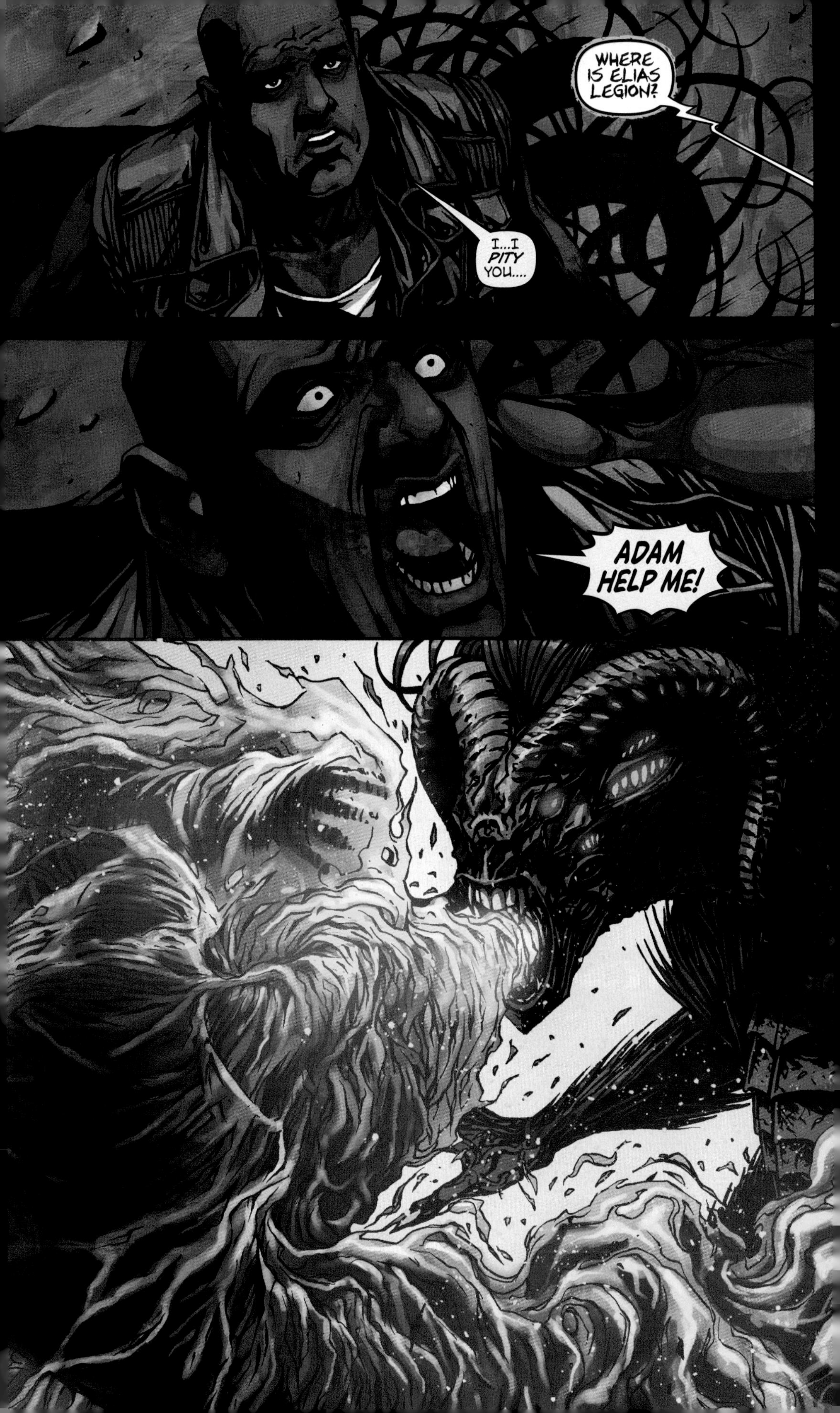
WHERE IS ELIAS LEGION?
I...I PITY YOU....
ADAM HELP ME!

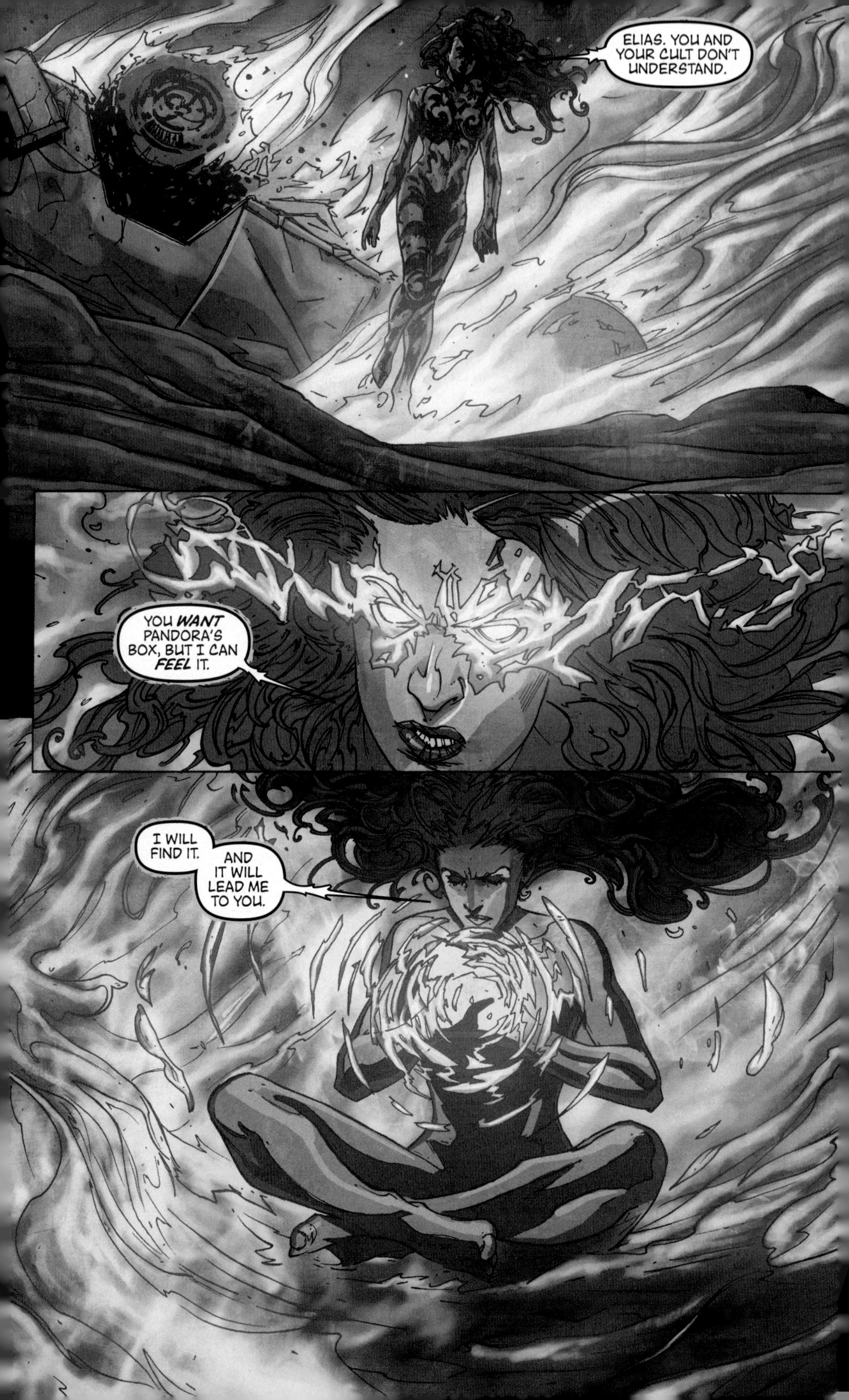
ELIAS. YOU AND YOUR CULT DON'T UNDERSTAND.
YOU ***WANT*** PANDORA'S BOX, BUT I CAN ***FEEL*** IT.
I WILL FIND IT.
AND IT WILL LEAD ME TO YOU.

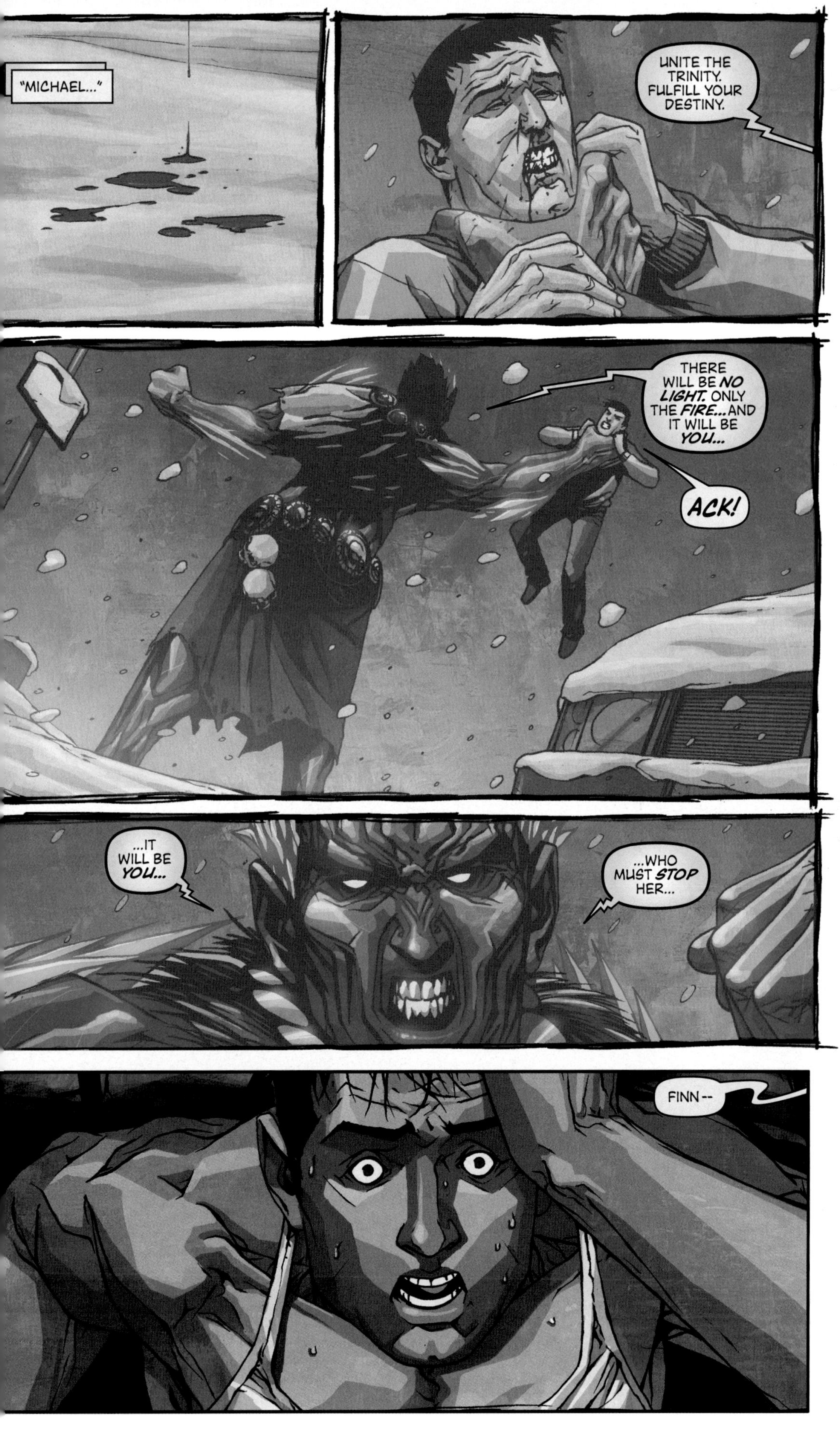
"MICHAEL..."
UNITE THE TRINITY. FULFILL YOUR DESTINY.
THERE WILL BE NO LIGHT. ONLY THE FIRE...AND IT WILL BE YOU...
ACK!
...IT WILL BE YOU...
...WHO MUST STOP HER...
FINN--

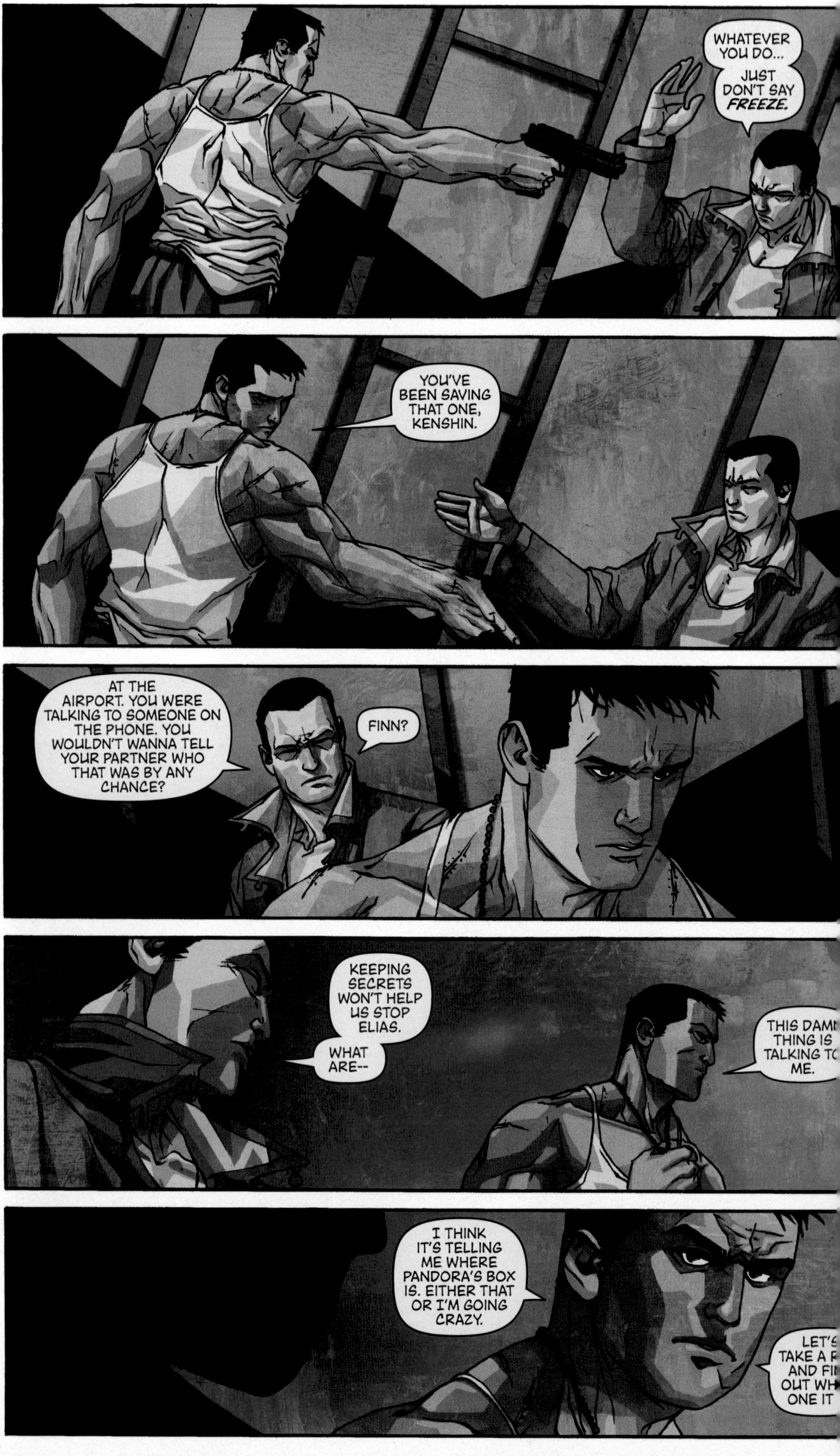
WHATEVER YOU DO... JUST DON'T SAY *FREEZE.*
YOU'VE BEEN SAVING THAT ONE, KENSHIN.
AT THE AIRPORT. YOU WERE TALKING TO SOMEONE ON THE PHONE. YOU WOULDN'T WANNA TELL YOUR PARTNER WHO THAT WAS BY ANY CHANCE?
FINN?
KEEPING SECRETS WON'T HELP US STOP ELIAS.
WHAT ARE--
THIS DAMN THING IS TALKING TO ME.
I THINK IT'S TELLING ME WHERE PANDORA'S BOX IS. EITHER THAT OR I'M GOING CRAZY.

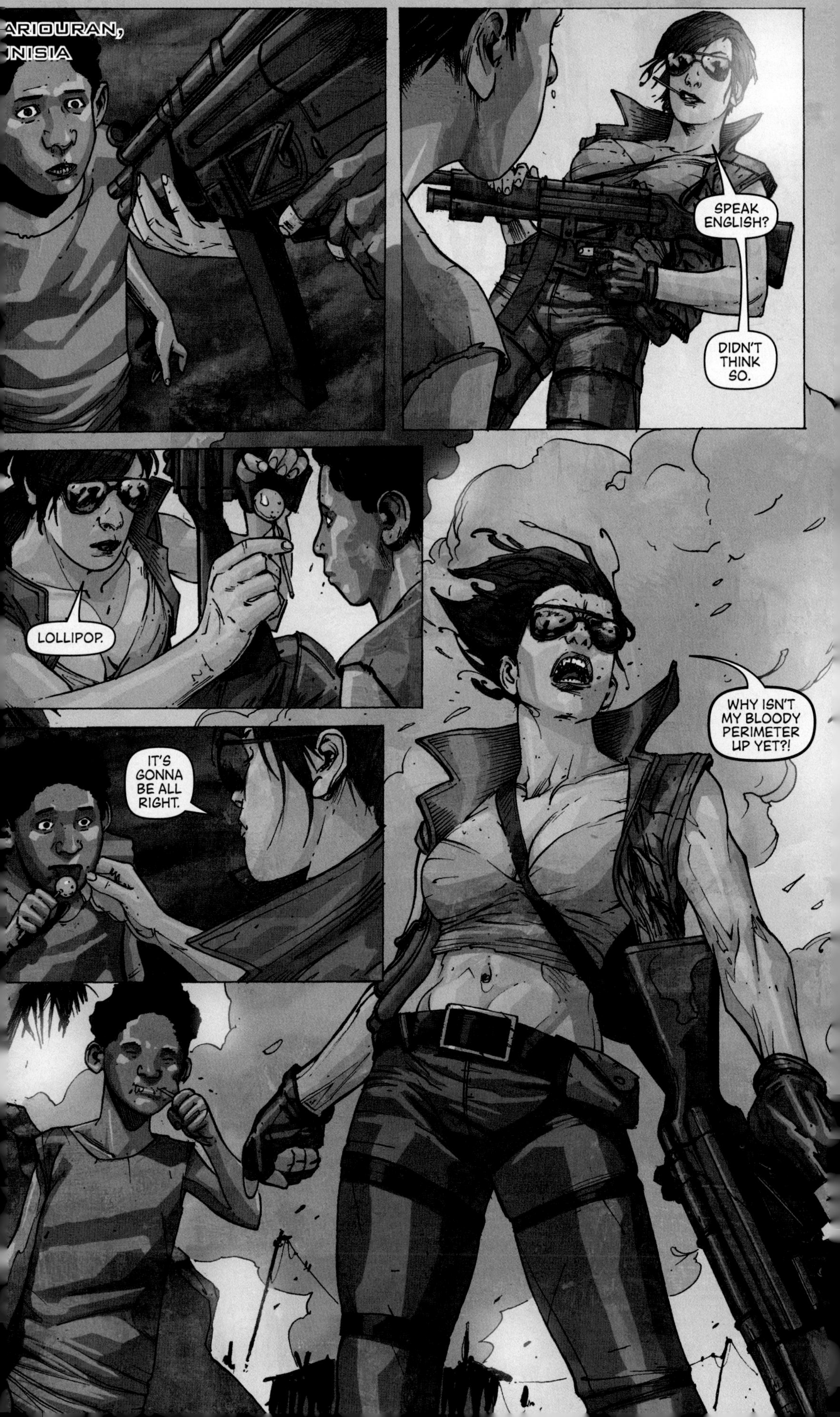

ARIOURAN,
UNISIA
SPEAK ENGLISH?
DIDN'T THINK SO.
LOLLIPOP.
IT'S GONNA BE ALL RIGHT.
WHY ISN'T MY BLOODY PERIMETER UP YET?!

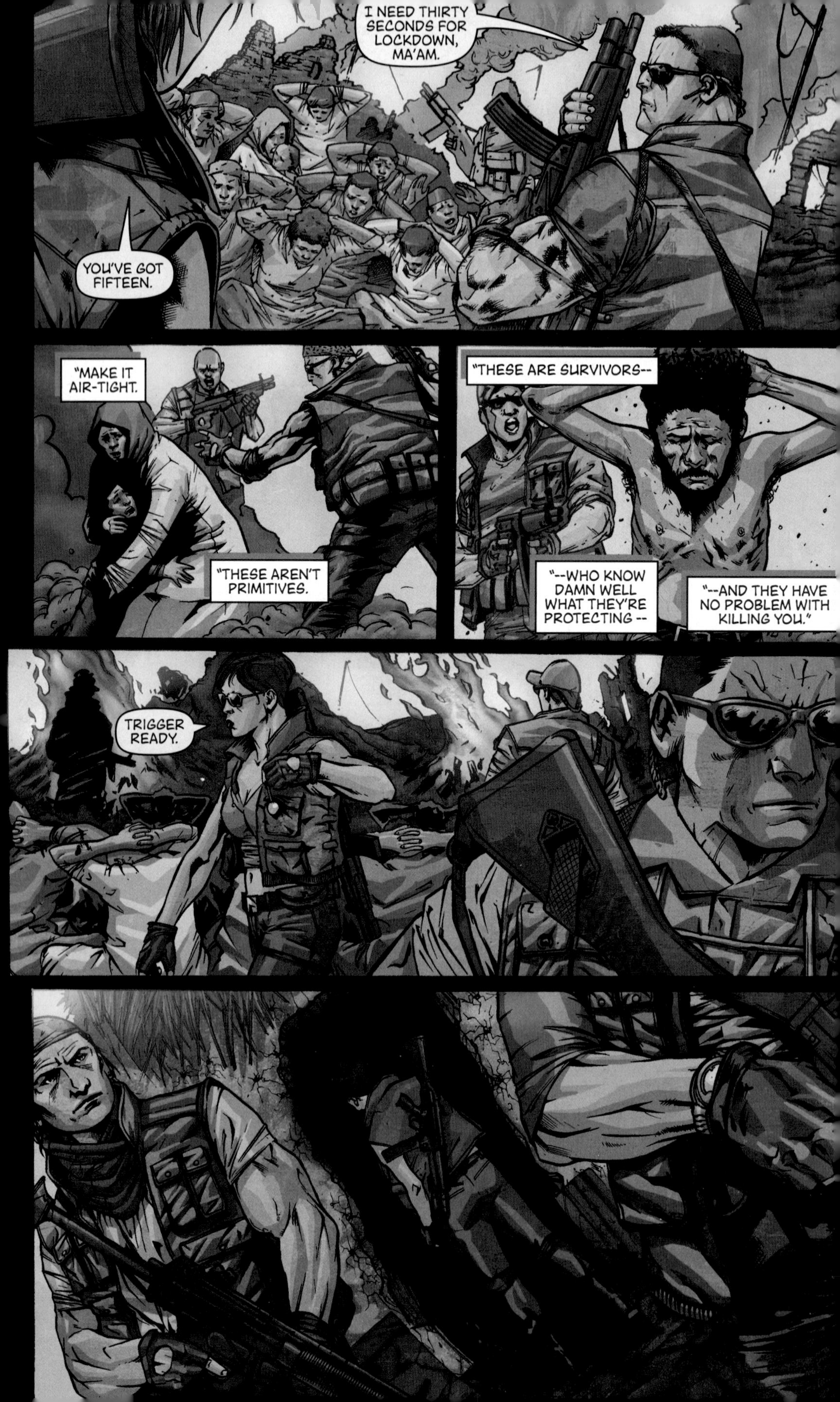
I NEED THIRTY SECONDS FOR LOCKDOWN, MA'AM.
YOU'VE GOT FIFTEEN.
"MAKE IT AIR-TIGHT.
"THESE AREN'T PRIMITIVES.
"THESE ARE SURVIVORS--
"--WHO KNOW DAMN WELL WHAT THEY'RE PROTECTING --
"--AND THEY HAVE NO PROBLEM WITH KILLING YOU."
TRIGGER READY.

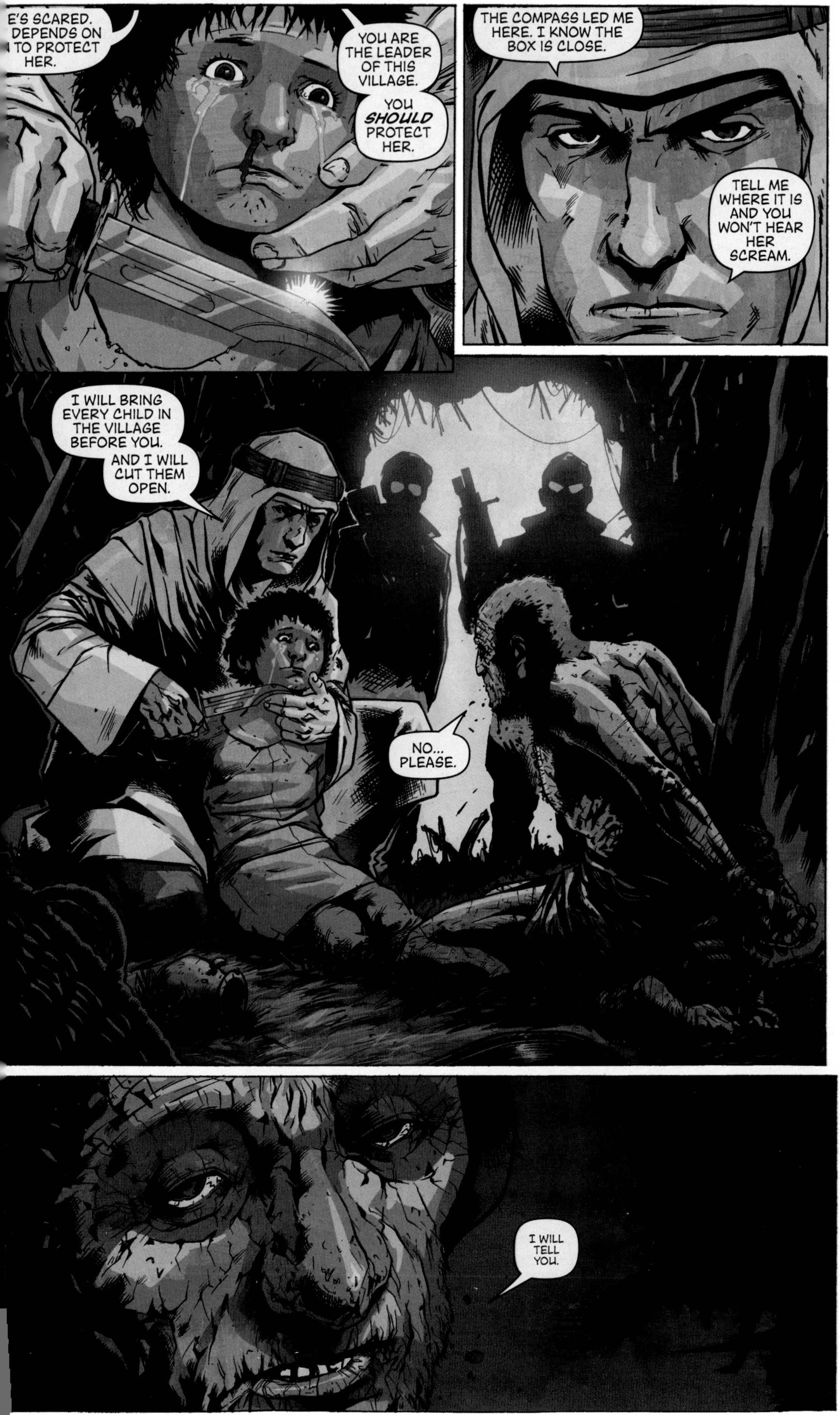
E'S SCARED.
DEPENDS ON
TO PROTECT
HER.
YOU ARE THE LEADER OF THIS VILLAGE.
YOU SHOULD PROTECT HER.
THE COMPASS LED ME HERE. I KNOW THE BOX IS CLOSE.
TELL ME WHERE IT IS AND YOU WON'T HEAR HER SCREAM.
I WILL BRING EVERY CHILD IN THE VILLAGE BEFORE YOU.
AND I WILL CUT THEM OPEN.
NO... PLEASE.
I WILL TELL YOU.

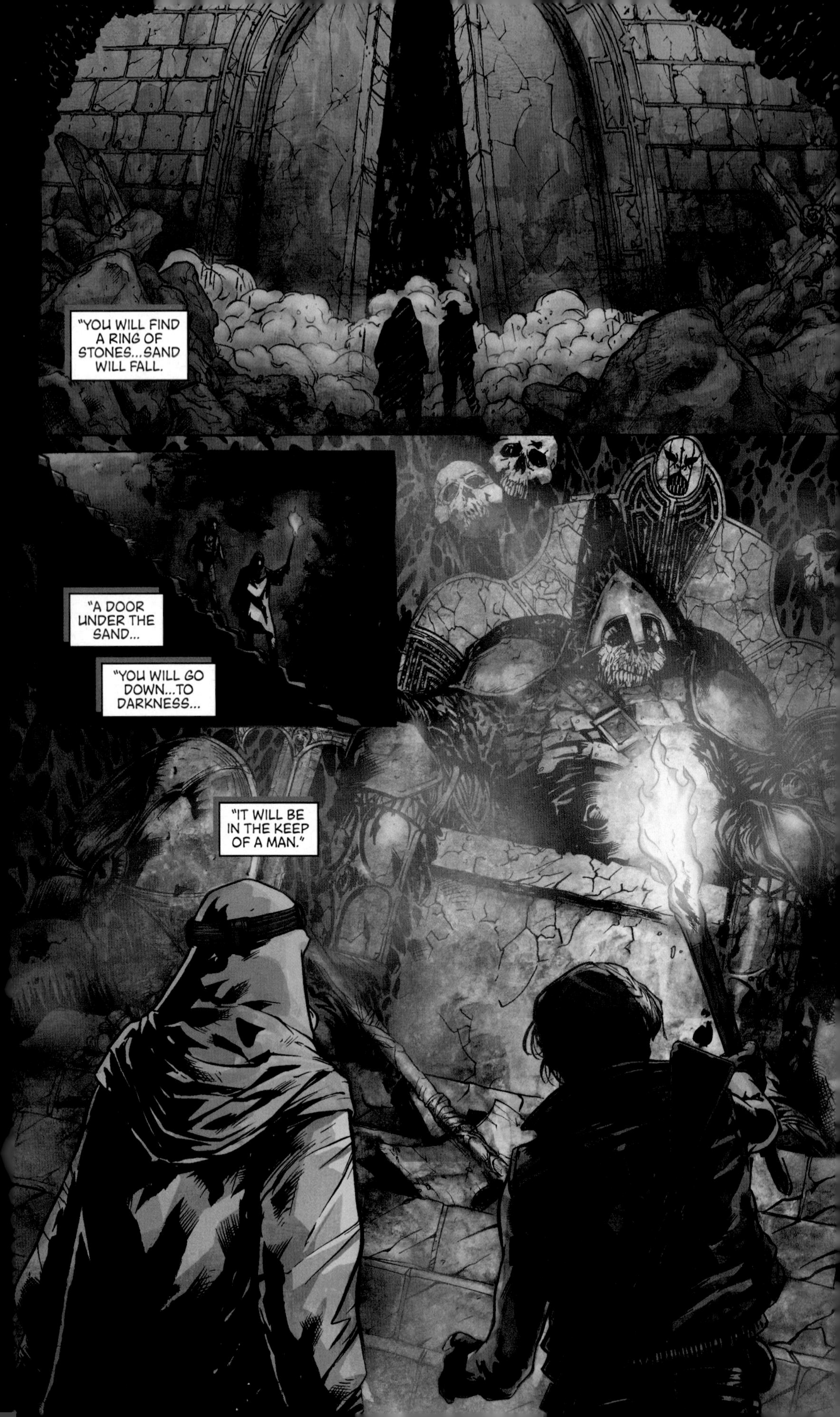
"YOU WILL FIND A RING OF STONES...SAND WILL FALL.
"A DOOR UNDER THE SAND...
"YOU WILL GO DOWN...TO DARKNESS...
"IT WILL BE IN THE KEEP OF A MAN."

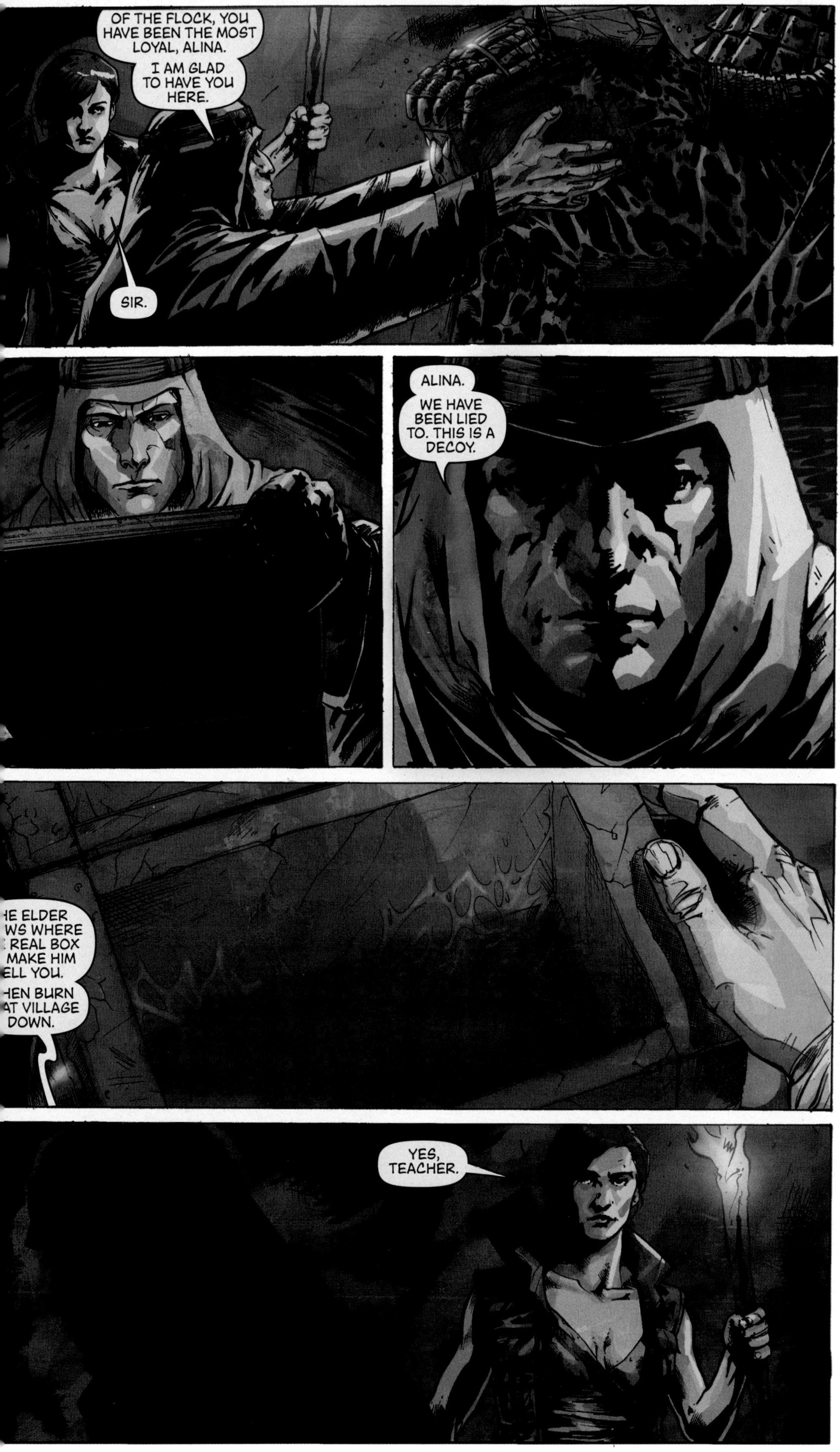
OF THE FLOCK, YOU HAVE BEEN THE MOST LOYAL, ALINA.
I AM GLAD TO HAVE YOU HERE.
SIR.
ALINA.
WE HAVE BEEN LIED TO. THIS IS A DECOY.
HE ELDER WS WHERE REAL BOX MAKE HIM ELL YOU.
HEN BURN AT VILLAGE DOWN.
YES, TEACHER.

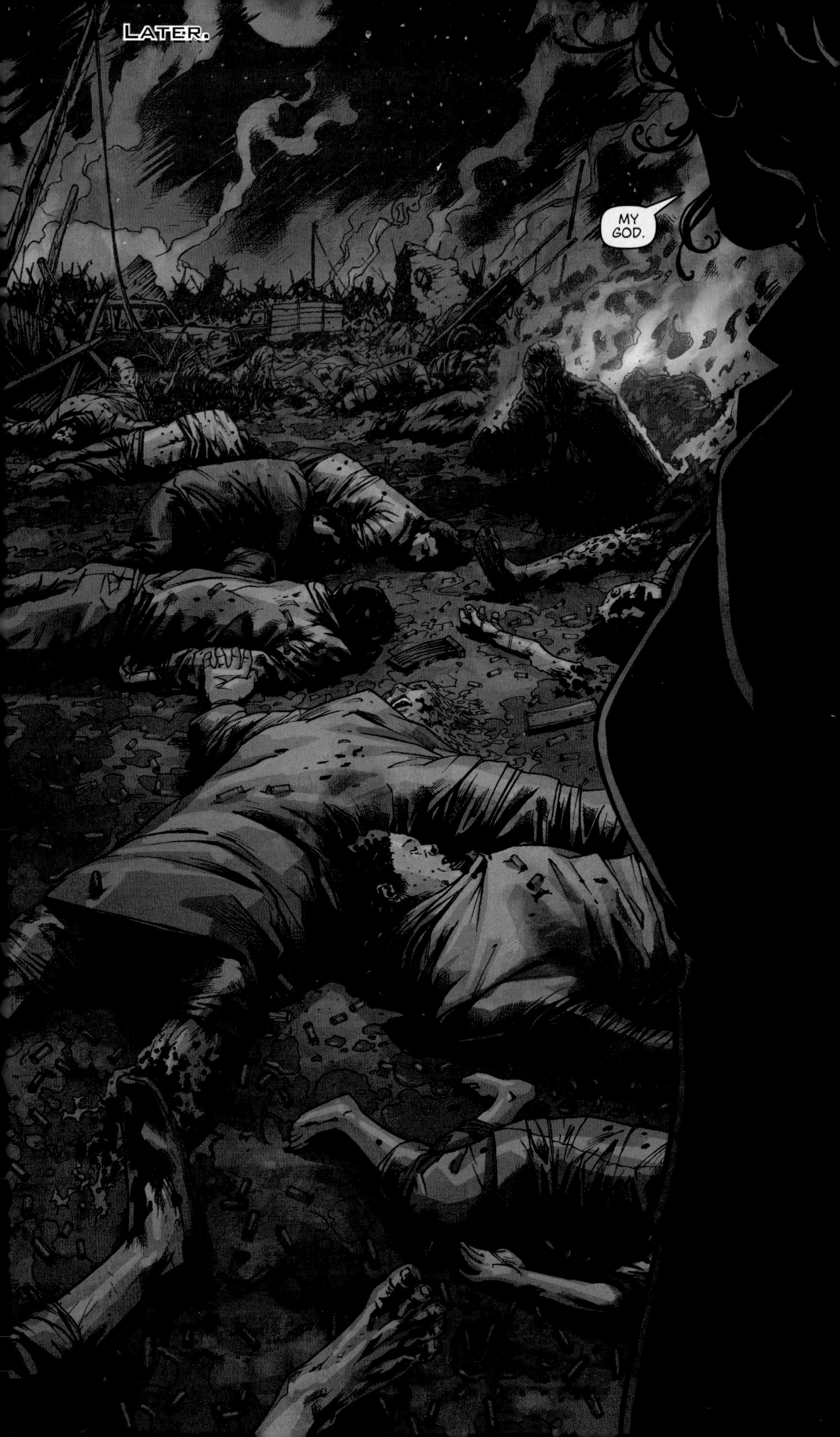
LATER.
MY GOD.

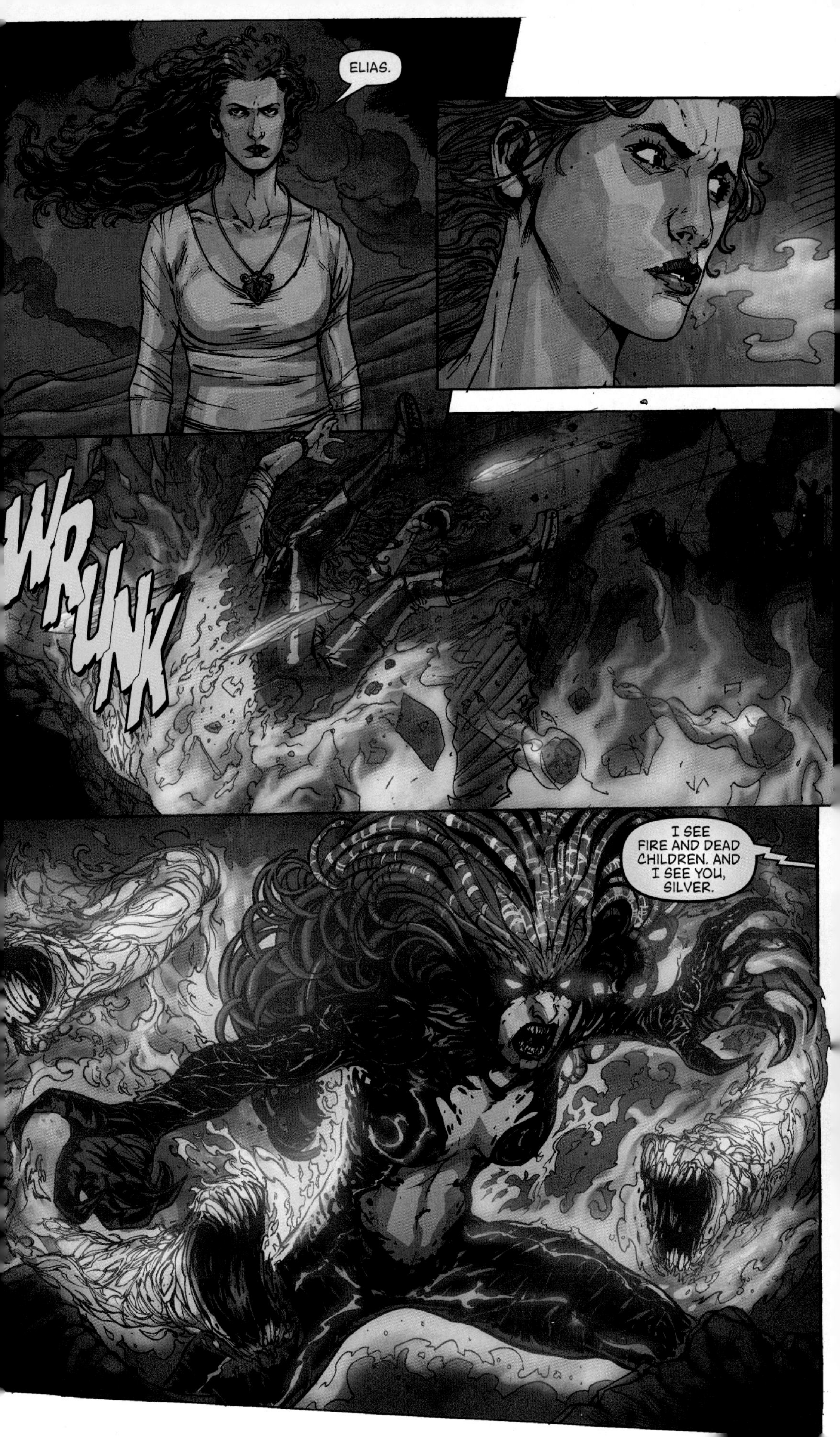
ELIAS.
WRUNK
I SEE FIRE AND DEAD CHILDREN. AND I SEE YOU, SILVER.

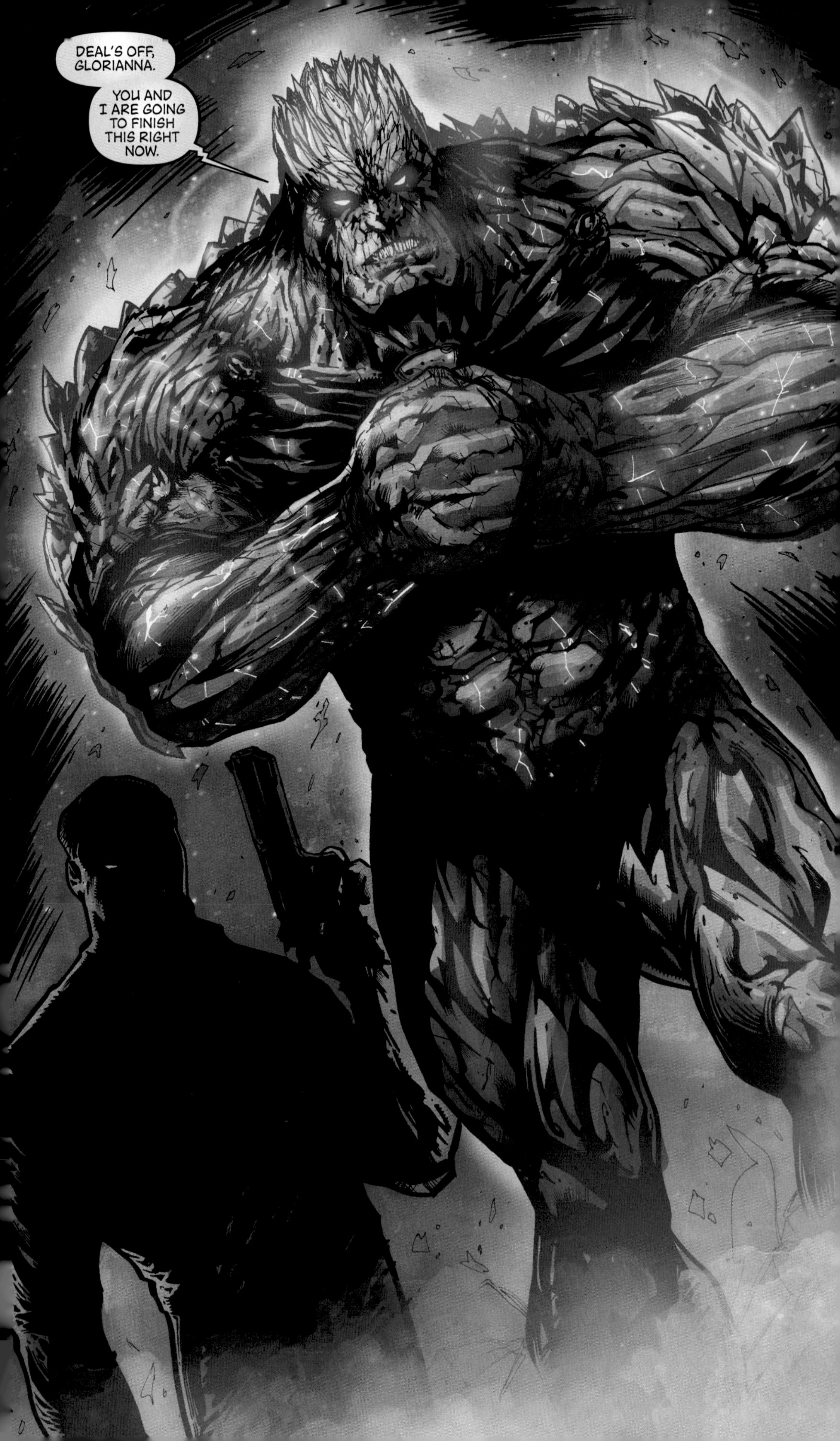
DEAL'S OFF, GLORIANNA.
YOU AND I ARE GOING TO FINISH THIS RIGHT NOW.

BROKEN TRINITY

"PANDORA'S BOX" Part 4

written by: **Bryan Edward Hill & Rob Levin**
art by: **Facundo Percio**
colors by: **Imaginary Friends Studios**
letters by: **Troy Peteri**

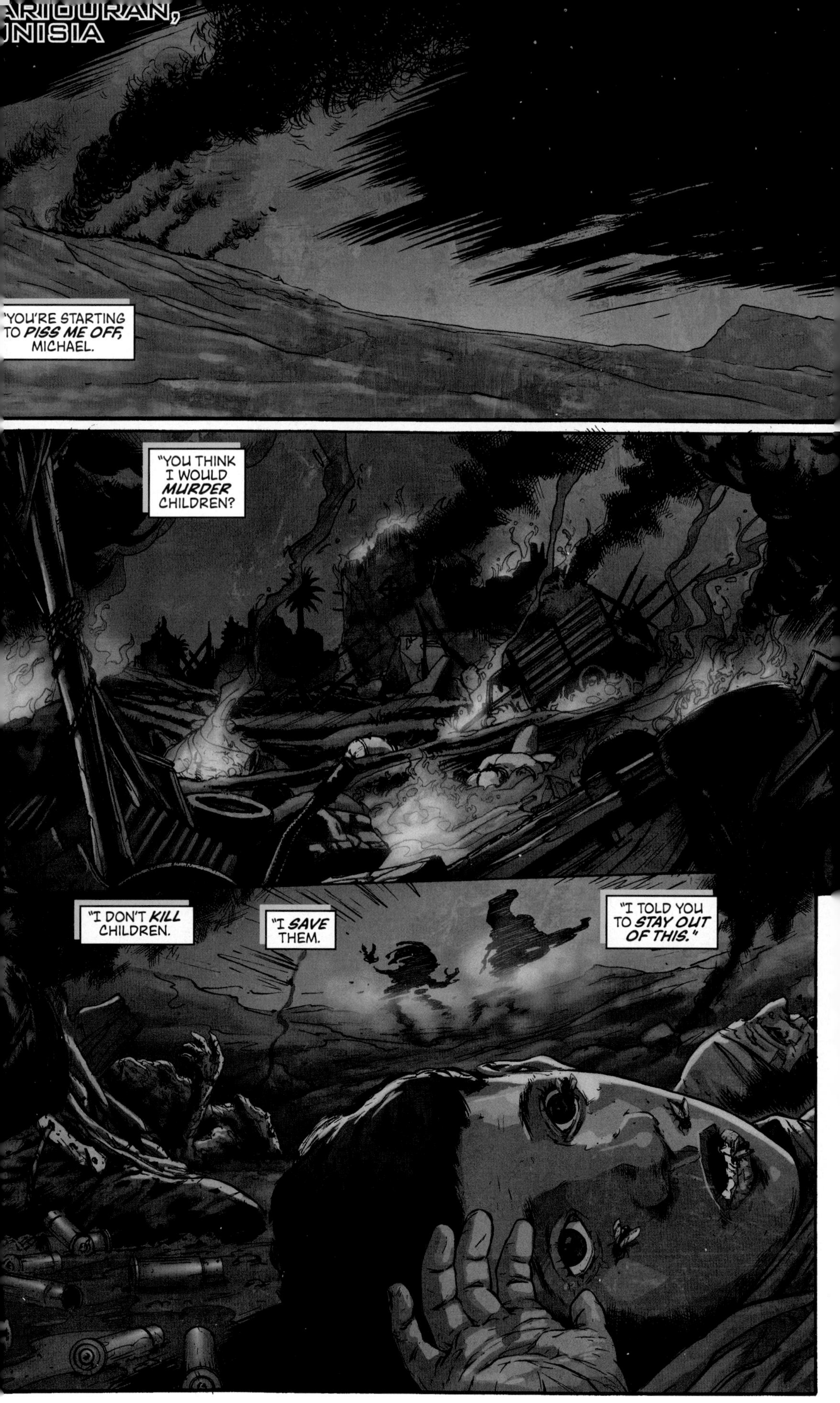
ARIOURAN,
NISIA
"YOU'RE STARTING TO PISS ME OFF, MICHAEL.
"YOU THINK I WOULD MURDER CHILDREN?
"I DON'T KILL CHILDREN.
"I SAVE THEM.
"I TOLD YOU TO STAY OUT OF THIS."

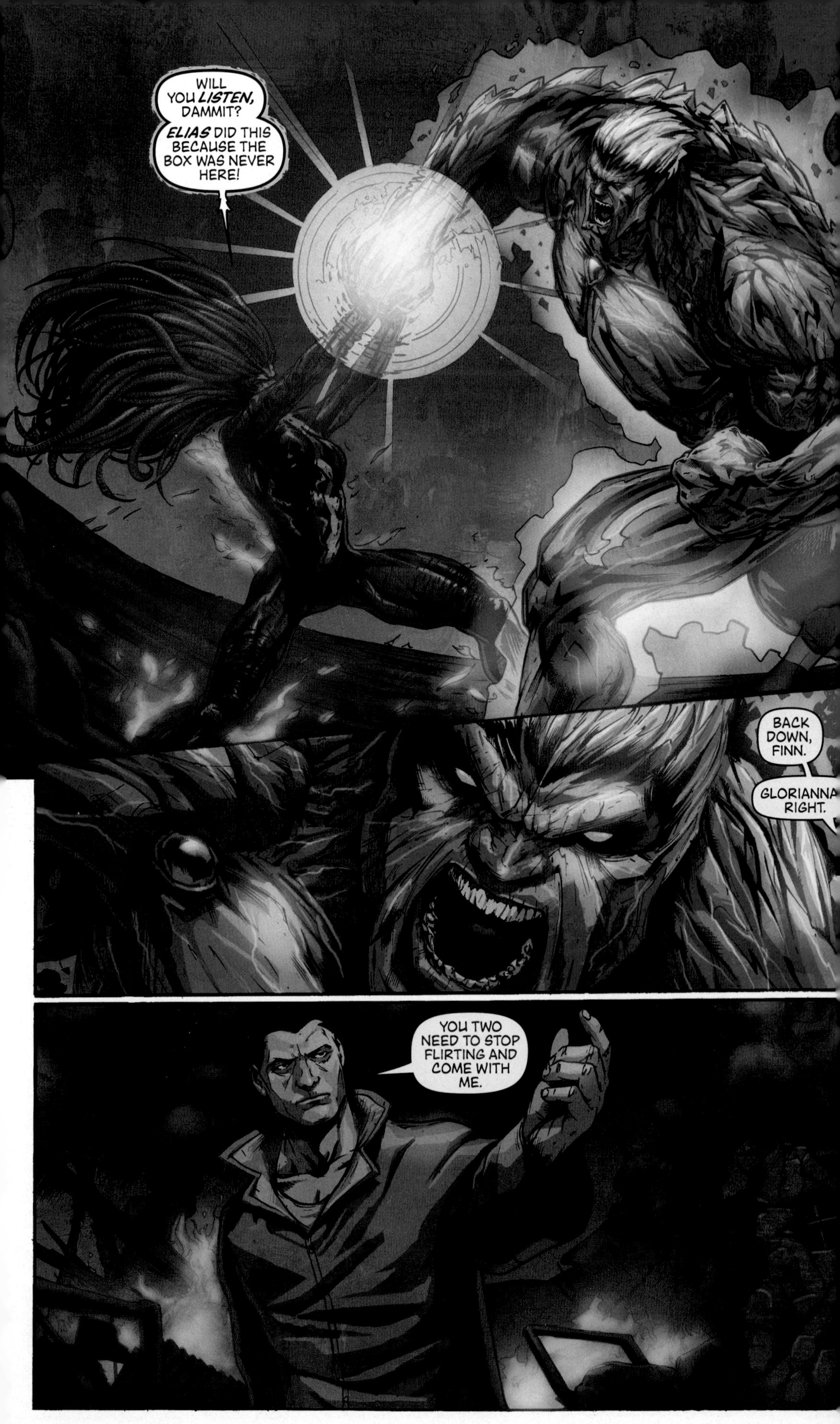
WILL YOU *LISTEN,* DAMMIT?
ELIAS DID THIS BECAUSE THE BOX WAS NEVER HERE!
BACK DOWN, FINN.
GLORIANNA RIGHT.
YOU TWO NEED TO STOP FLIRTING AND COME WITH ME.

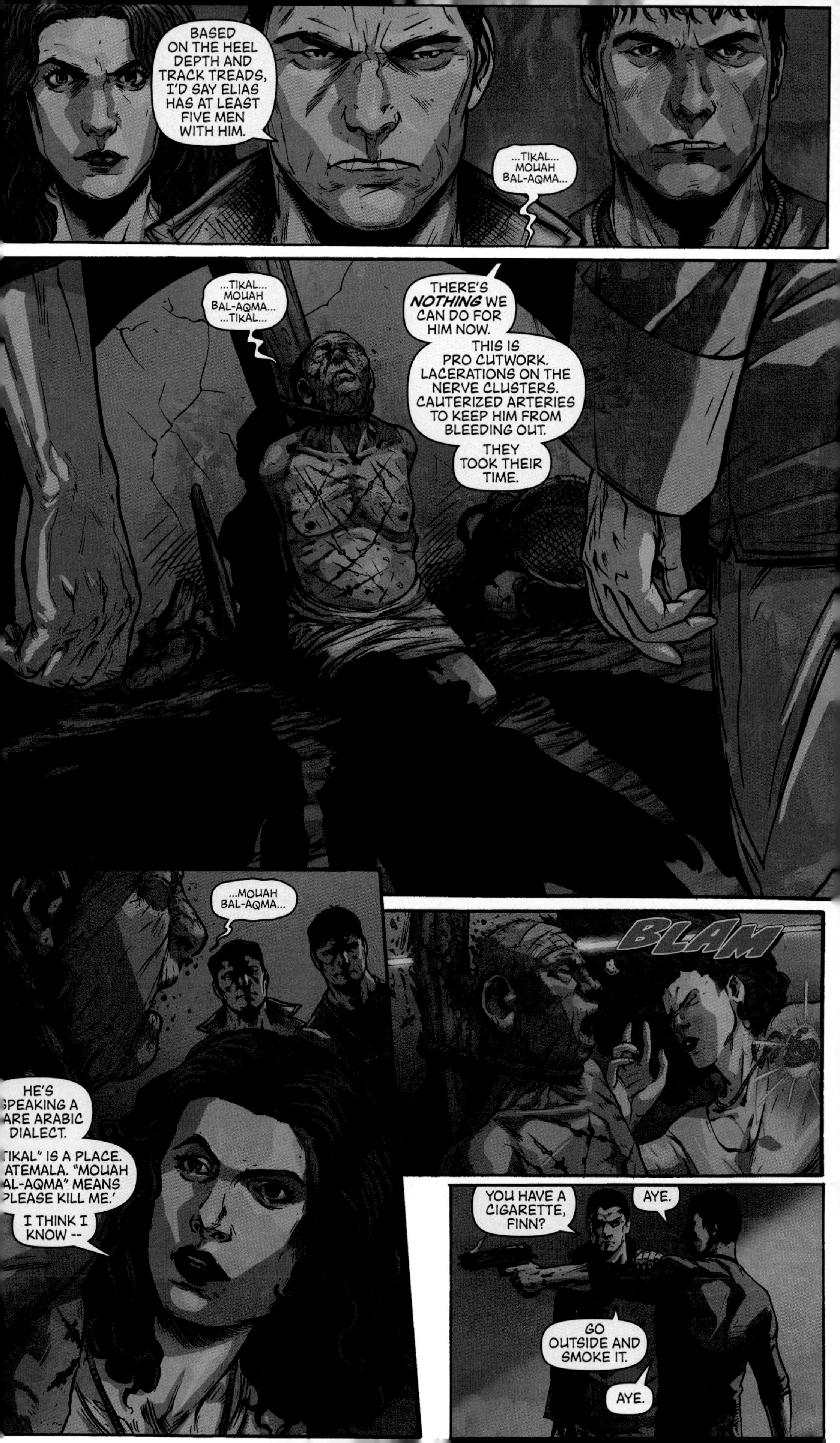
BASED ON THE HEEL DEPTH AND TRACK TREADS, I'D SAY ELIAS HAS AT LEAST FIVE MEN WITH HIM.
...TIKAL... MOUAH BAL-AQMA...
...TIKAL... MOUAH BAL-AQMA... ...TIKAL...
THERE'S *NOTHING* WE CAN DO FOR HIM NOW.
THIS IS PRO CUTWORK. LACERATIONS ON THE NERVE CLUSTERS. CAUTERIZED ARTERIES TO KEEP HIM FROM BLEEDING OUT.
THEY TOOK THEIR TIME.
...MOUAH BAL-AQMA...
HE'S SPEAKING A ARE ARABIC DIALECT.
TIKAL" IS A PLACE. ATEMALA. "MOUAH AL-AQMA" MEANS PLEASE KILL ME.'
I THINK I KNOW --
BLAM
YOU HAVE A CIGARETTE, FINN?
AYE.
GO OUTSIDE AND SMOKE IT.
AYE.

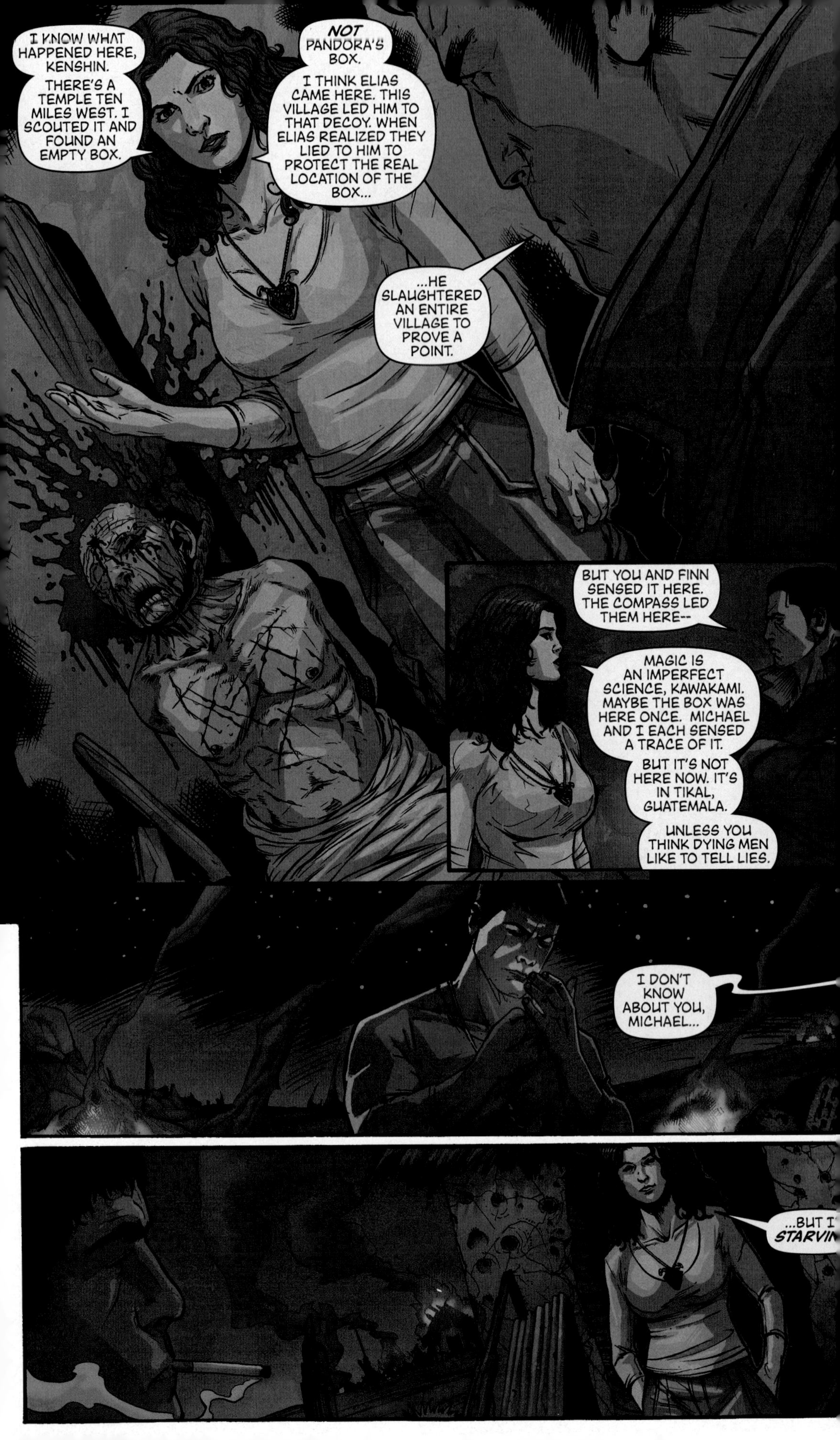
I KNOW WHAT HAPPENED HERE, KENSHIN.
THERE'S A TEMPLE TEN MILES WEST. I SCOUTED IT AND FOUND AN EMPTY BOX.
NOT PANDORA'S BOX.
I THINK ELIAS CAME HERE. THIS VILLAGE LED HIM TO THAT DECOY. WHEN ELIAS REALIZED THEY LIED TO HIM TO PROTECT THE REAL LOCATION OF THE BOX...
...HE SLAUGHTERED AN ENTIRE VILLAGE TO PROVE A POINT.
BUT YOU AND FINN SENSED IT HERE. THE COMPASS LED THEM HERE--
MAGIC IS AN IMPERFECT SCIENCE, KAWAKAMI. MAYBE THE BOX WAS HERE ONCE. MICHAEL AND I EACH SENSED A TRACE OF IT.
BUT IT'S NOT HERE NOW. IT'S IN TIKAL, GUATEMALA.
UNLESS YOU THINK DYING MEN LIKE TO TELL LIES.
I DON'T KNOW ABOUT YOU, MICHAEL...
...BUT I'
STARVIN

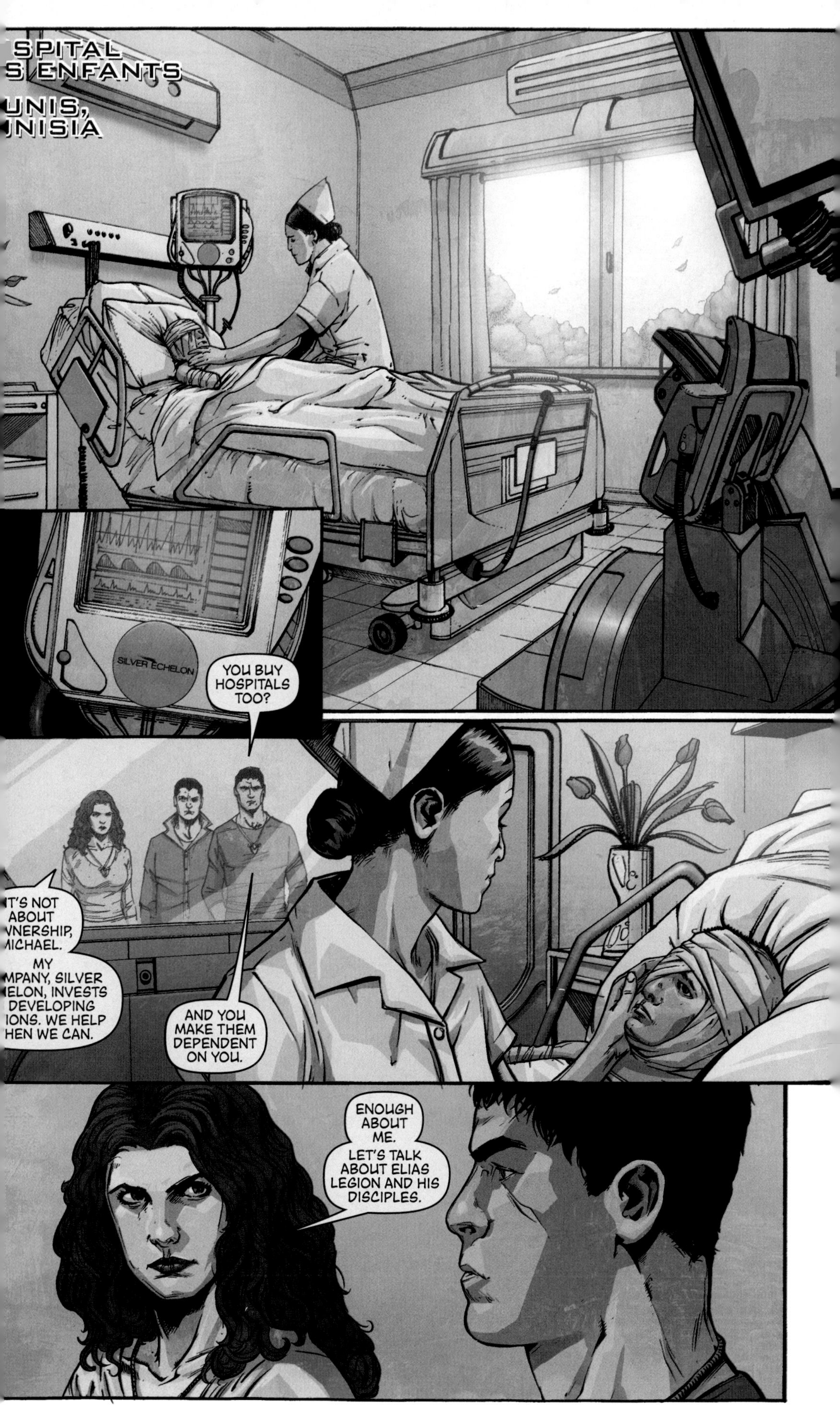

SPITAL
S ENFANTS
UNIS,
NISIA
SILVER ECHELON
YOU BUY HOSPITALS TOO?
T'S NOT ABOUT WNERSHIP, MICHAEL.
MY MPANY, SILVER HELON, INVESTS DEVELOPING IONS. WE HELP HEN WE CAN.
AND YOU MAKE THEM DEPENDENT ON YOU.
ENOUGH ABOUT ME.
LET'S TALK ABOUT ELIAS LEGION AND HIS DISCIPLES.

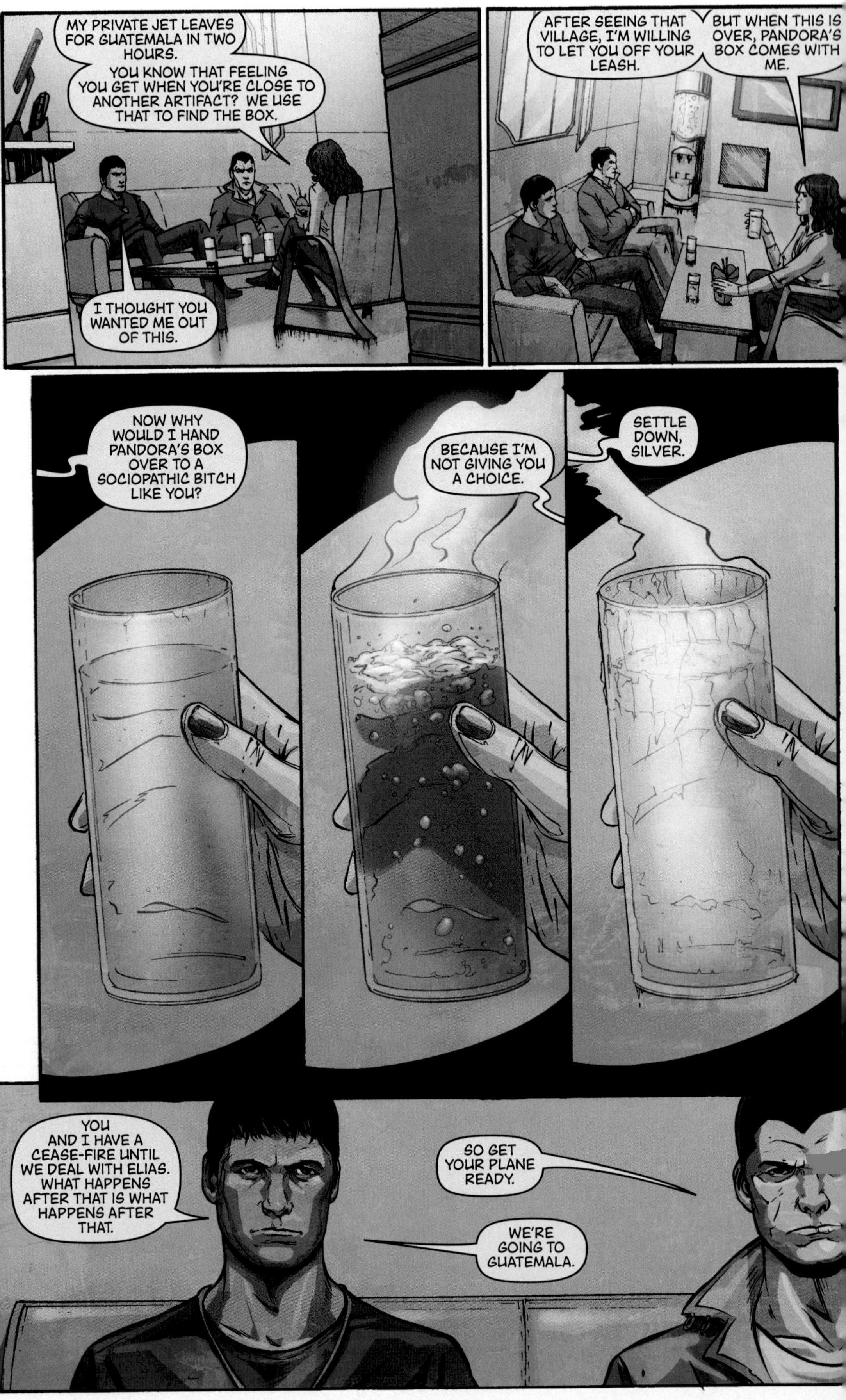
MY PRIVATE JET LEAVES FOR GUATEMALA IN TWO HOURS.
YOU KNOW THAT FEELING YOU GET WHEN YOU'RE CLOSE TO ANOTHER ARTIFACT? WE USE THAT TO FIND THE BOX.
I THOUGHT YOU WANTED ME OUT OF THIS.
AFTER SEEING THAT VILLAGE, I'M WILLING TO LET YOU OFF YOUR LEASH.
BUT WHEN THIS IS OVER, PANDORA'S BOX COMES WITH ME.
NOW WHY WOULD I HAND PANDORA'S BOX OVER TO A SOCIOPATHIC BITCH LIKE YOU?
BECAUSE I'M NOT GIVING YOU A CHOICE.
SETTLE DOWN, SILVER.
YOU AND I HAVE A CEASE-FIRE UNTIL WE DEAL WITH ELIAS. WHAT HAPPENS AFTER THAT IS WHAT HAPPENS AFTER THAT.
SO GET YOUR PLANE READY.
WE'RE GOING TO GUATEMALA.

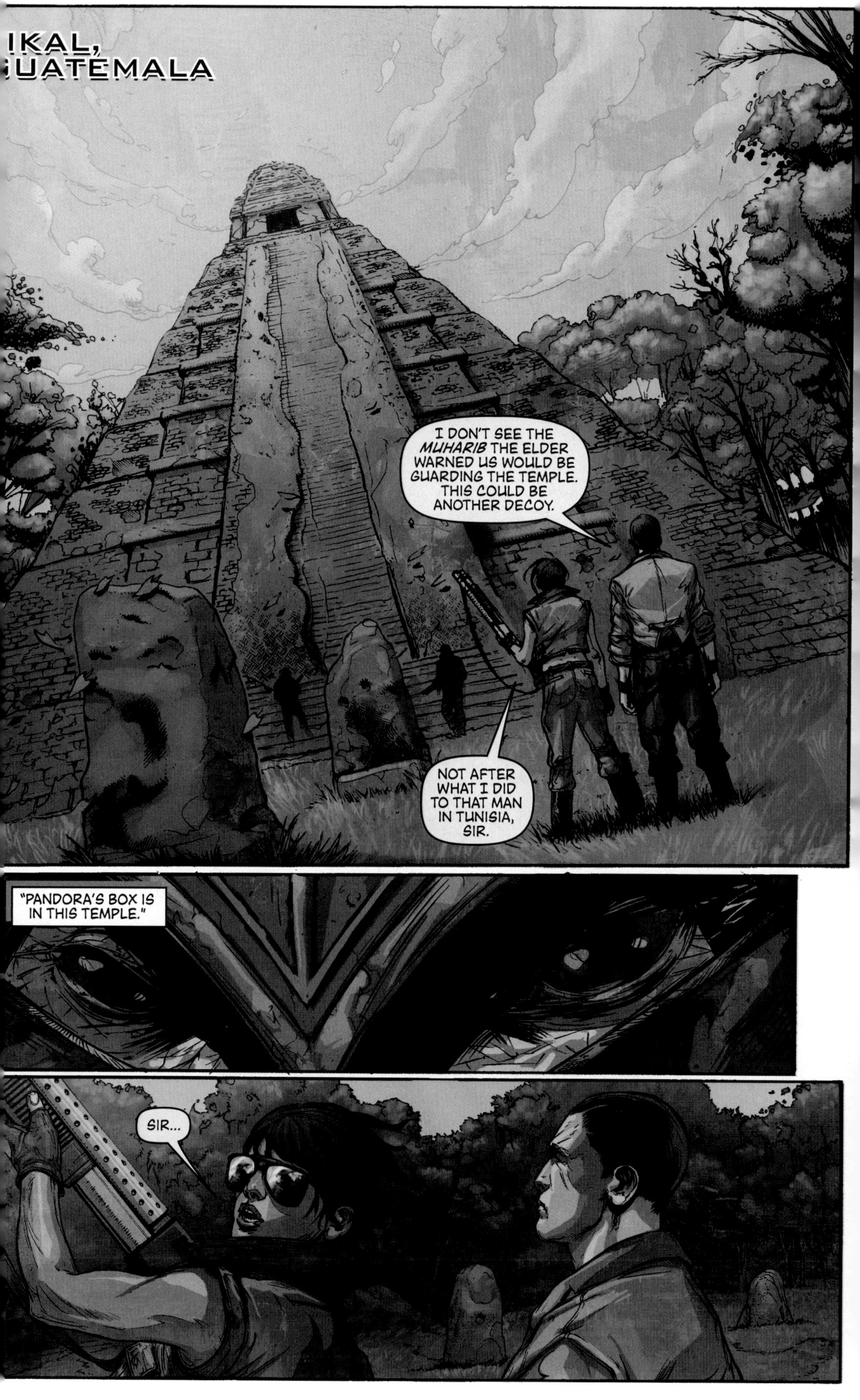
IKAL,
UATEMALA
I DON'T SEE THE *MUHARIB* THE ELDER WARNED US WOULD BE GUARDING THE TEMPLE. THIS COULD BE ANOTHER DECOY.
NOT AFTER WHAT I DID TO THAT MAN IN TUNISIA, SIR.
"PANDORA'S BOX IS IN THIS TEMPLE."
SIR...

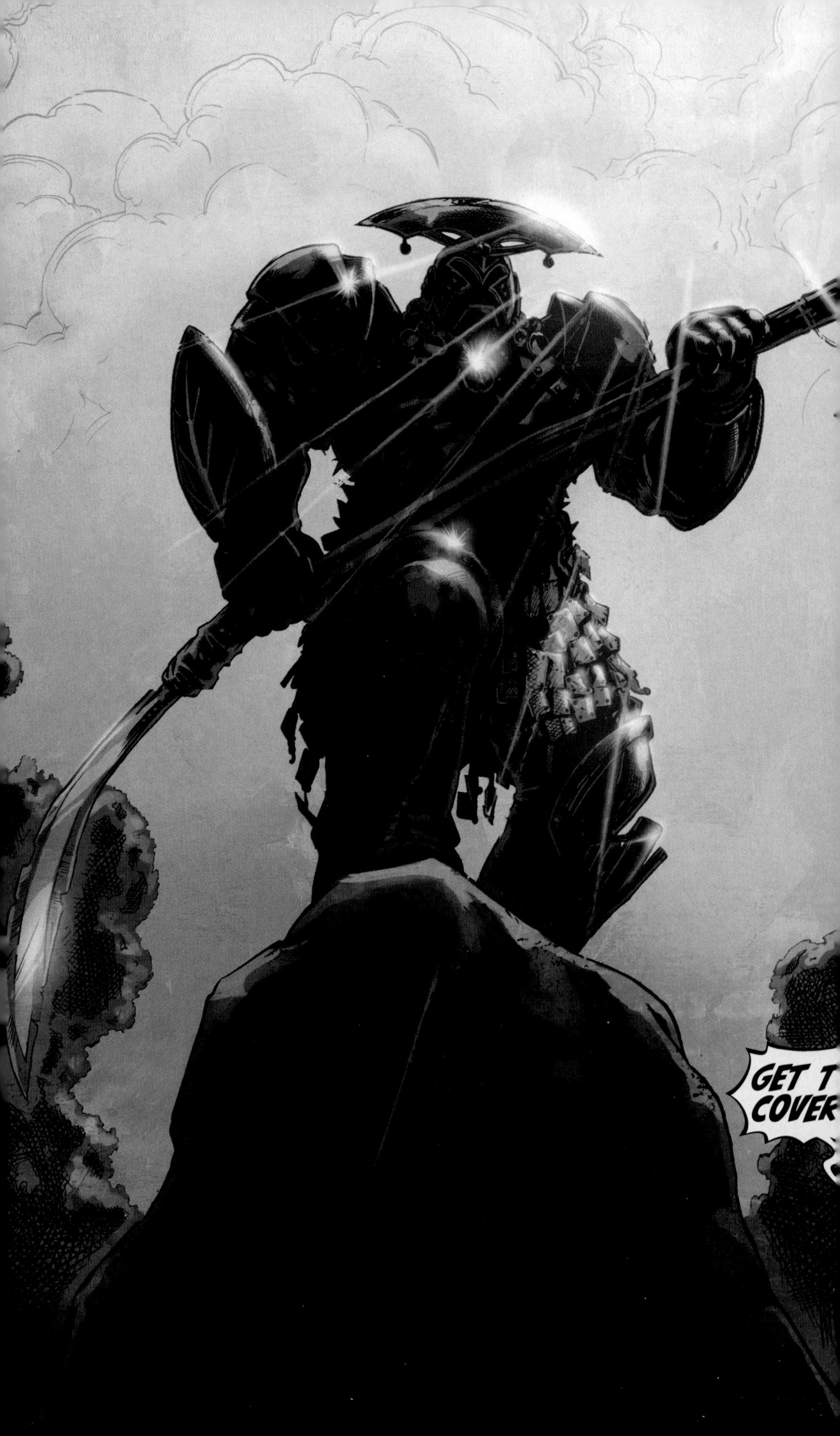
GET T
COVER

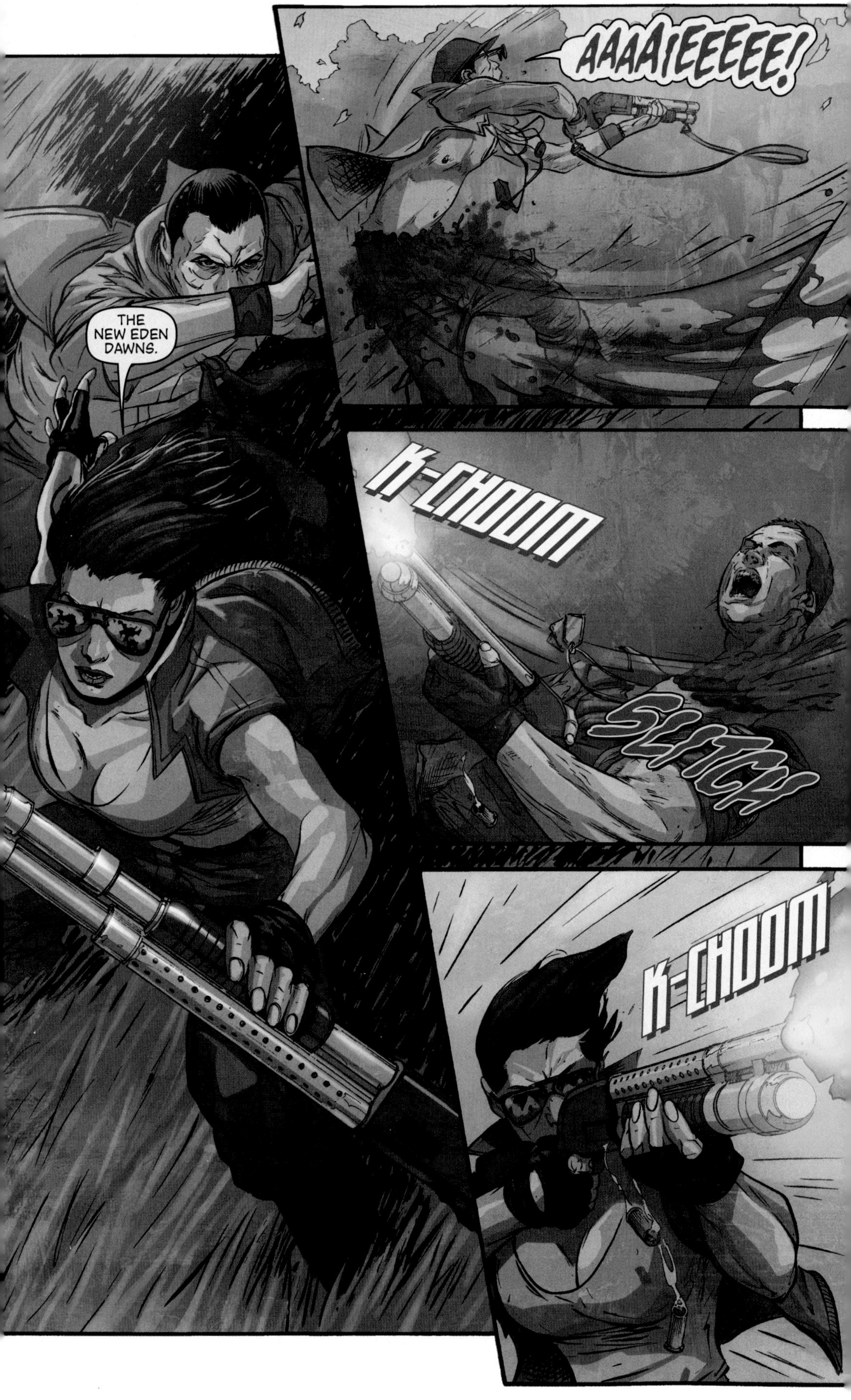
THE NEW EDEN DAWNS.
AAAAIEEEEE!
K-CHOOM
SLITCH
K-CHOOM

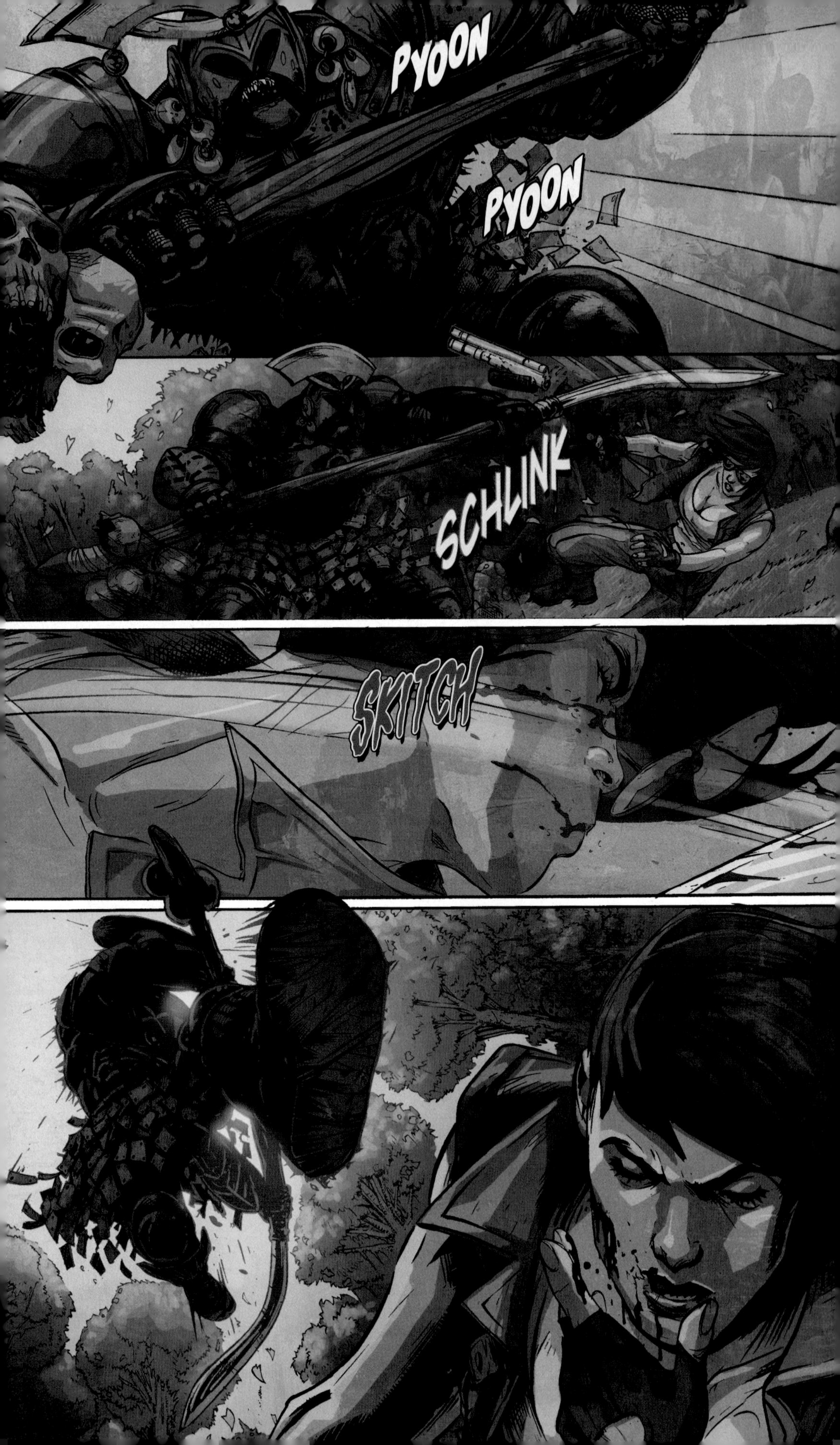
PYOON
PYOON
SCHLINK
SKITCH

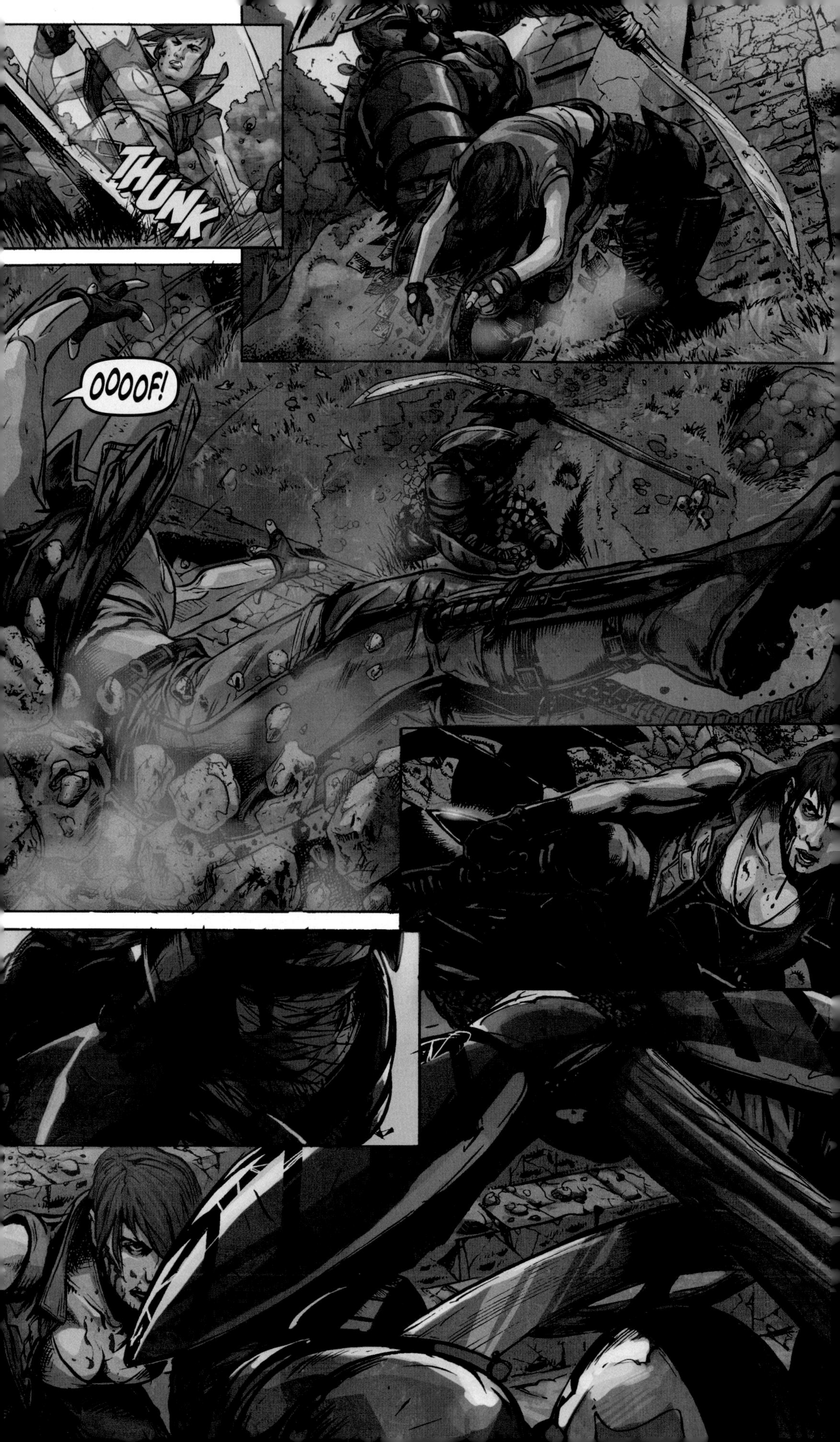
THUNK
OOOOF!

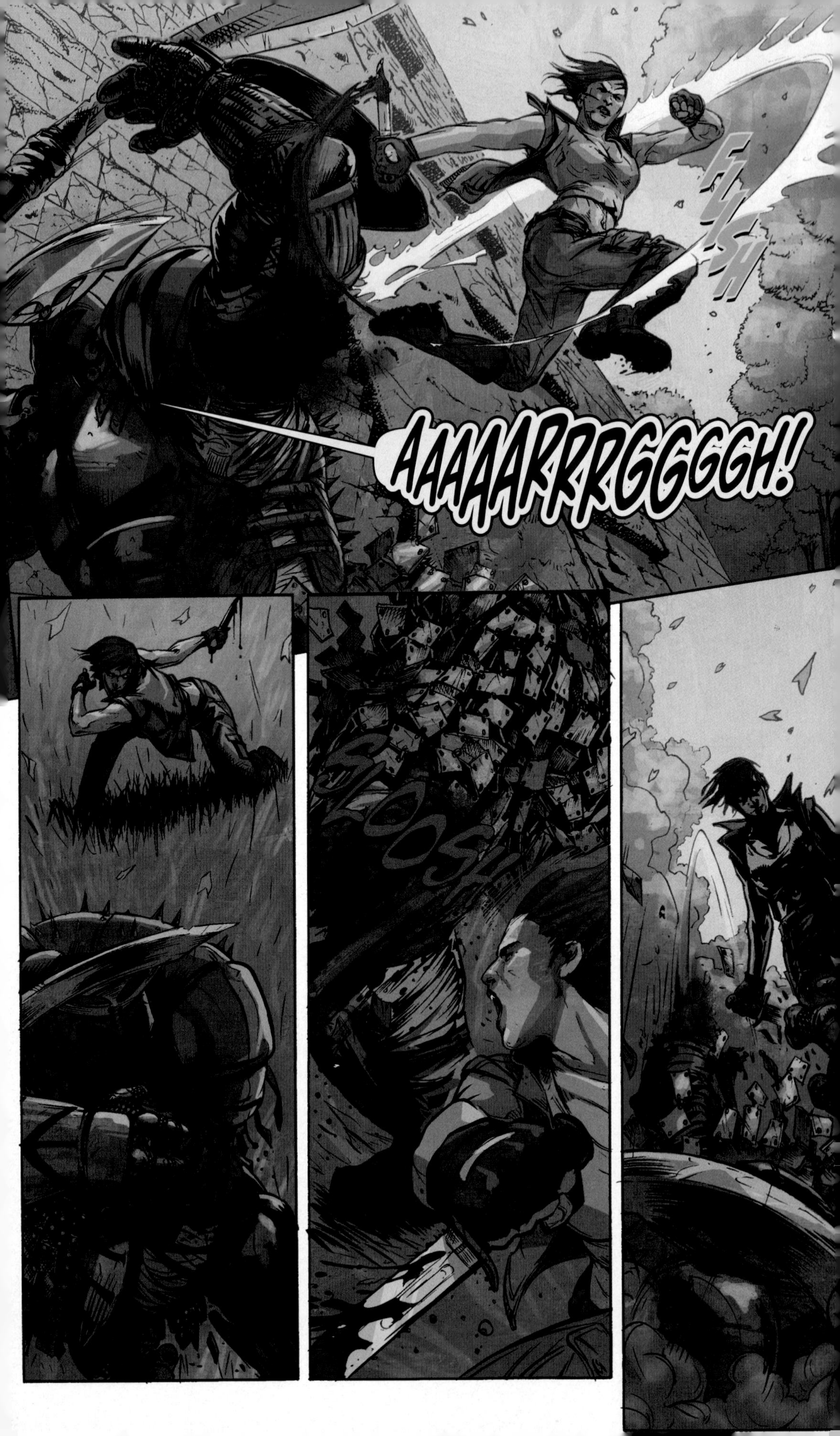
AAAAARRRGGGGH!
SHOOSH!

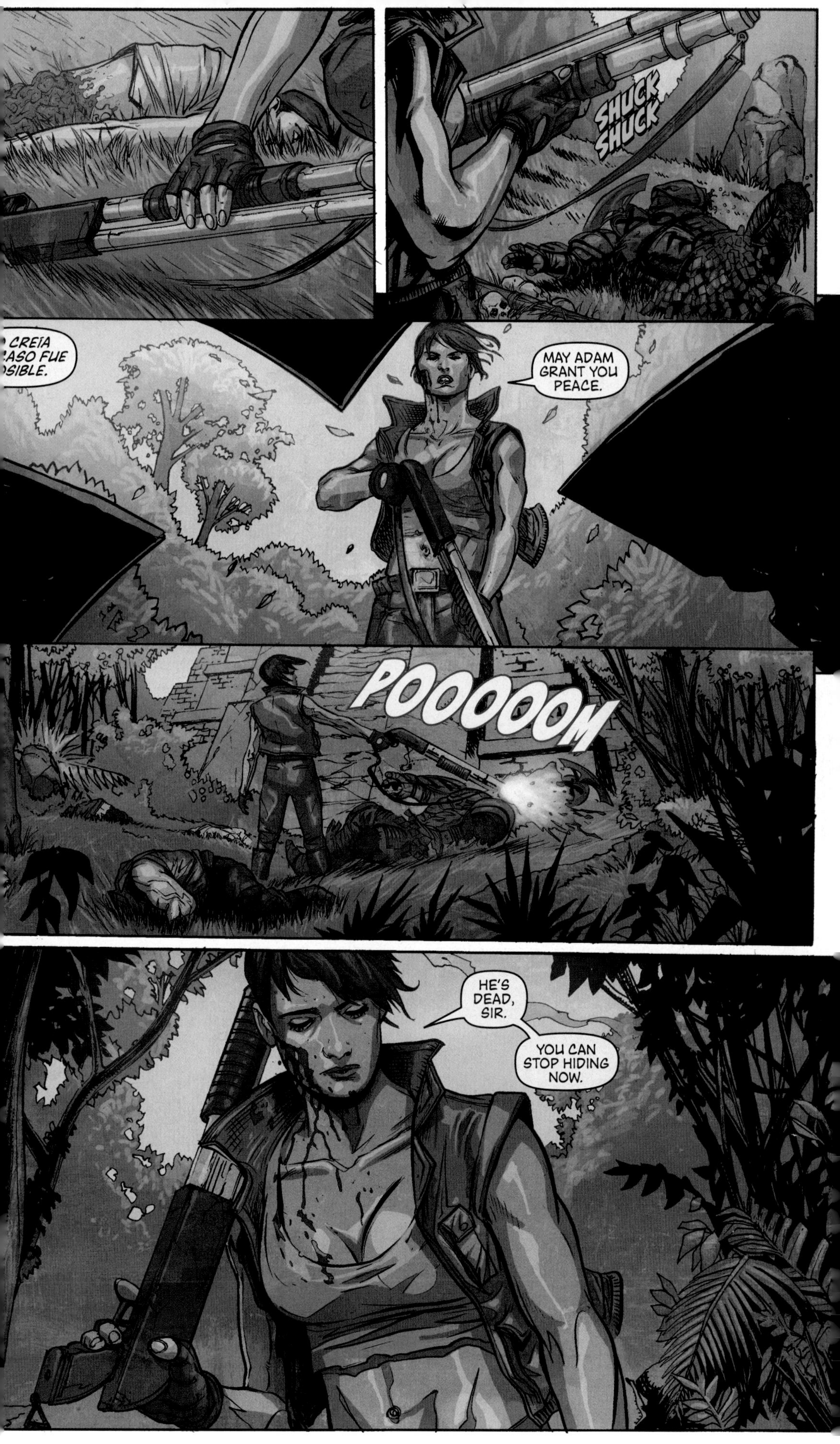
SHUCK SHUCK
CREÍA CASO FUE SIBLE.
MAY ADAM GRANT YOU PEACE.
POOOOOM
HE'S DEAD, SIR.
YOU CAN STOP HIDING NOW.

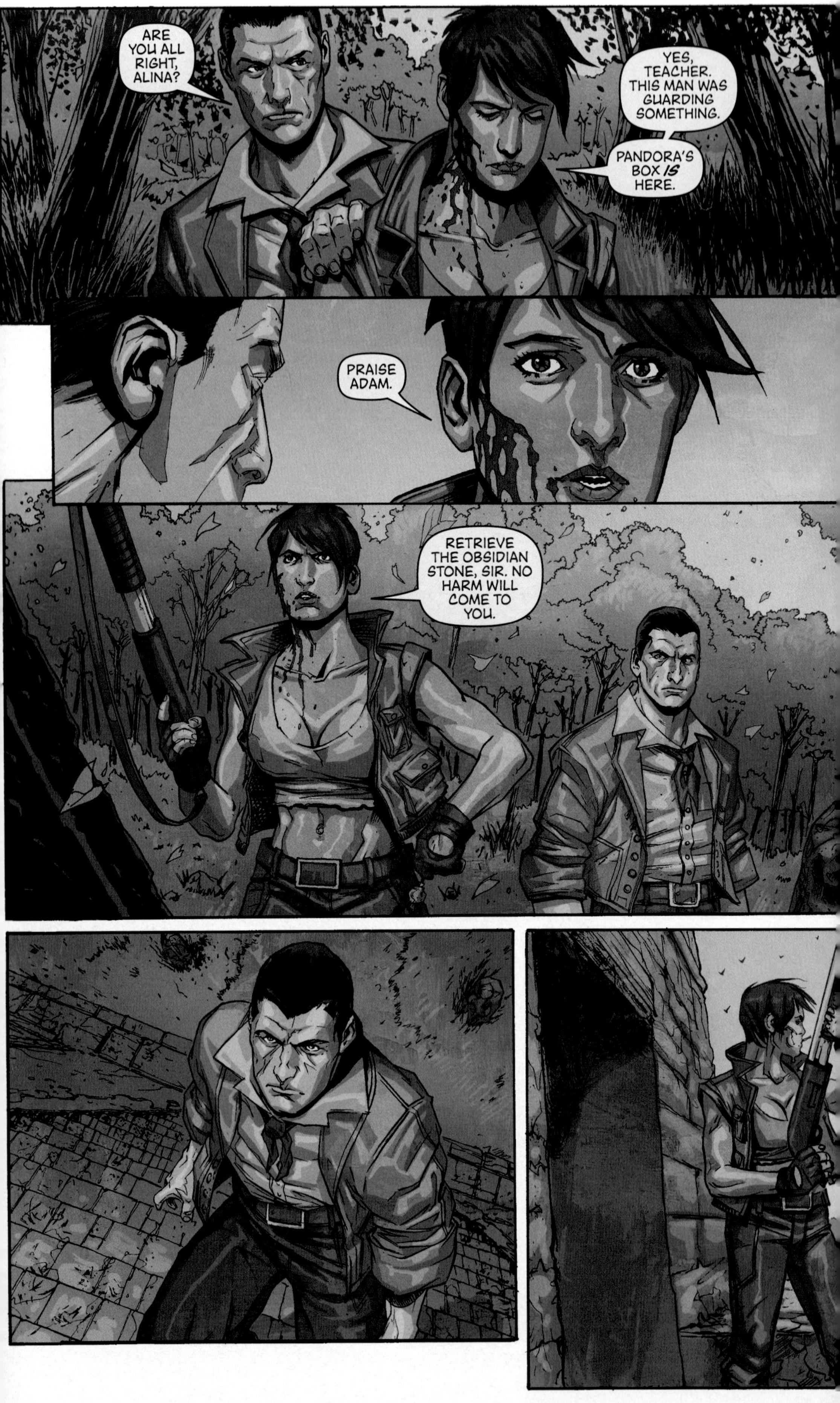
ARE YOU ALL RIGHT, ALINA?
YES, TEACHER. THIS MAN WAS GUARDING SOMETHING.
PANDORA'S BOX *IS* HERE.
PRAISE ADAM.
RETRIEVE THE OBSIDIAN STONE, SIR. NO HARM WILL COME TO YOU.

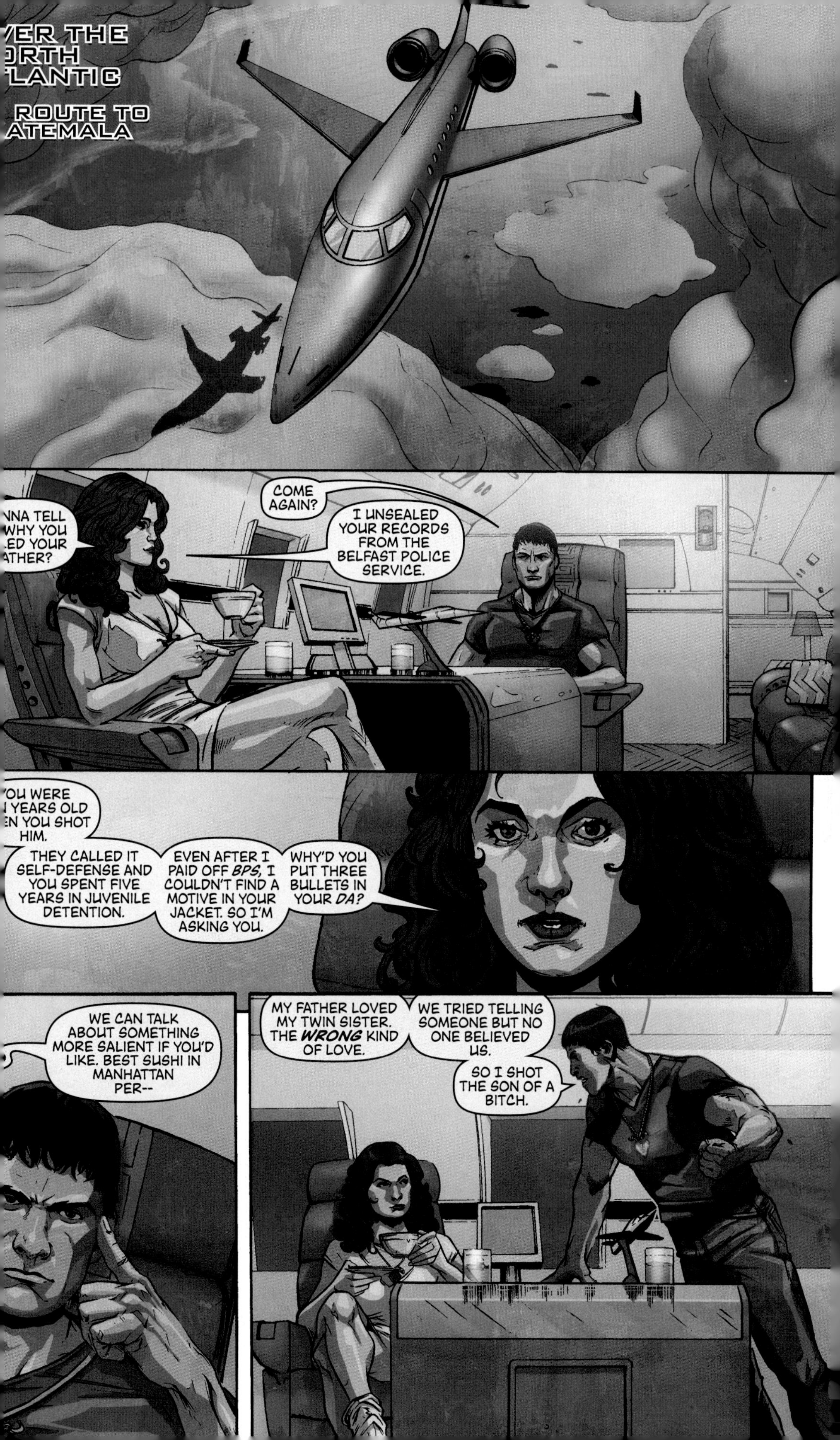

VER THE
ORTH
LANTIC
ROUTE TO
ATEMALA
NNA TELL
WHY YOU
ED YOUR
ATHER?
COME AGAIN?
I UNSEALED YOUR RECORDS FROM THE BELFAST POLICE SERVICE.
OU WERE
YEARS OLD
EN YOU SHOT
HIM.
THEY CALLED IT SELF-DEFENSE AND YOU SPENT FIVE YEARS IN JUVENILE DETENTION.
EVEN AFTER I PAID OFF BPS, I COULDN'T FIND A MOTIVE IN YOUR JACKET. SO I'M ASKING YOU.
WHY'D YOU PUT THREE BULLETS IN YOUR DA?
WE CAN TALK ABOUT SOMETHING MORE SALIENT IF YOU'D LIKE. BEST SUSHI IN MANHATTAN PER--
MY FATHER LOVED MY TWIN SISTER. THE WRONG KIND OF LOVE.
WE TRIED TELLING SOMEONE BUT NO ONE BELIEVED US.
SO I SHOT THE SON OF A BITCH.

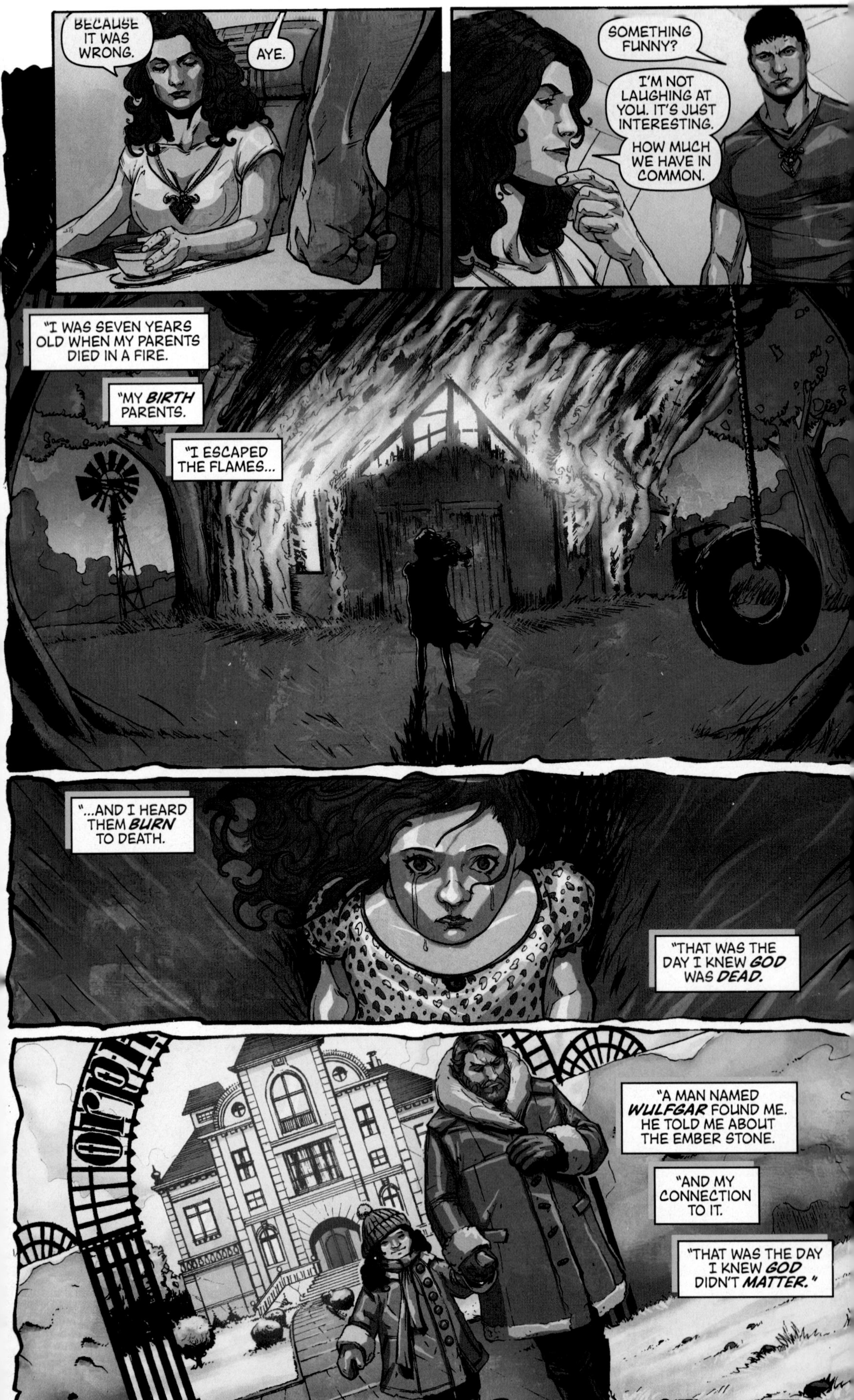
BECAUSE IT WAS WRONG.
AYE.
SOMETHING FUNNY?
I'M NOT LAUGHING AT YOU. IT'S JUST INTERESTING.
HOW MUCH WE HAVE IN COMMON.
"I WAS SEVEN YEARS OLD WHEN MY PARENTS DIED IN A FIRE.
"MY BIRTH PARENTS.
"I ESCAPED THE FLAMES...
"...AND I HEARD THEM BURN TO DEATH.
"THAT WAS THE DAY I KNEW GOD WAS DEAD.
"A MAN NAMED WULFGAR FOUND ME. HE TOLD ME ABOUT THE EMBER STONE.
"AND MY CONNECTION TO IT.
"THAT WAS THE DAY I KNEW GOD DIDN'T MATTER."

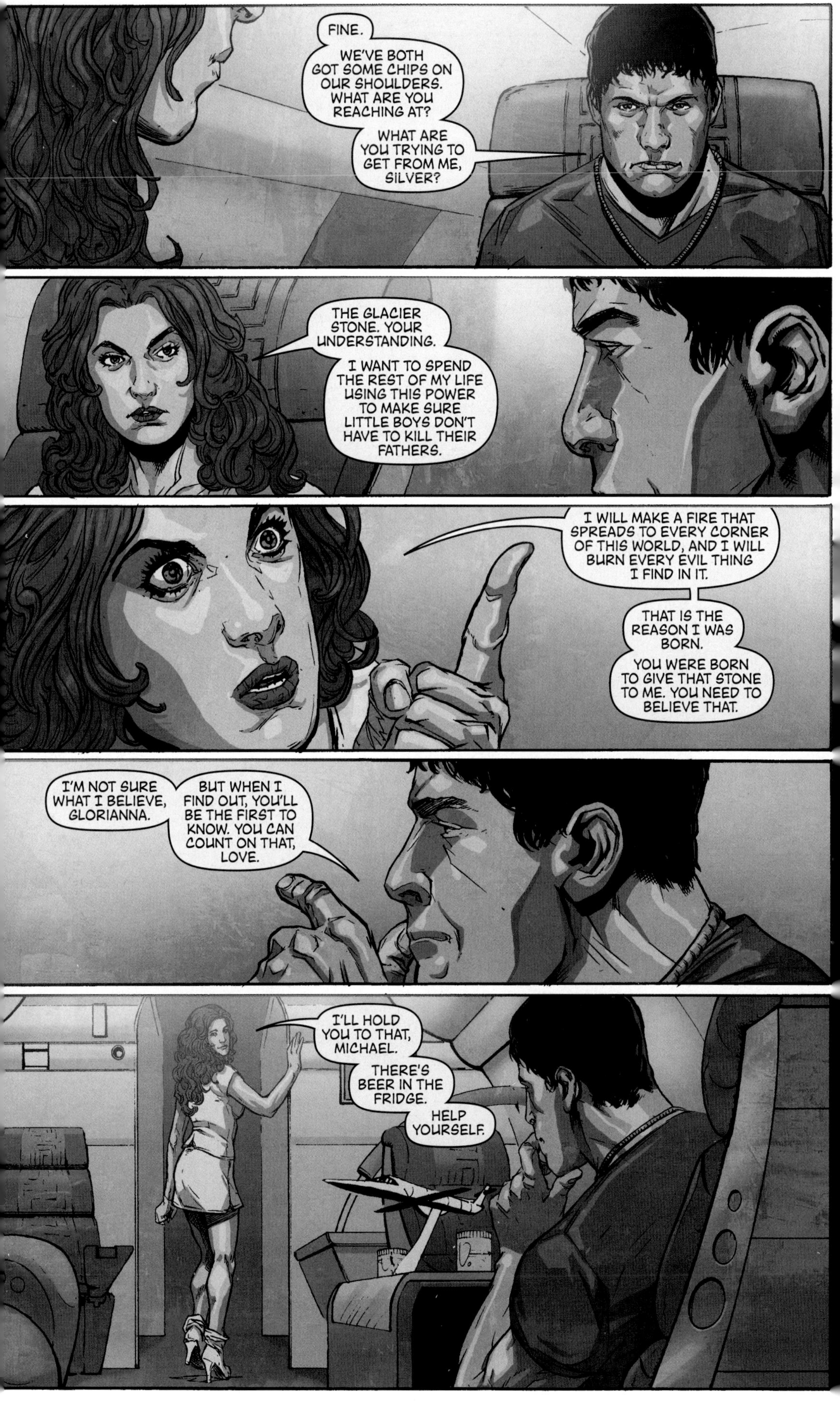
FINE.
WE'VE BOTH GOT SOME CHIPS ON OUR SHOULDERS. WHAT ARE YOU REACHING AT?
WHAT ARE YOU TRYING TO GET FROM ME, SILVER?
THE GLACIER STONE. YOUR UNDERSTANDING.
I WANT TO SPEND THE REST OF MY LIFE USING THIS POWER TO MAKE SURE LITTLE BOYS DON'T HAVE TO KILL THEIR FATHERS.
I WILL MAKE A FIRE THAT SPREADS TO EVERY CORNER OF THIS WORLD, AND I WILL BURN EVERY EVIL THING I FIND IN IT.
THAT IS THE REASON I WAS BORN.
YOU WERE BORN TO GIVE THAT STONE TO ME. YOU NEED TO BELIEVE THAT.
I'M NOT SURE WHAT I BELIEVE, GLORIANNA.
BUT WHEN I FIND OUT, YOU'LL BE THE FIRST TO KNOW. YOU CAN COUNT ON THAT, LOVE.
I'LL HOLD YOU TO THAT, MICHAEL.
THERE'S BEER IN THE FRIDGE.
HELP YOURSELF.

SHOULDN'T YOU BE MEDITATIN' OR SOMETHING?

DO YOU HAVE ANY IDEA HOW LONG IT'S BEEN SINCE I'VE PLAYED A VIDEO GAME?

THIS IS A *NICE PLANE*, FINN.

KENSHIN. SHE'S GETTING TO ME A BIT.

PRETTY GIRLS CAN DO THAT.

IN JAPAN, SHE OFFERED ME TEN MILLION DOLLARS FOR THIS STONE.

AND I TOLD HER I'D TAKE IT.

GLORI MIGHT BE A NUTTER, BUT SHE'S NOT THE BLOODY DEVIL. IF ESTACADO CAN BE WHAT HE IS, THEN THE WORLD'S GOT NOTHING TO FEAR FROM HER.

WE'RE ABOUT TO HAVE A MOMENT, AREN'T WE.

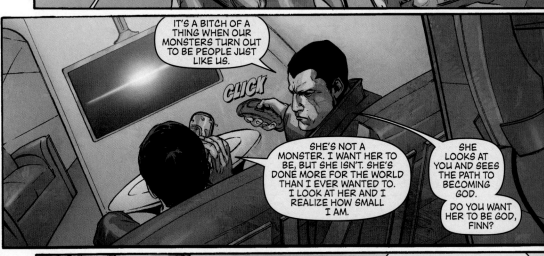

IT'S A BITCH OF A THING WHEN OUR MONSTERS TURN OUT TO BE PEOPLE JUST LIKE US.

CLICK

SHE'S NOT A MONSTER. I WANT HER TO BE, BUT SHE ISN'T. SHE'S DONE MORE FOR THE WORLD THAN I EVER WANTED TO. I LOOK AT HER AND I REALIZE HOW SMALL I AM.

SHE LOOKS AT YOU AND SEES THE PATH TO BECOMING GOD.

DO YOU WANT HER TO BE GOD, FINN?

GOD'S A PAINTING ON MY MOTHER'S WALL THAT I NEVER SAW DO A FECKIN' THING.

GLORI SILVER THINKS SHE CAN DO BETTER THAN THAT.

I MIGHT BE WILLING TO LET HER TRY.

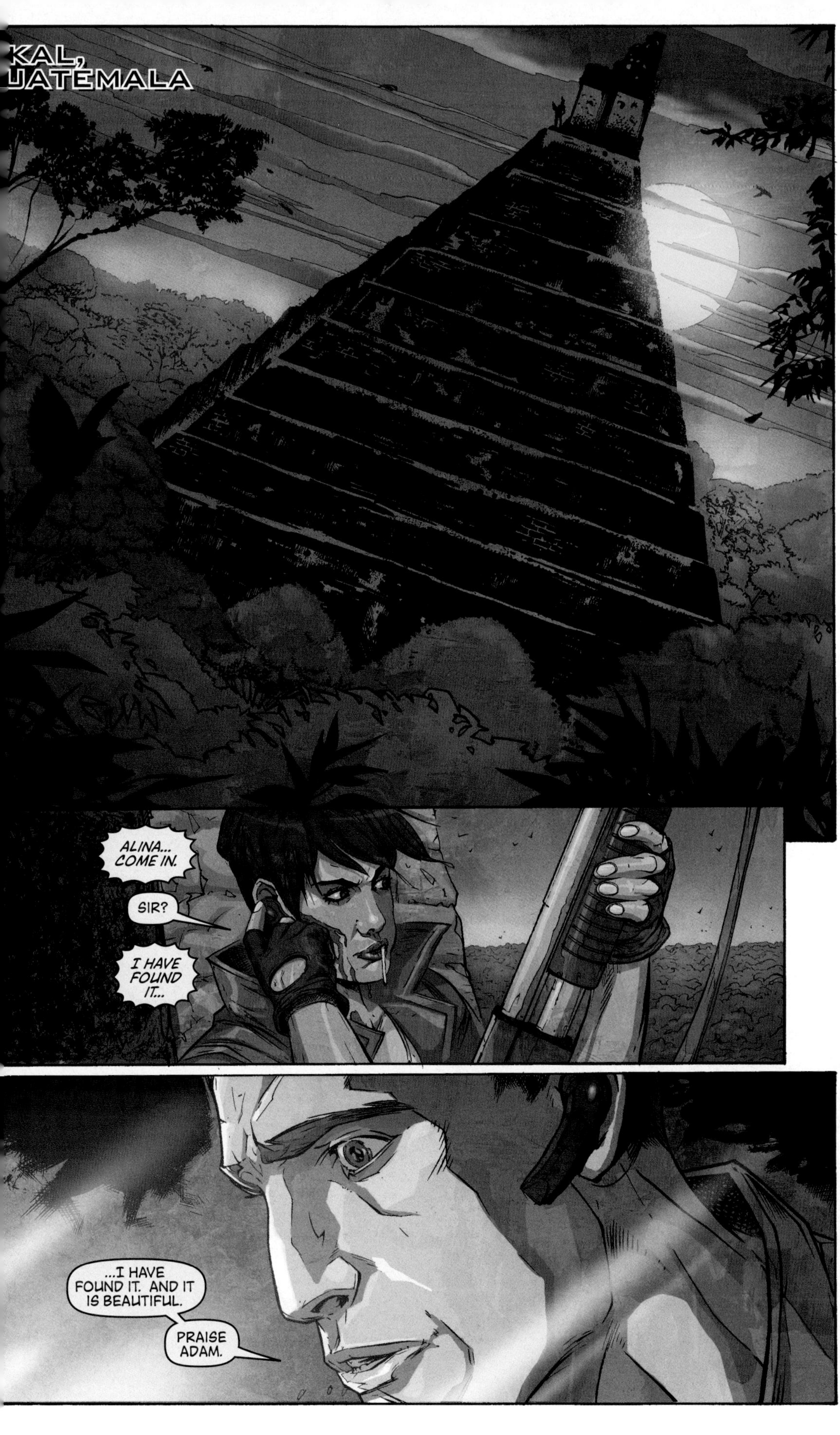

KAL,
UATEMALA
ALINA... COME IN.
SIR?
I HAVE FOUND IT...
...I HAVE FOUND IT. AND IT IS BEAUTIFUL.
PRAISE ADAM.

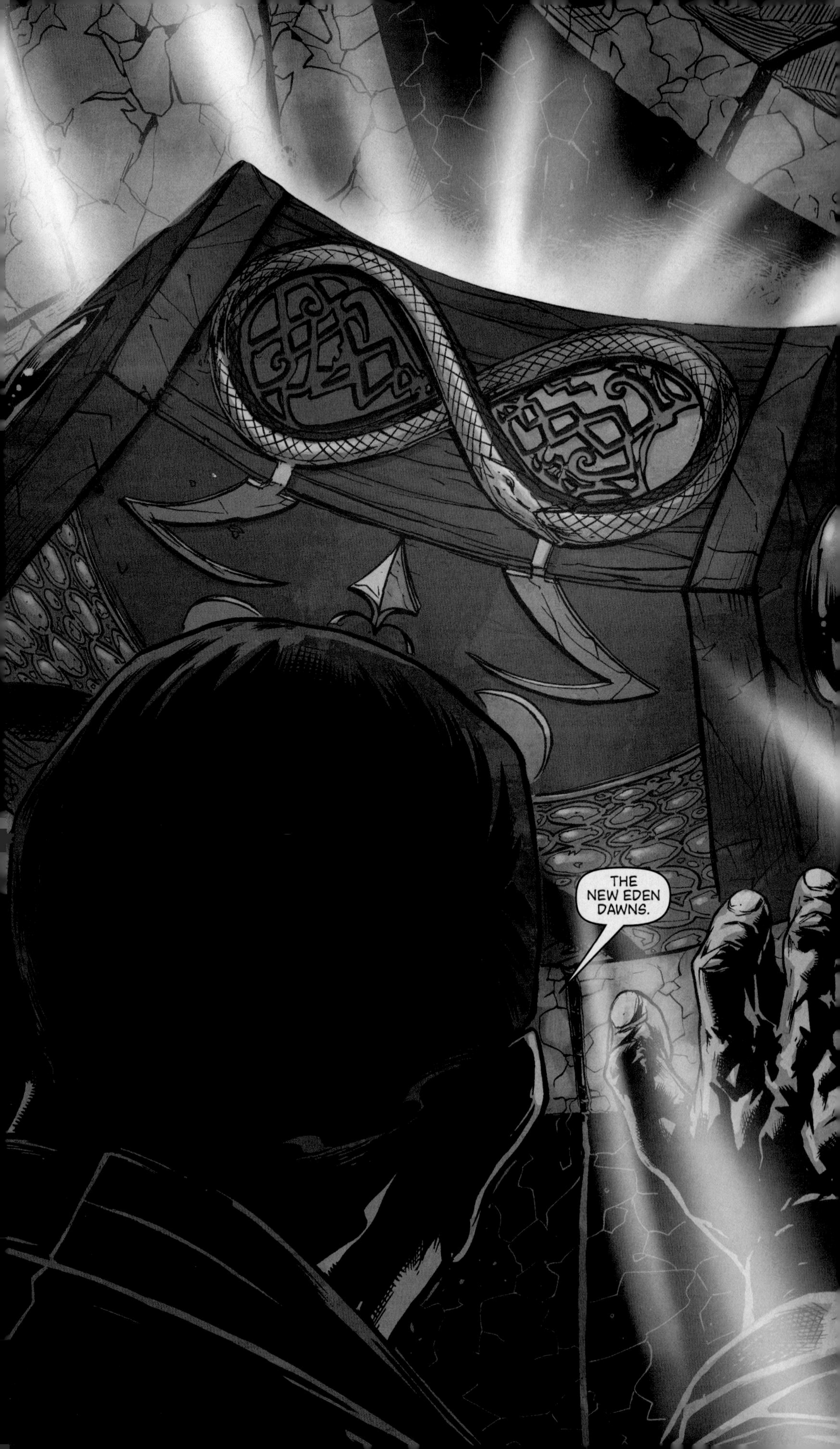
THE NEW EDEN DAWNS.

BROKEN TRINITY

"PANDORA'S BOX" Part 5

{
written by: **Bryan Edward Hill & Rob Levin**
art by: **Facundo Percio**
colors by: **Imaginary Friends Studios**
letters by: **Troy Peteri**
}

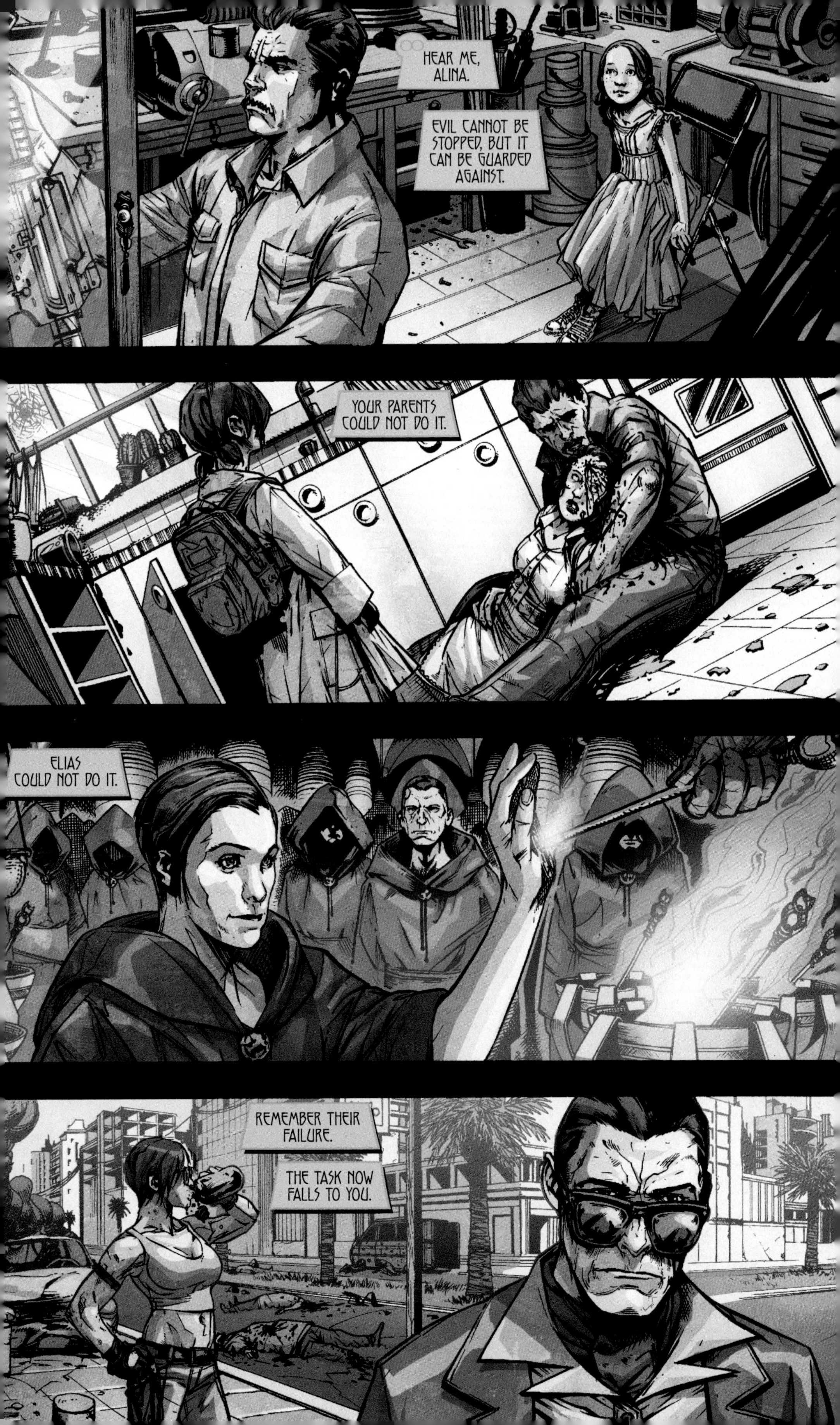
HEAR ME, ALINA.
EVIL CANNOT BE STOPPED, BUT IT CAN BE GUARDED AGAINST.
YOUR PARENTS COULD NOT DO IT.
ELIAS COULD NOT DO IT.
REMEMBER THEIR FAILURE.
THE TASK NOW FALLS TO YOU.

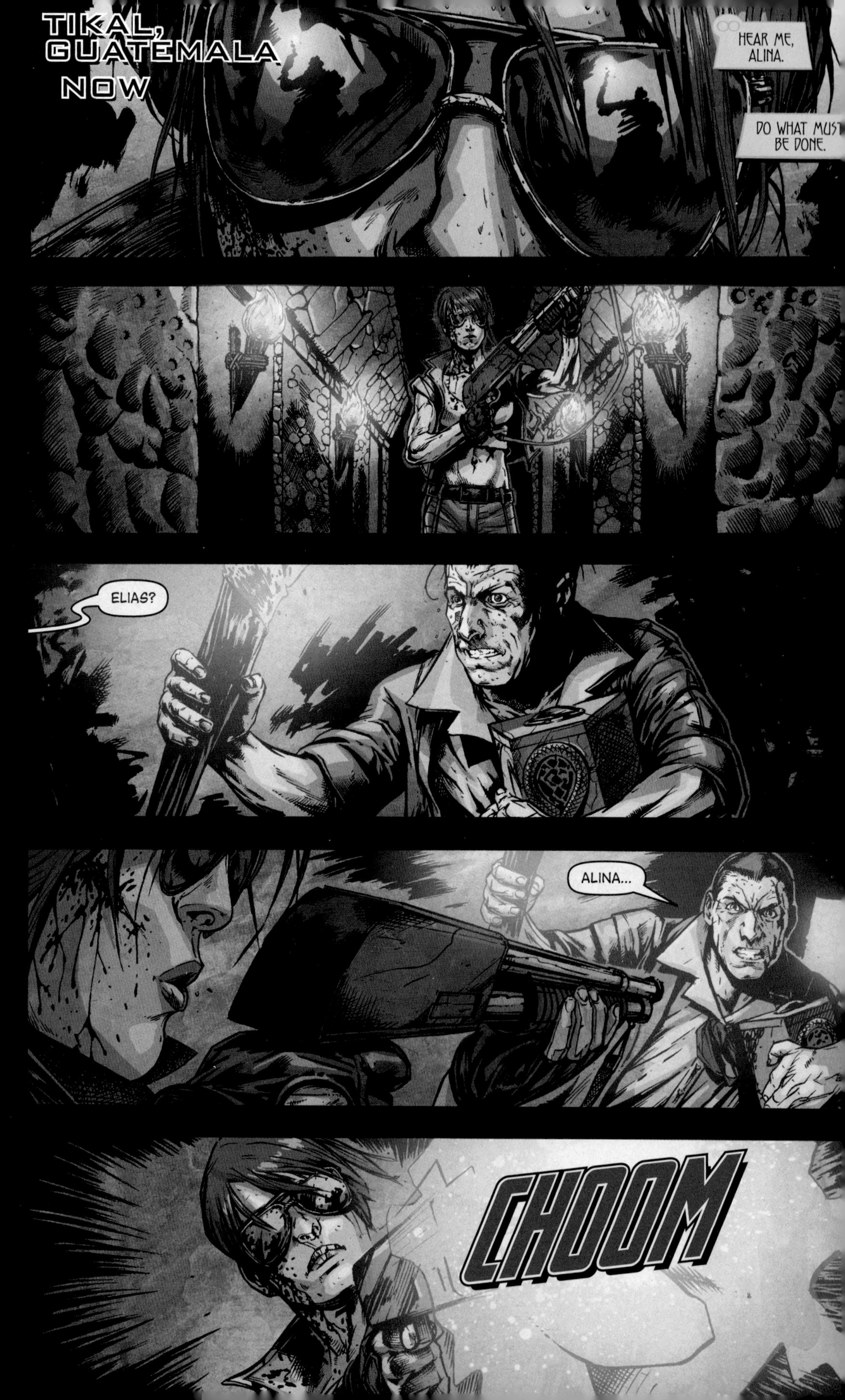
TIKAL, GUATEMALA
NOW
HEAR ME, ALINA.
DO WHAT MUST BE DONE.
ELIAS?
ALINA...
CHOOM

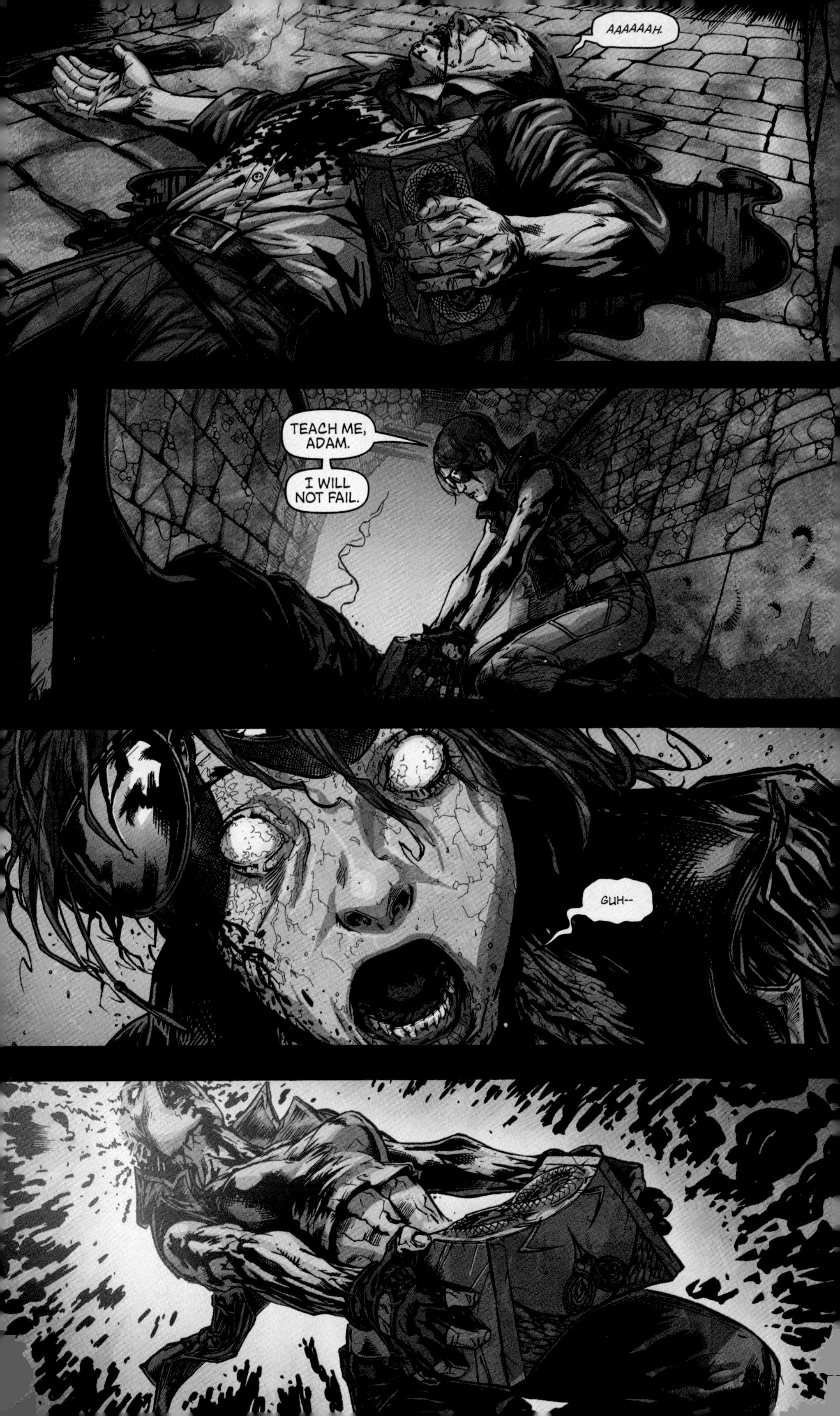
AAAAAAH.
TEACH ME, ADAM.
I WILL NOT FAIL.
GUH--

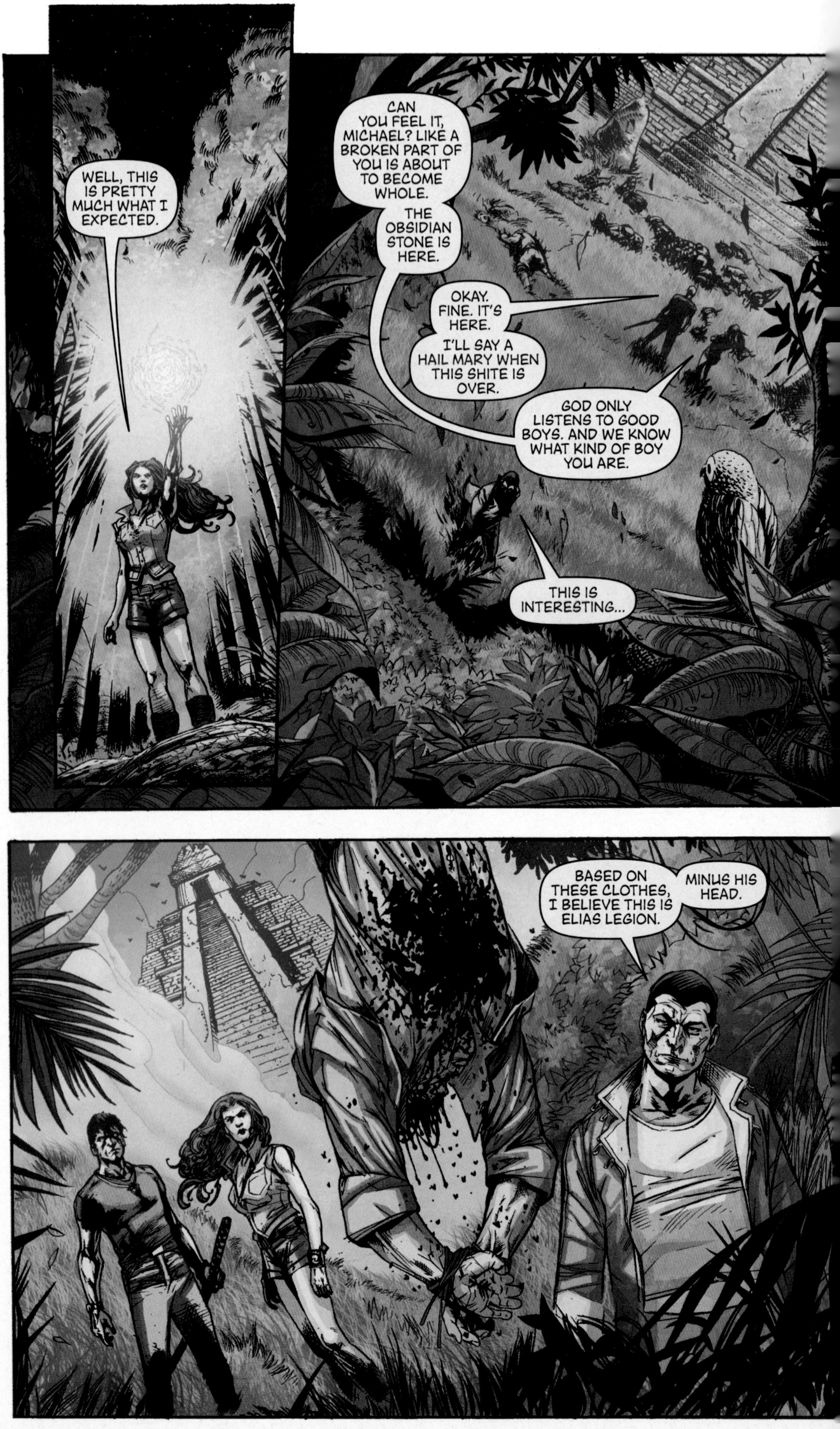
WELL, THIS IS PRETTY MUCH WHAT I EXPECTED.
CAN YOU FEEL IT, MICHAEL? LIKE A BROKEN PART OF YOU IS ABOUT TO BECOME WHOLE.
THE OBSIDIAN STONE IS HERE.
OKAY. FINE. IT'S HERE.
I'LL SAY A HAIL MARY WHEN THIS SHITE IS OVER.
GOD ONLY LISTENS TO GOOD BOYS. AND WE KNOW WHAT KIND OF BOY YOU ARE.
THIS IS INTERESTING...
BASED ON THESE CLOTHES, I BELIEVE THIS IS ELIAS LEGION.
MINUS HIS HEAD.

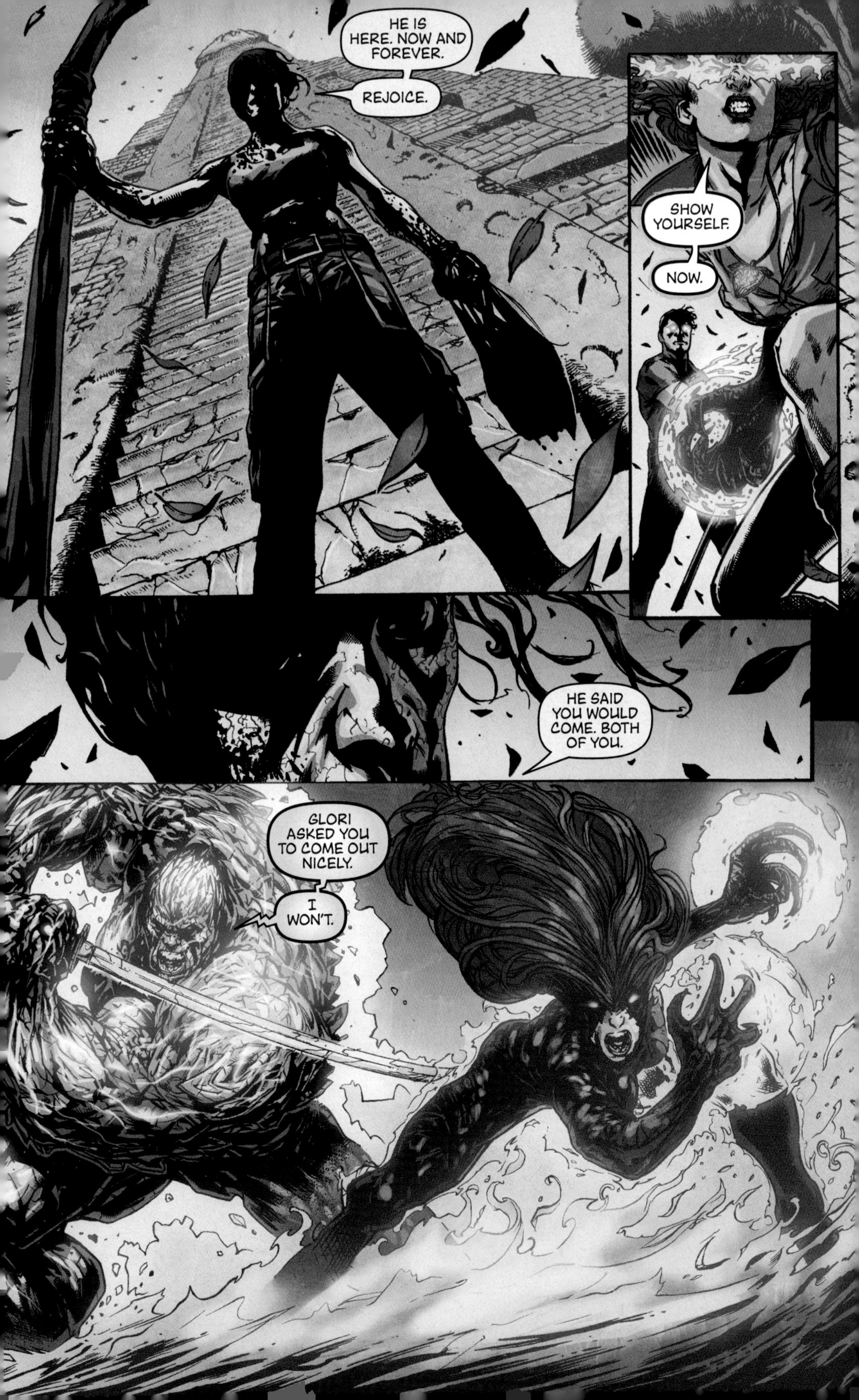
HE IS HERE. NOW AND FOREVER.
REJOICE.
SHOW YOURSELF.
NOW.
HE SAID YOU WOULD COME. BOTH OF YOU.
GLORI ASKED YOU TO COME OUT NICELY.
I WON'T.

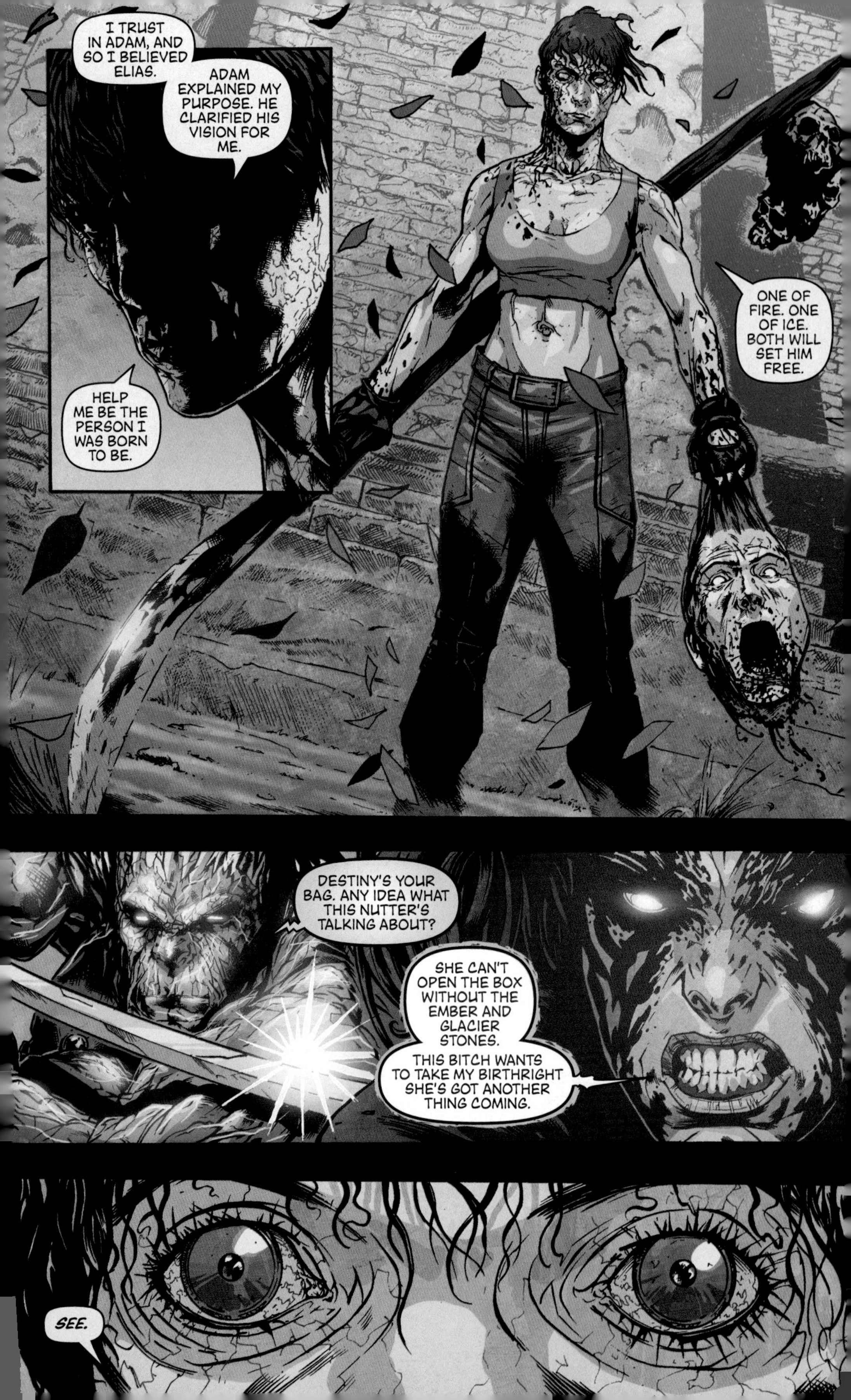

I TRUST IN ADAM, AND SO I BELIEVED ELIAS.
ADAM EXPLAINED MY PURPOSE. HE CLARIFIED HIS VISION FOR ME.
HELP ME BE THE PERSON I WAS BORN TO BE.
ONE OF FIRE. ONE OF ICE. BOTH WILL SET HIM FREE.
DESTINY'S YOUR BAG. ANY IDEA WHAT THIS NUTTER'S TALKING ABOUT?
SHE CAN'T OPEN THE BOX WITHOUT THE EMBER AND GLACIER STONES.
THIS BITCH WANTS TO TAKE MY BIRTHRIGHT SHE'S GOT ANOTHER THING COMING.
SEE.

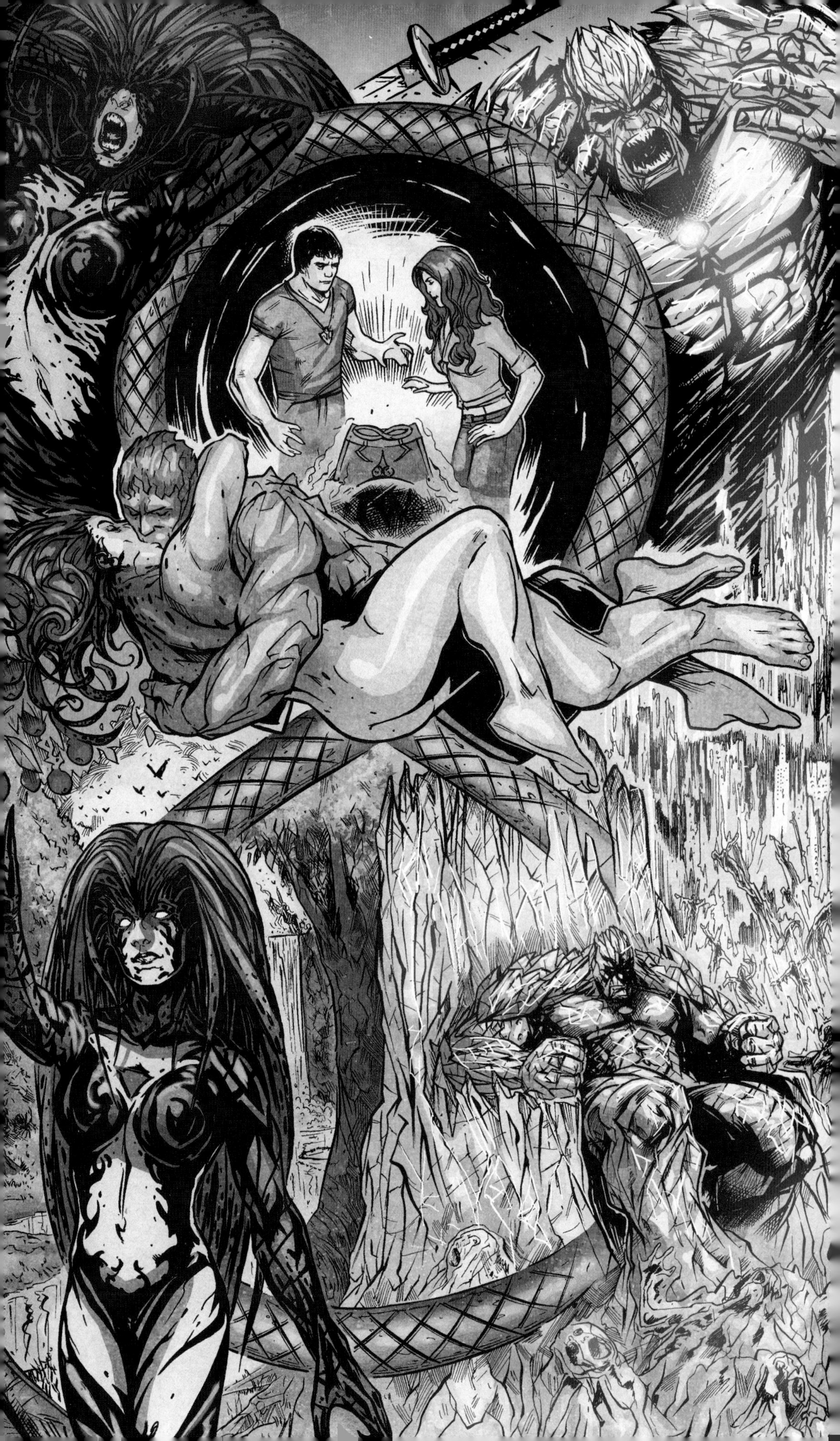

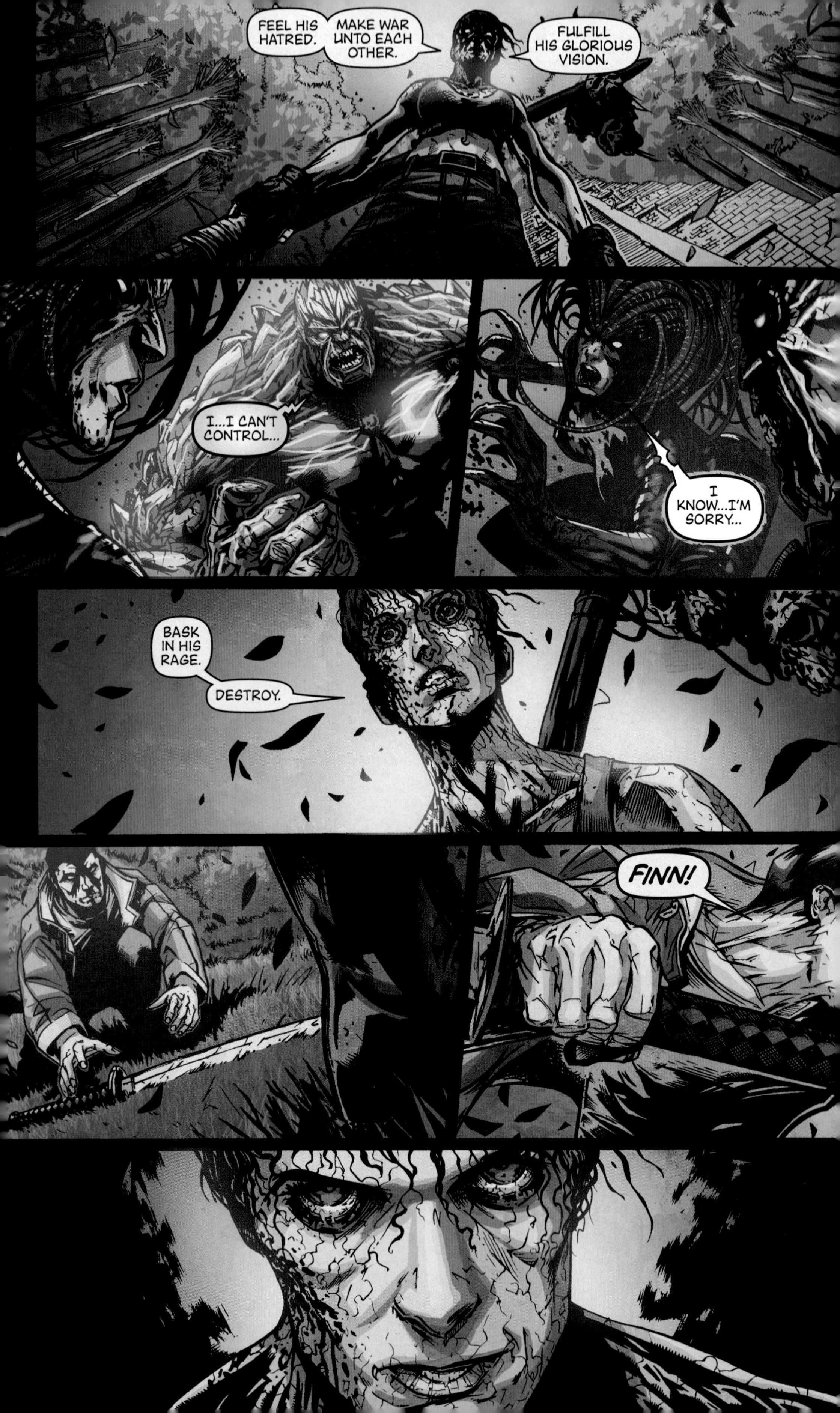
FEEL HIS HATRED.
MAKE WAR UNTO EACH OTHER.
FULFILL HIS GLORIOUS VISION.
I...I CAN'T CONTROL...
I KNOW...I'M SORRY...
BASK IN HIS RAGE.
DESTROY.
FINN!

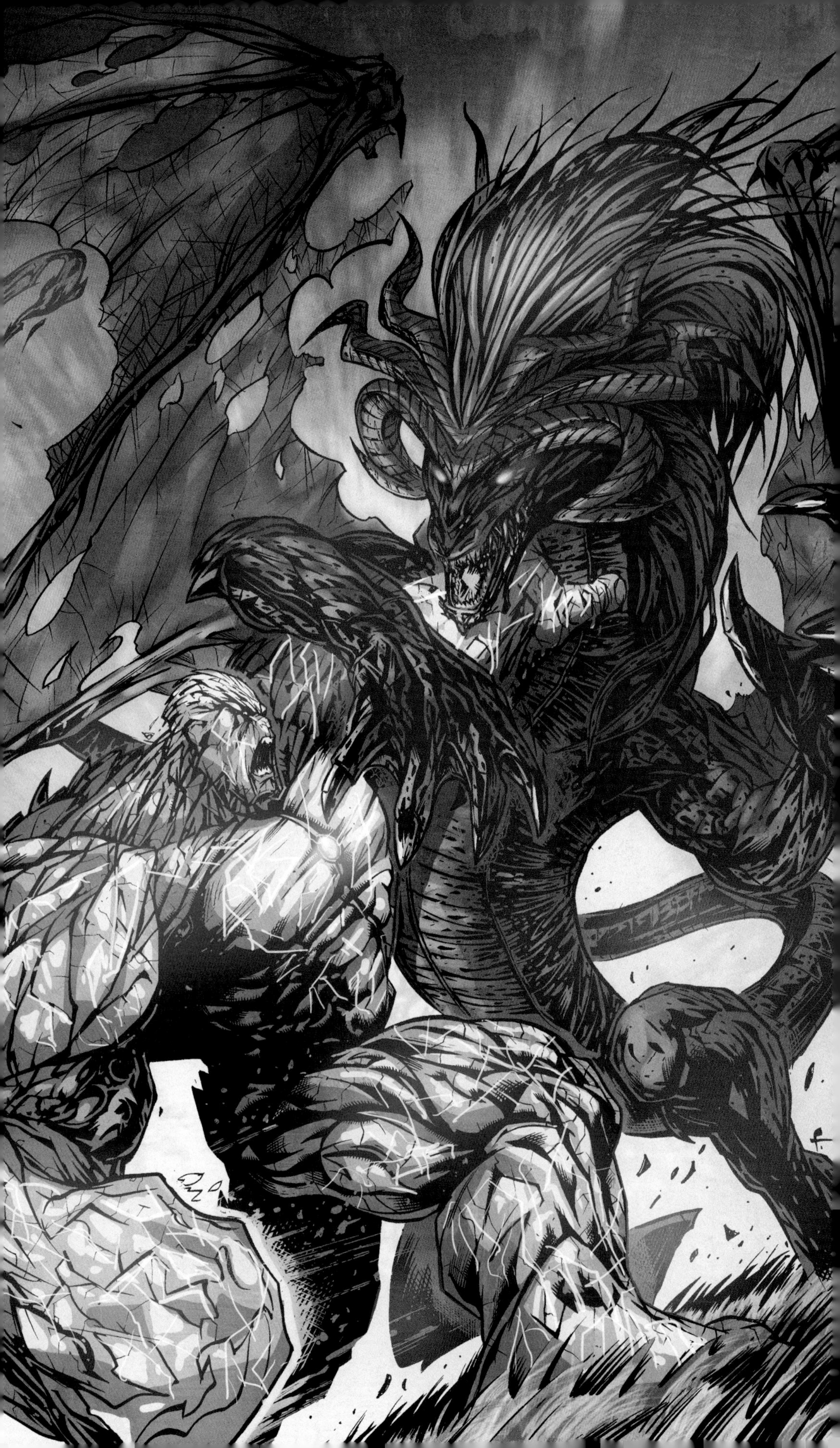

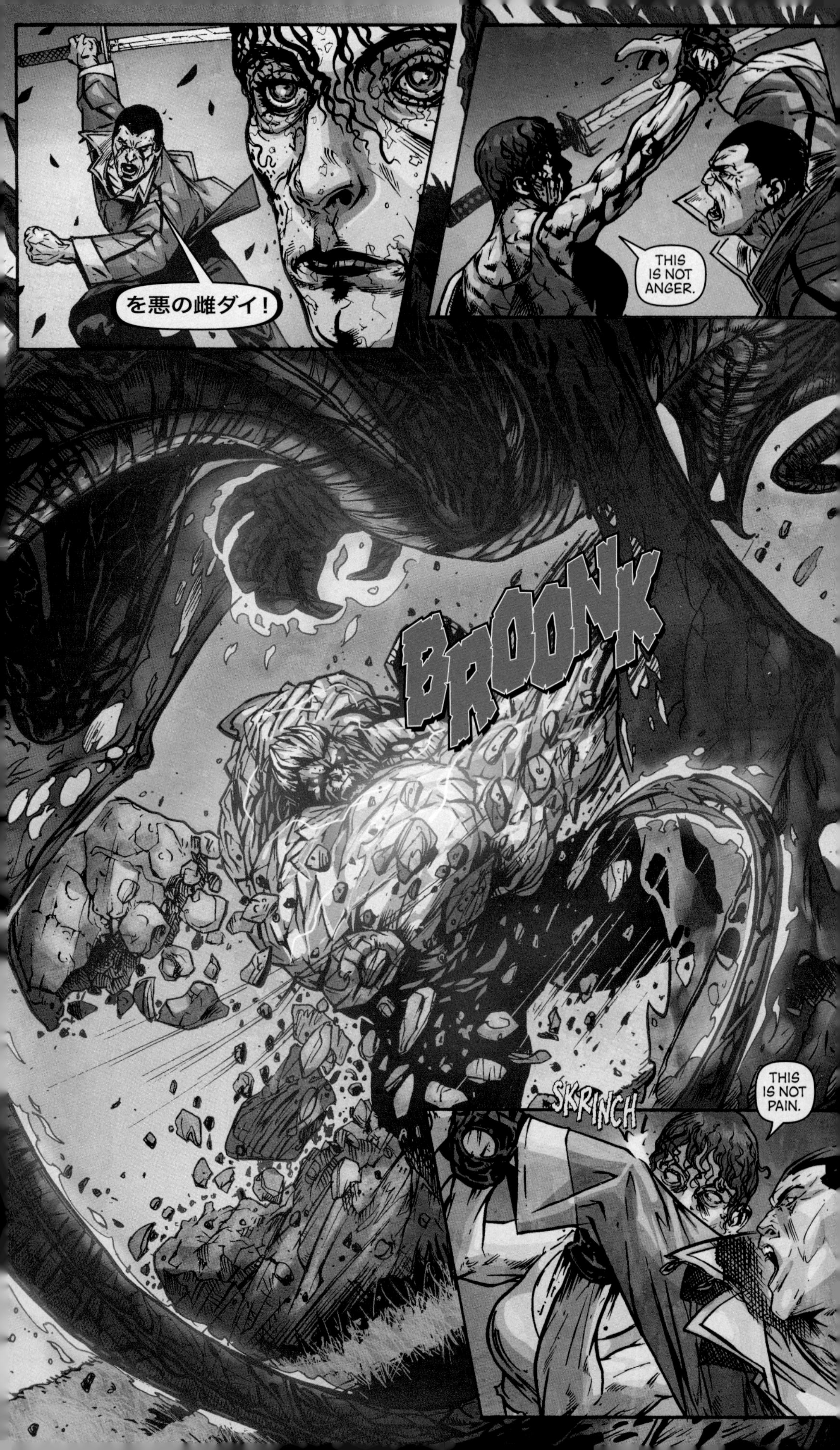
を悪の雌ダイ!
THIS IS NOT ANGER.
BROONK
SKRINCH
THIS IS NOT PAIN.

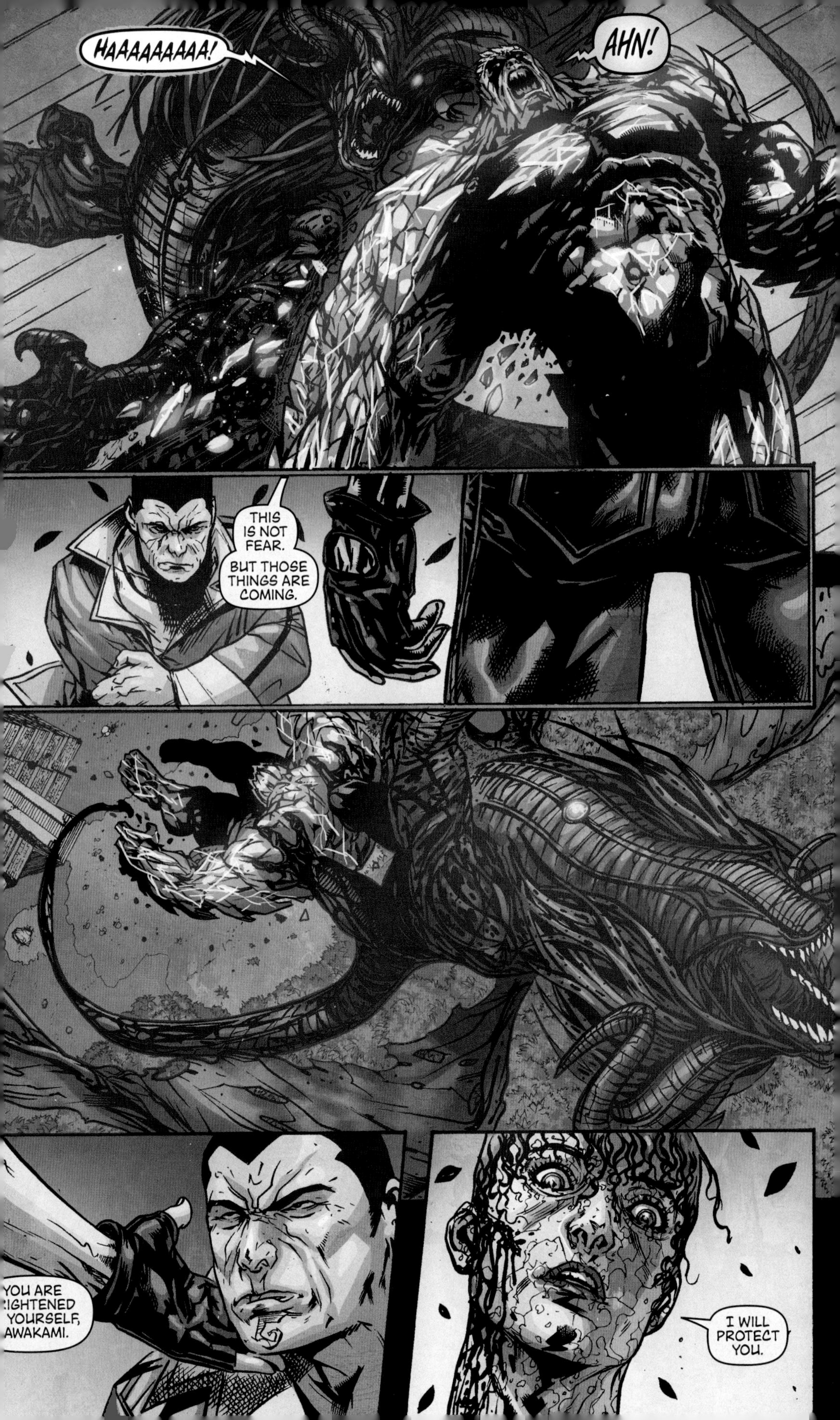
HAAAAAAAAA!
AHN!
THIS IS NOT FEAR.
BUT THOSE THINGS ARE COMING.
YOU ARE
IGHTENED YOURSELF,
AWAKAMI.
I WILL PROTECT YOU.

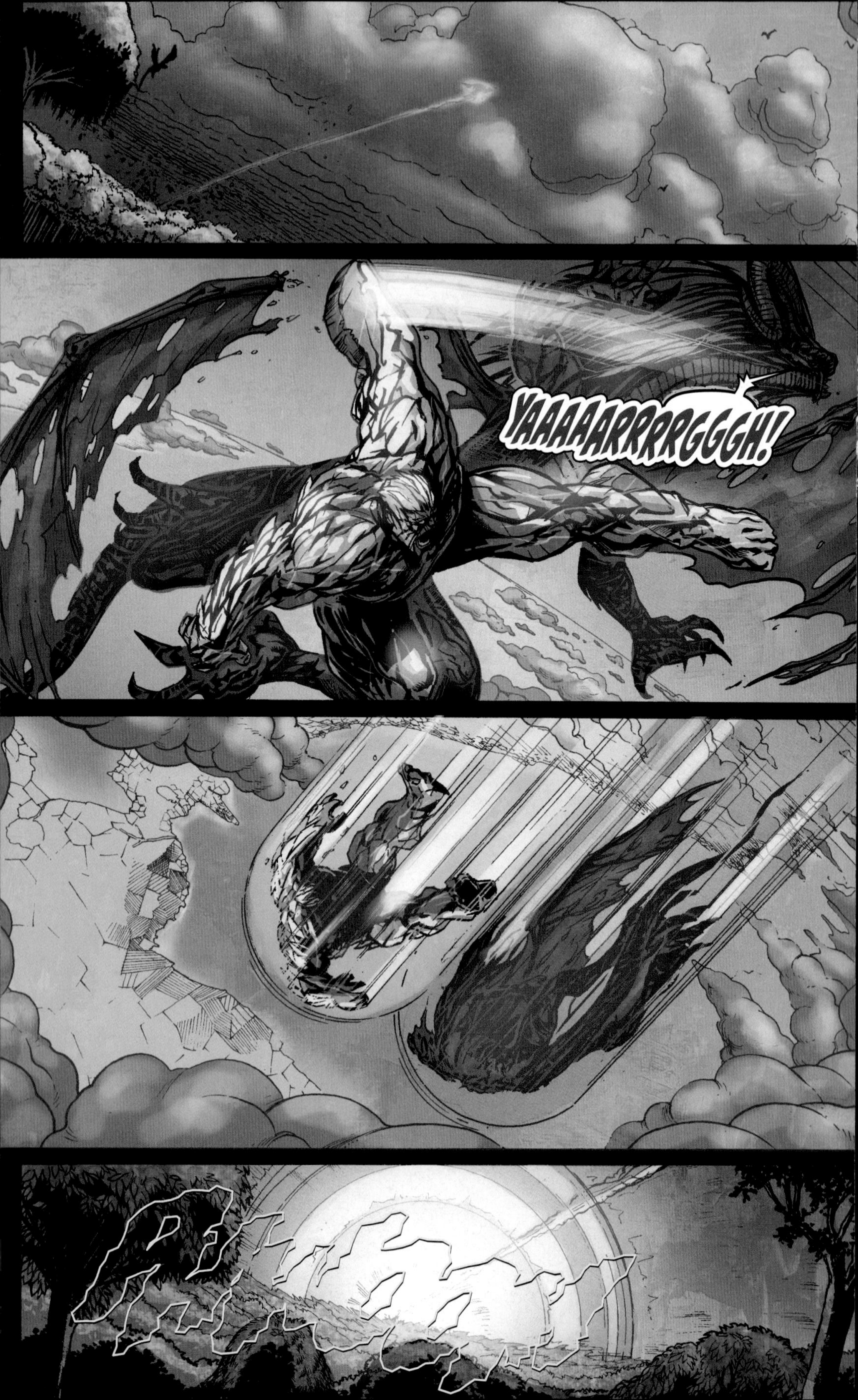
YAAAAARRRRGGGH!

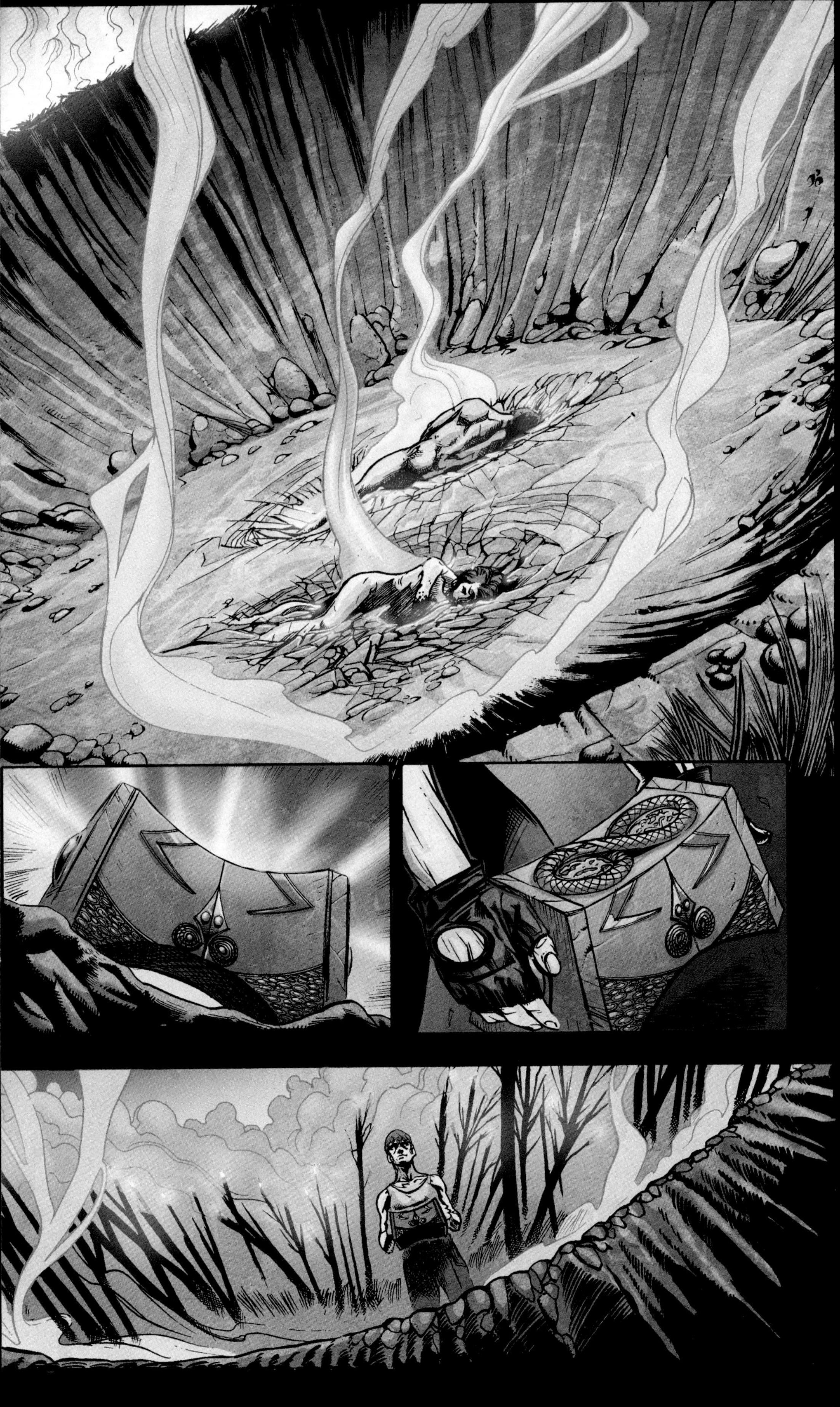

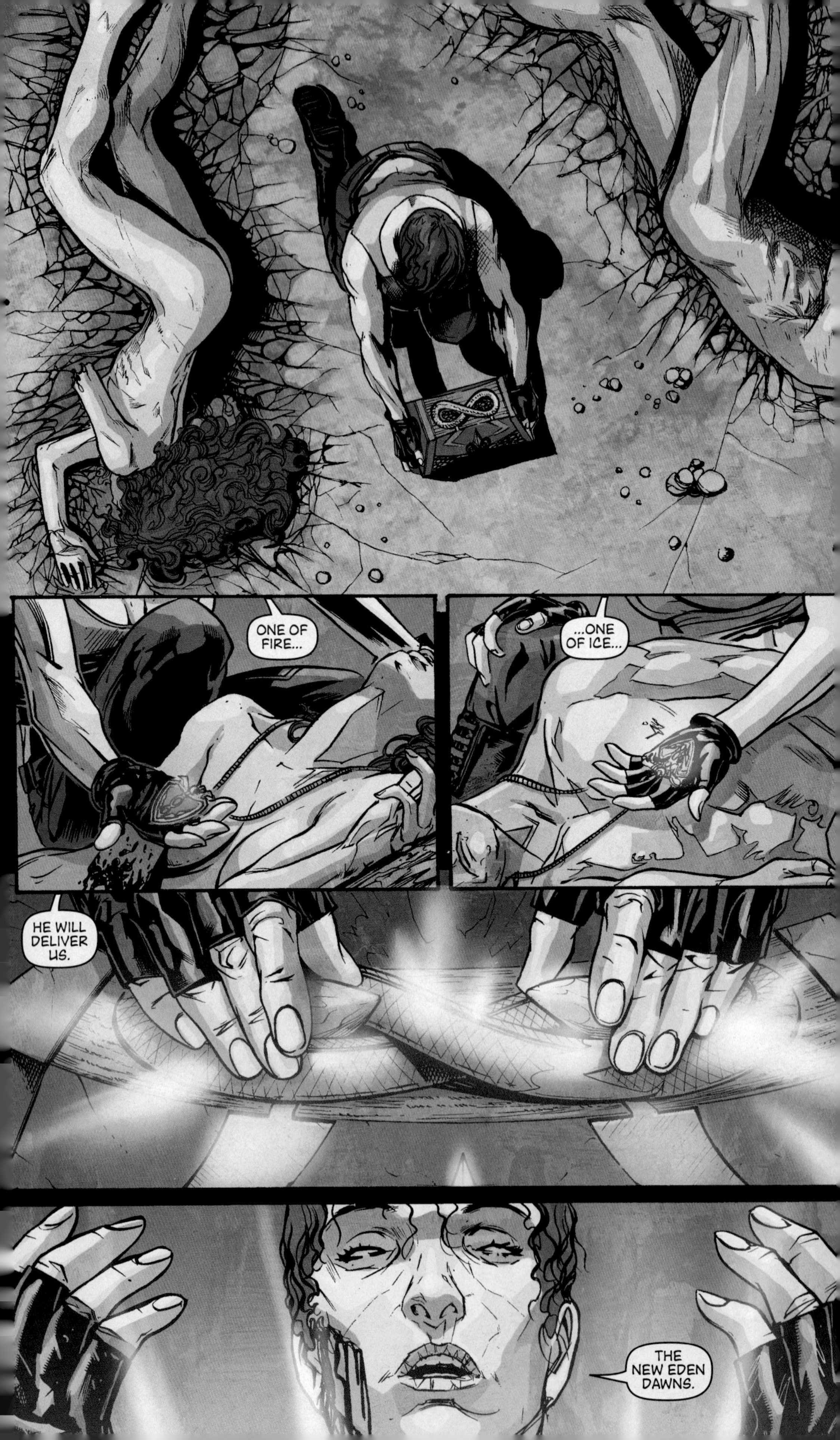
ONE OF FIRE...
...ONE OF ICE...
HE WILL DELIVER US.
THE NEW EDEN DAWNS.

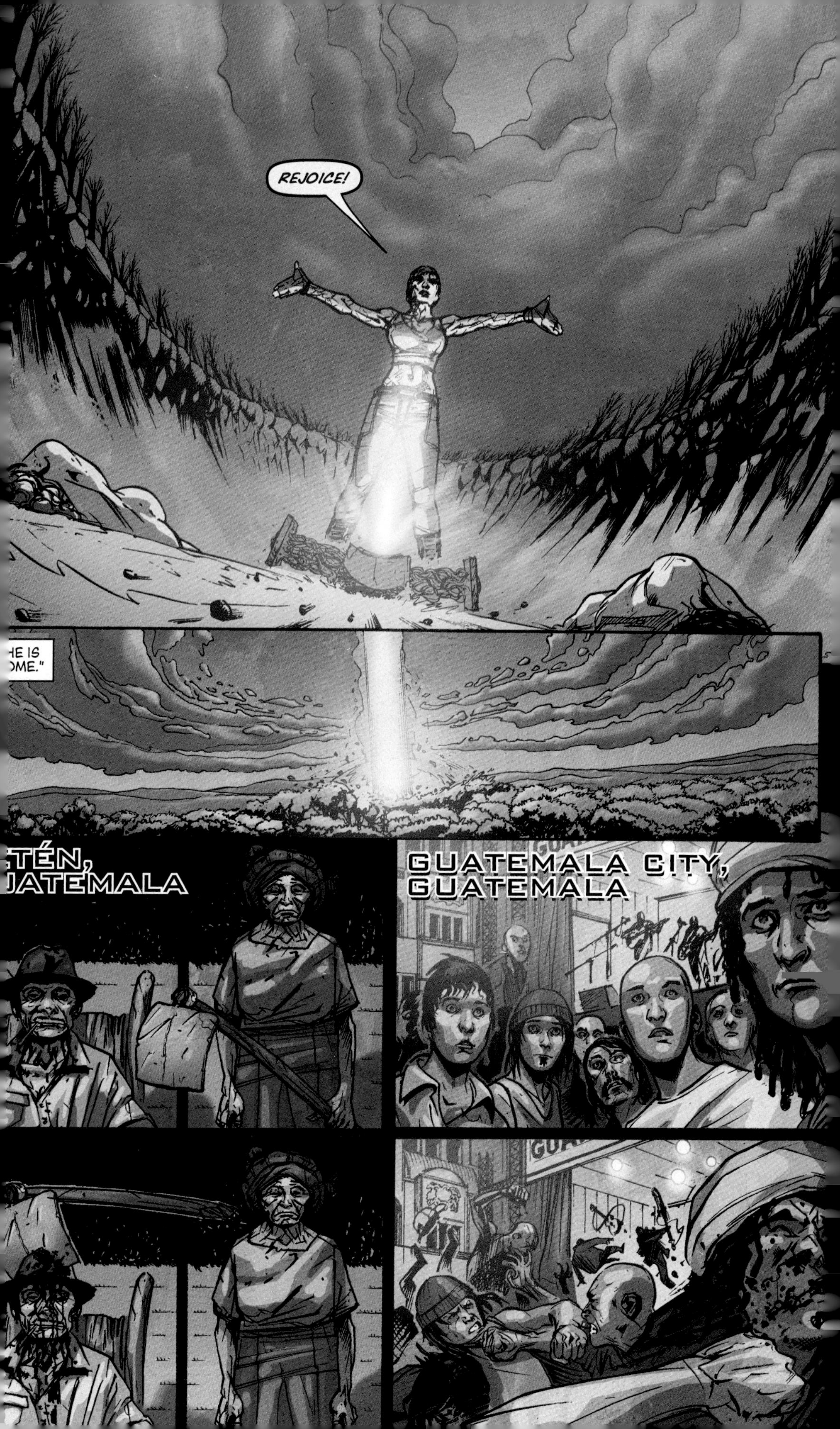
REJOICE!
HE IS
OME."
TÉN,
JATEMALA
GUATEMALA CITY,
GUATEMALA

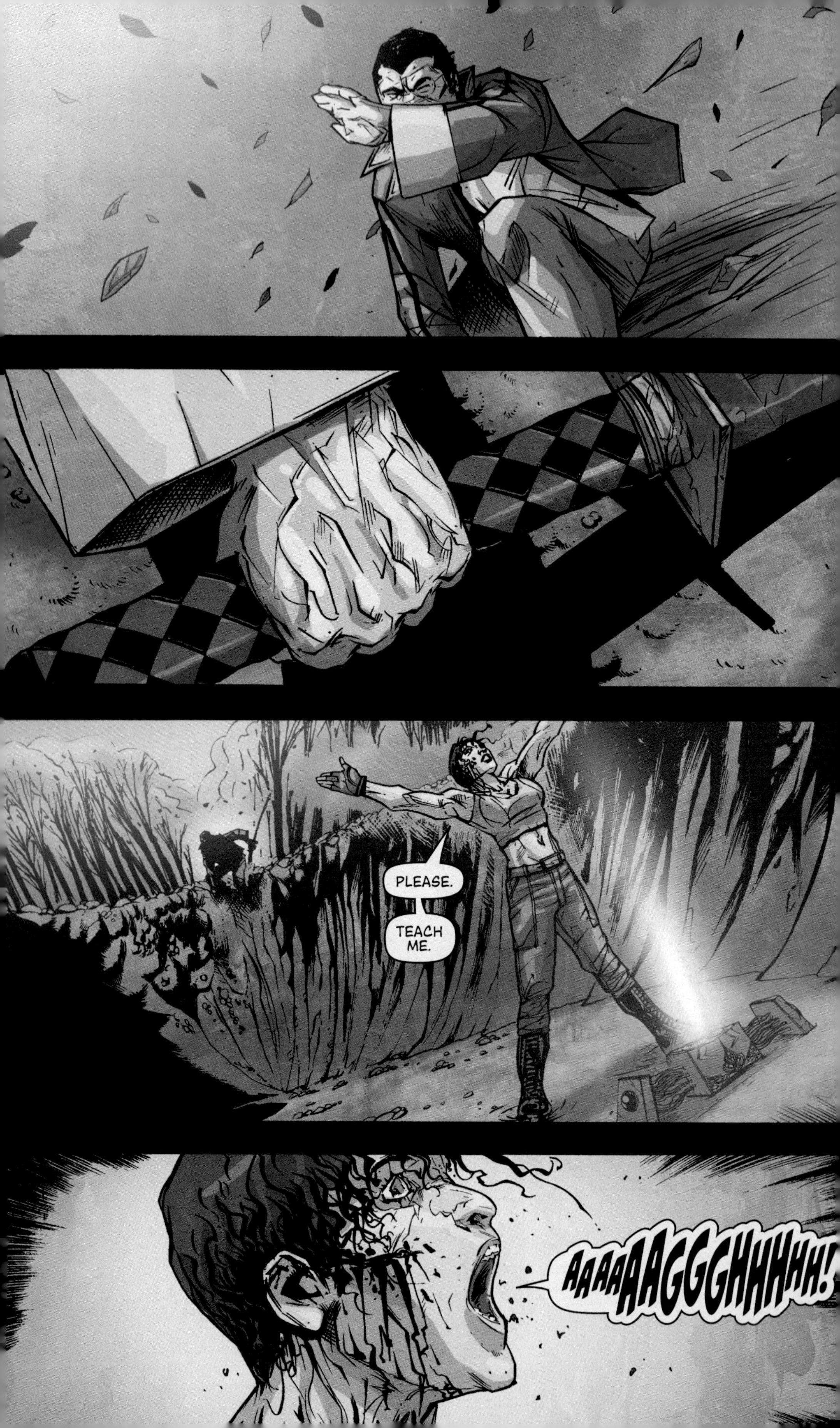
PLEASE.
TEACH ME.
AAAAAAGGGHHHHH!

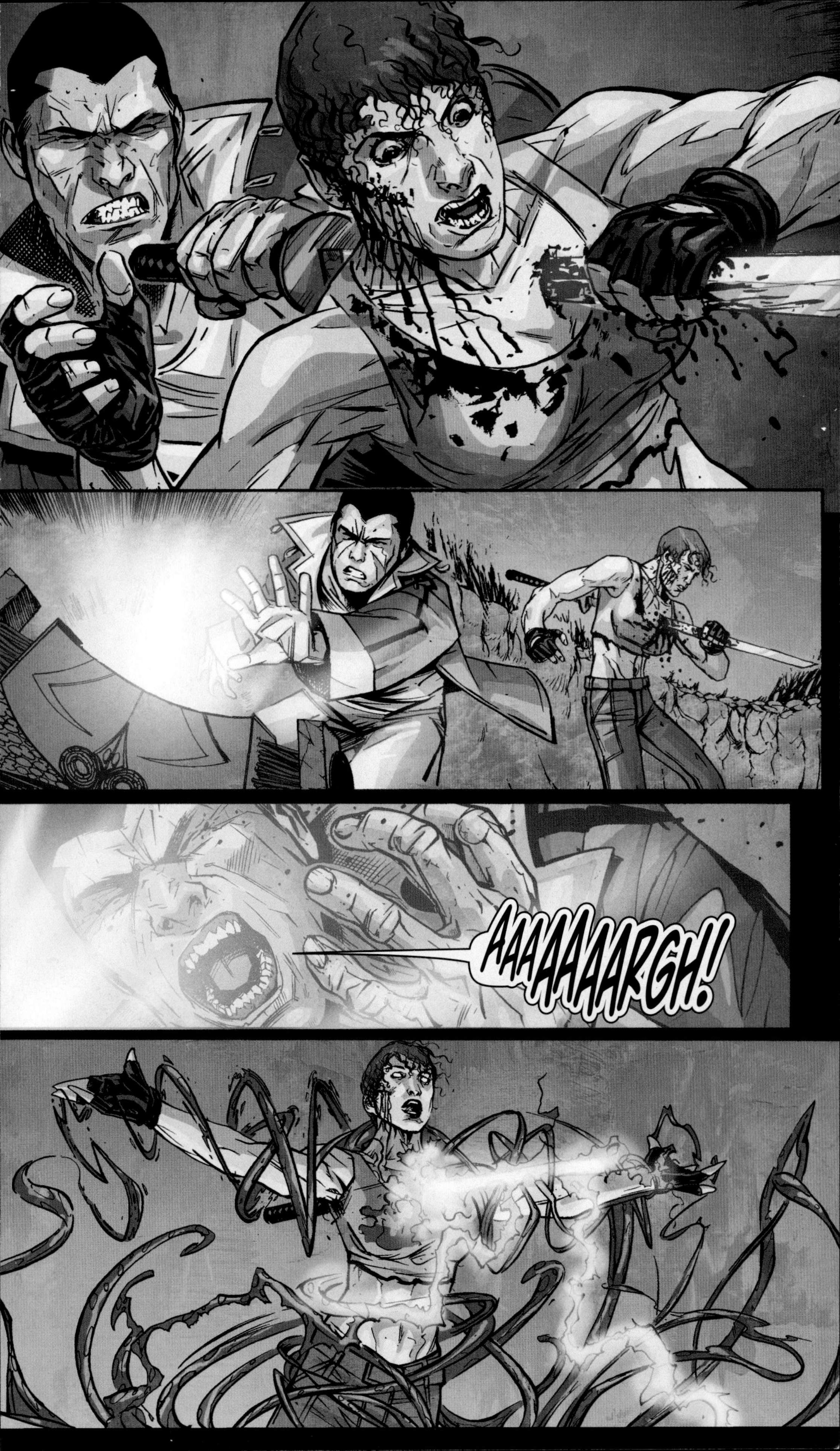
AAAAAAARGH!

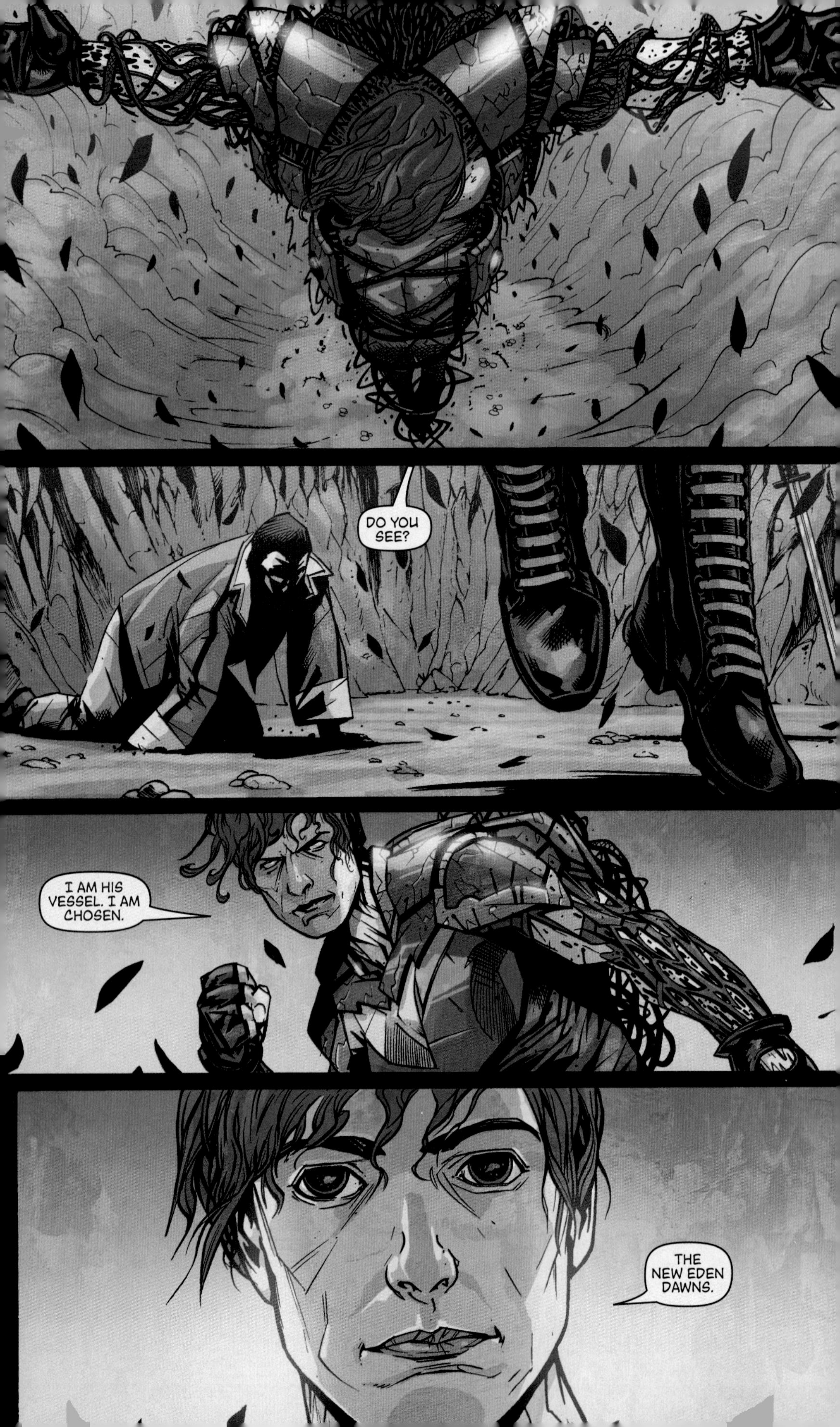
DO YOU SEE?
I AM HIS VESSEL. I AM CHOSEN.
THE NEW EDEN DAWNS.

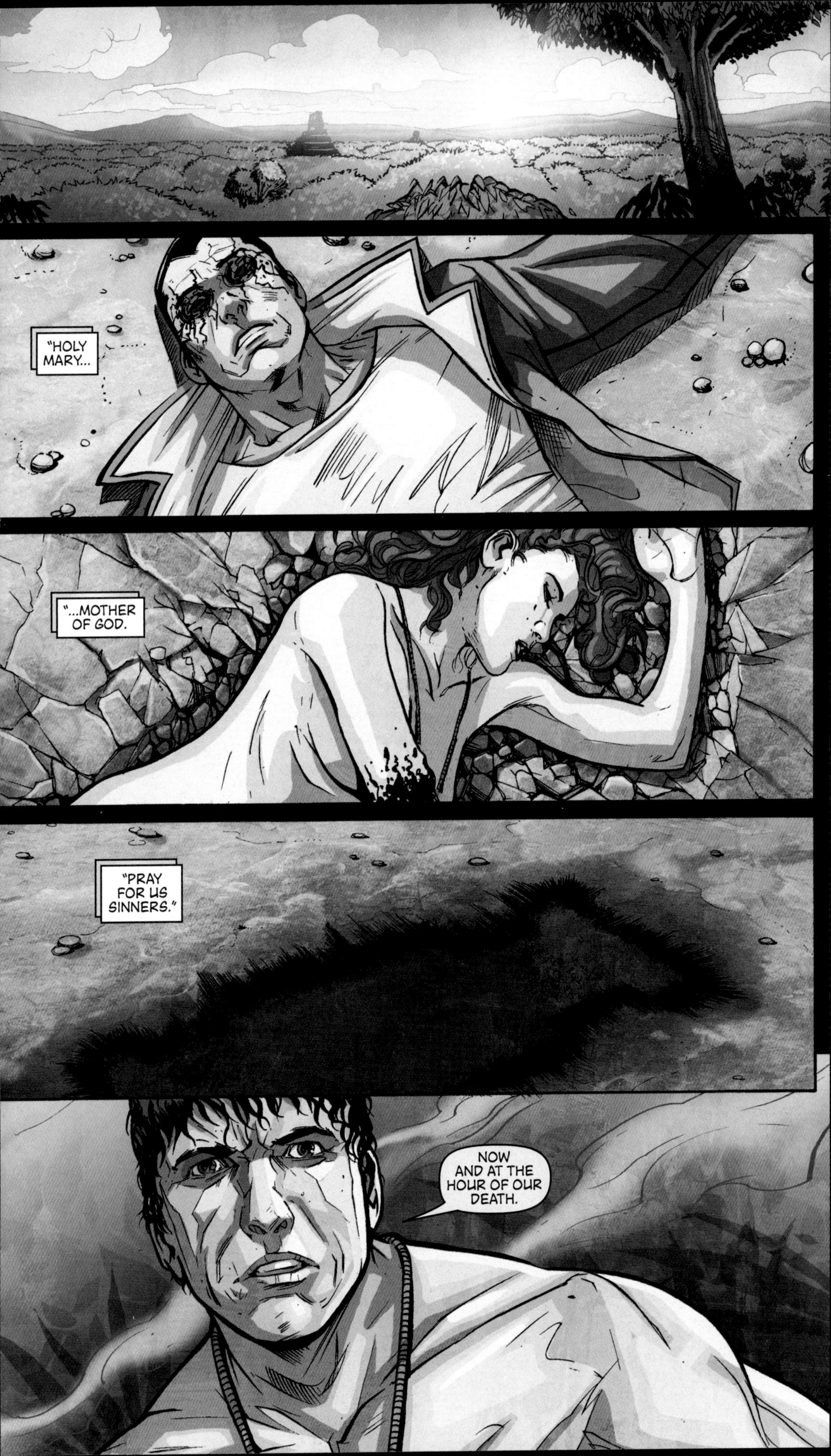
"HOLY MARY...
"...MOTHER OF GOD.
"PRAY FOR US SINNERS."
NOW AND AT THE HOUR OF OUR DEATH.

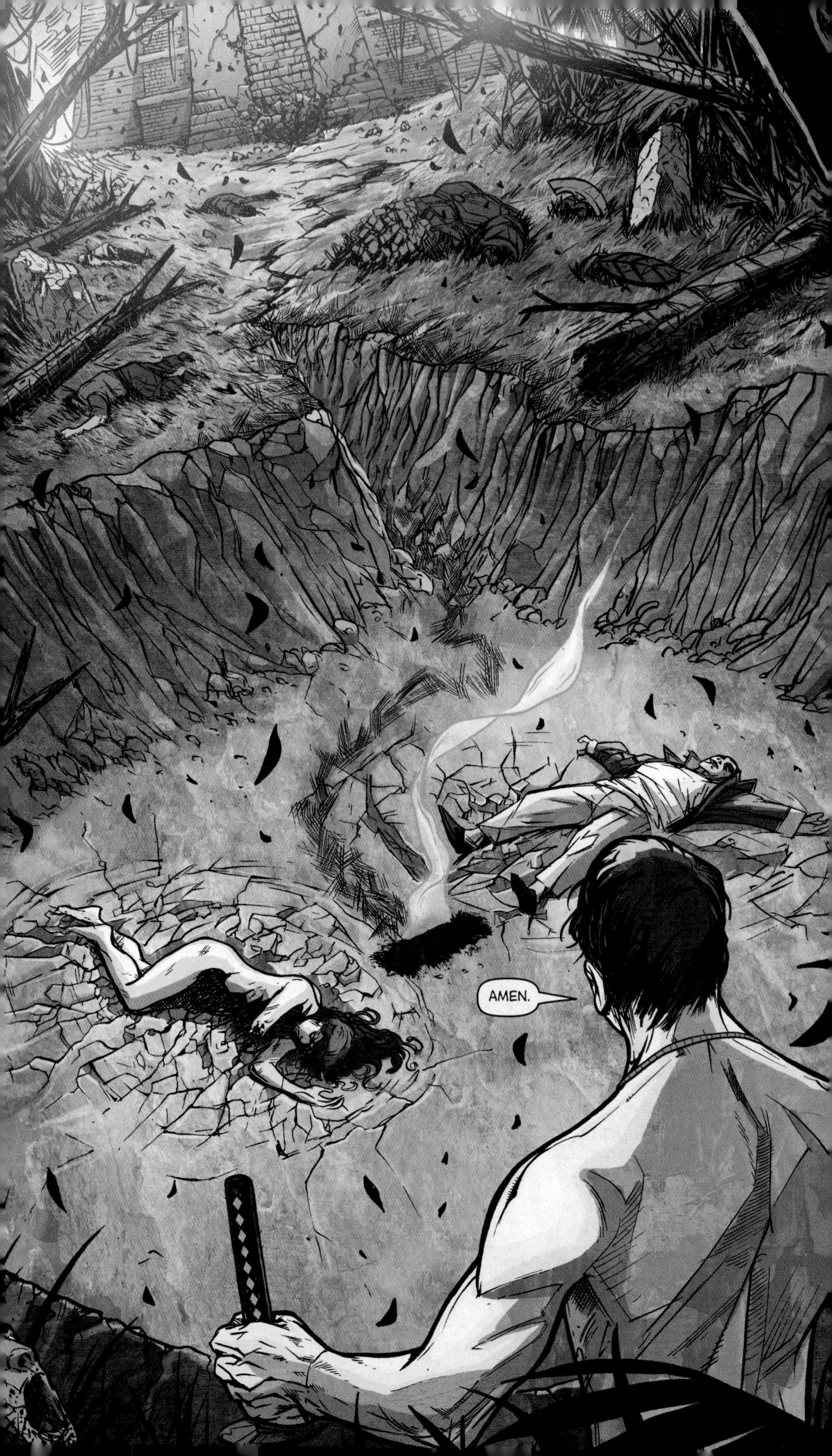
AMEN.

BROKEN TRINITY

"PANDORA'S BOX" Part 6

{
written by: **Bryan Edward Hill & Rob Levin**
art by: **Facundo Percio**
colors by: **Imaginary Friends Studios**
letters by: **Troy Peteri**
}

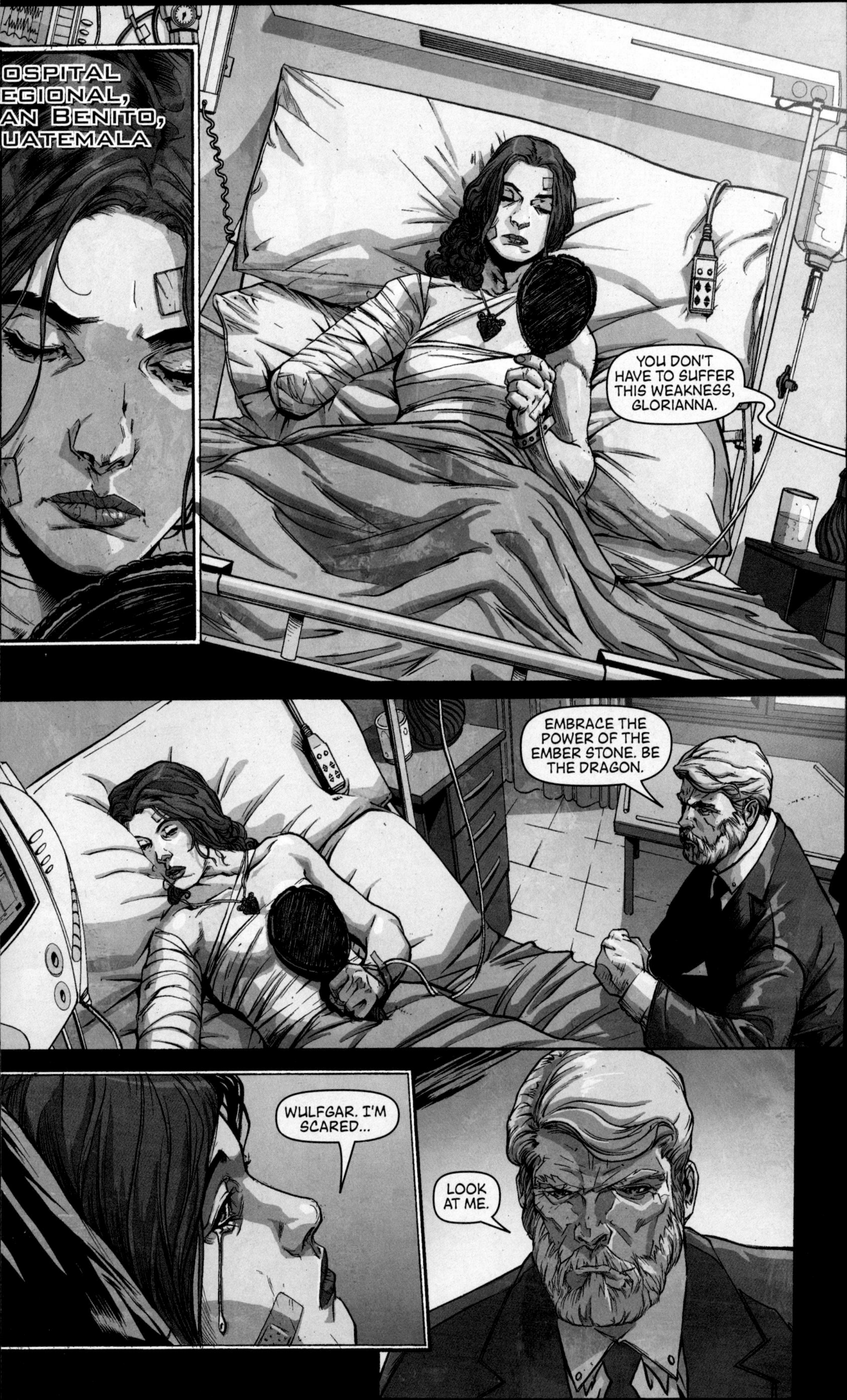
OSPITAL
EGIONAL,
AN BENITO,
UATEMALA
YOU DON'T HAVE TO SUFFER THIS WEAKNESS, GLORIANNA.
EMBRACE THE POWER OF THE EMBER STONE. BE THE DRAGON.
WULFGAR. I'M SCARED...
LOOK AT ME.

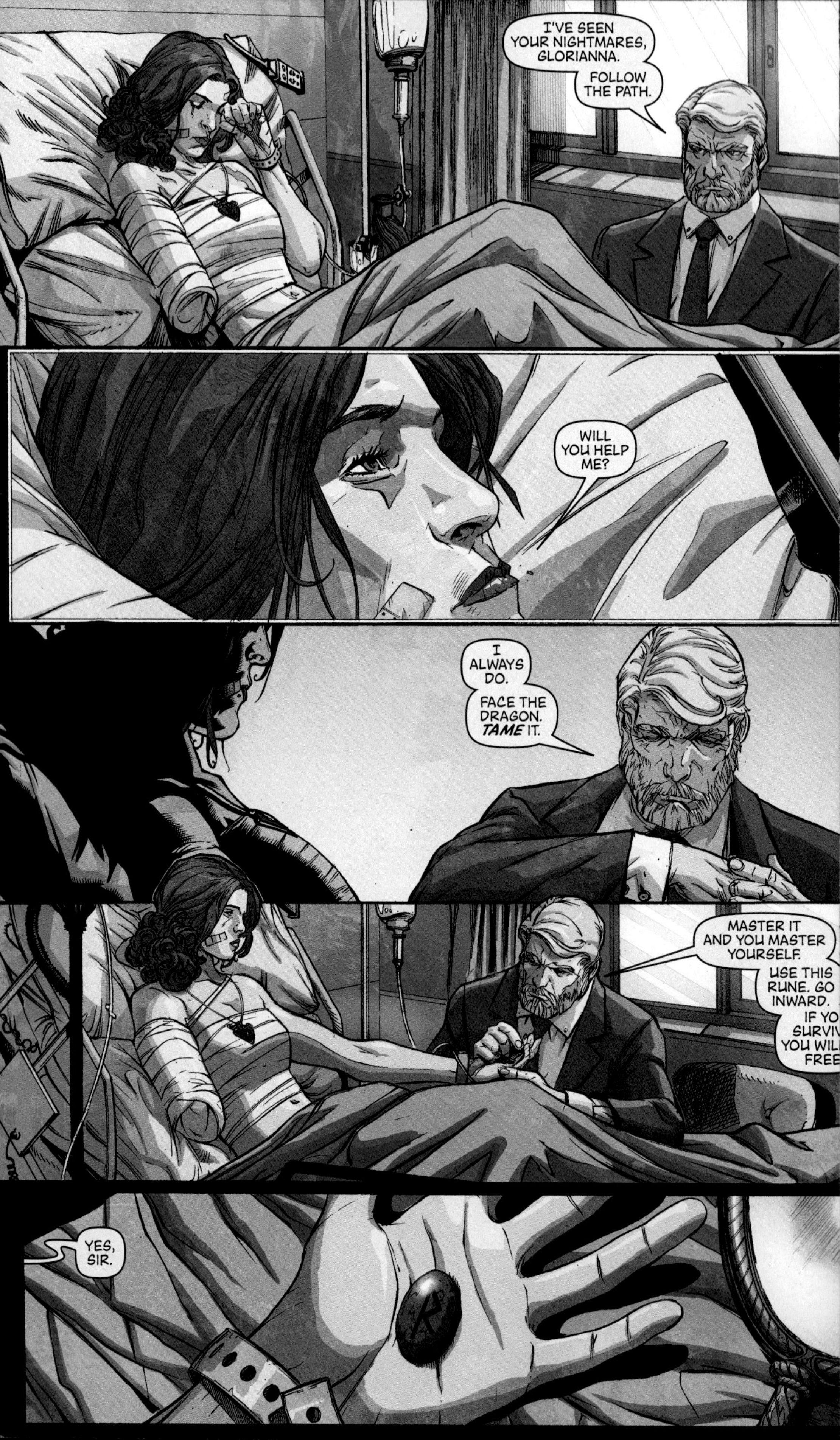
I'VE SEEN YOUR NIGHTMARES, GLORIANNA.
FOLLOW THE PATH.
WILL YOU HELP ME?
I ALWAYS DO.
FACE THE DRAGON. *TAME* IT.
MASTER IT AND YOU MASTER YOURSELF.
USE THIS RUNE. GO INWARD.
YES, SIR.

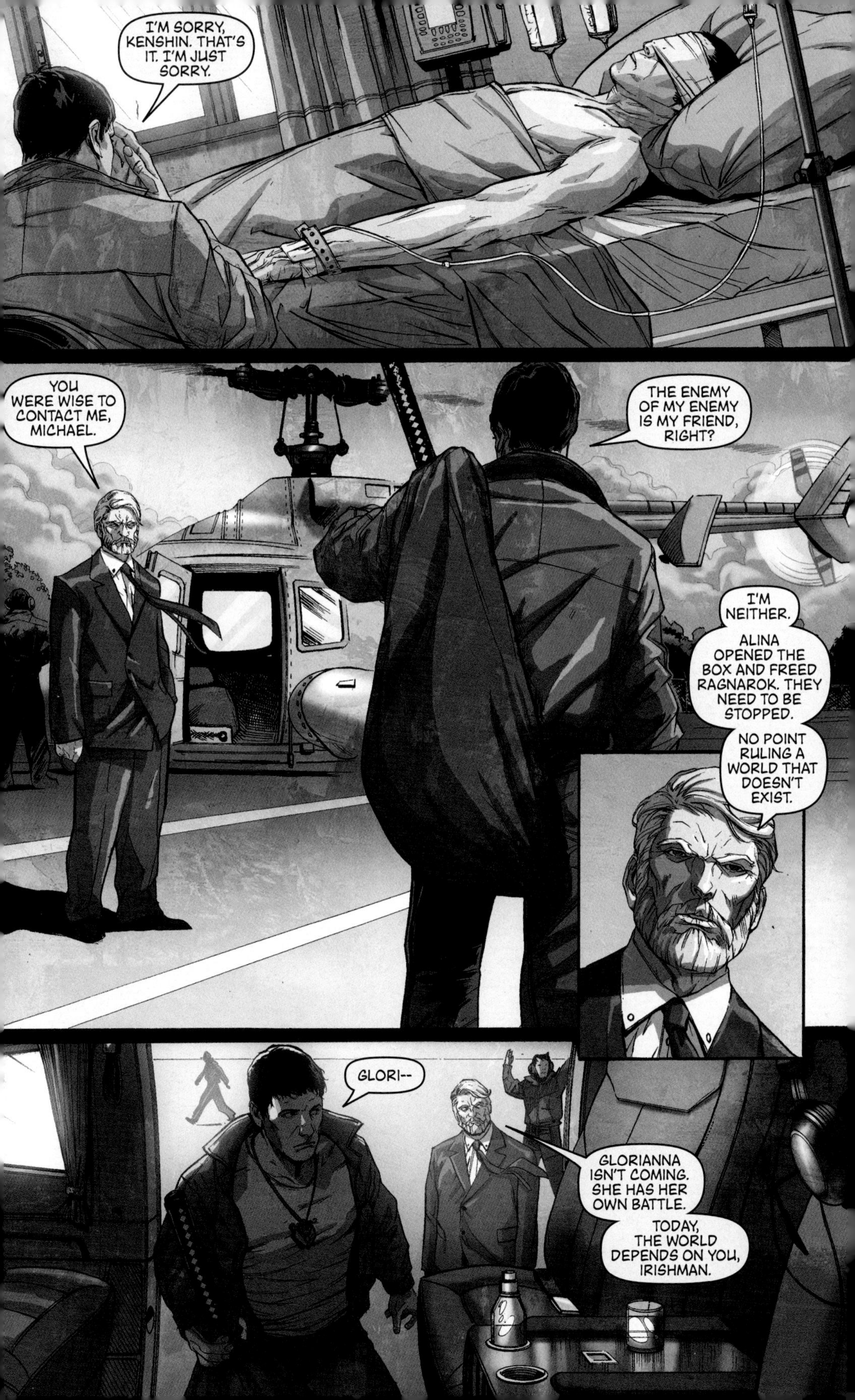

I'M SORRY, KENSHIN. THAT'S IT. I'M JUST SORRY.
YOU WERE WISE TO CONTACT ME, MICHAEL.
THE ENEMY OF MY ENEMY IS MY FRIEND, RIGHT?
I'M NEITHER.
ALINA OPENED THE BOX AND FREED RAGNAROK. THEY NEED TO BE STOPPED.
NO POINT RULING A WORLD THAT DOESN'T EXIST.
GLORI--
GLORIANNA ISN'T COMING. SHE HAS HER OWN BATTLE.
TODAY, THE WORLD DEPENDS ON YOU, IRISHMAN.

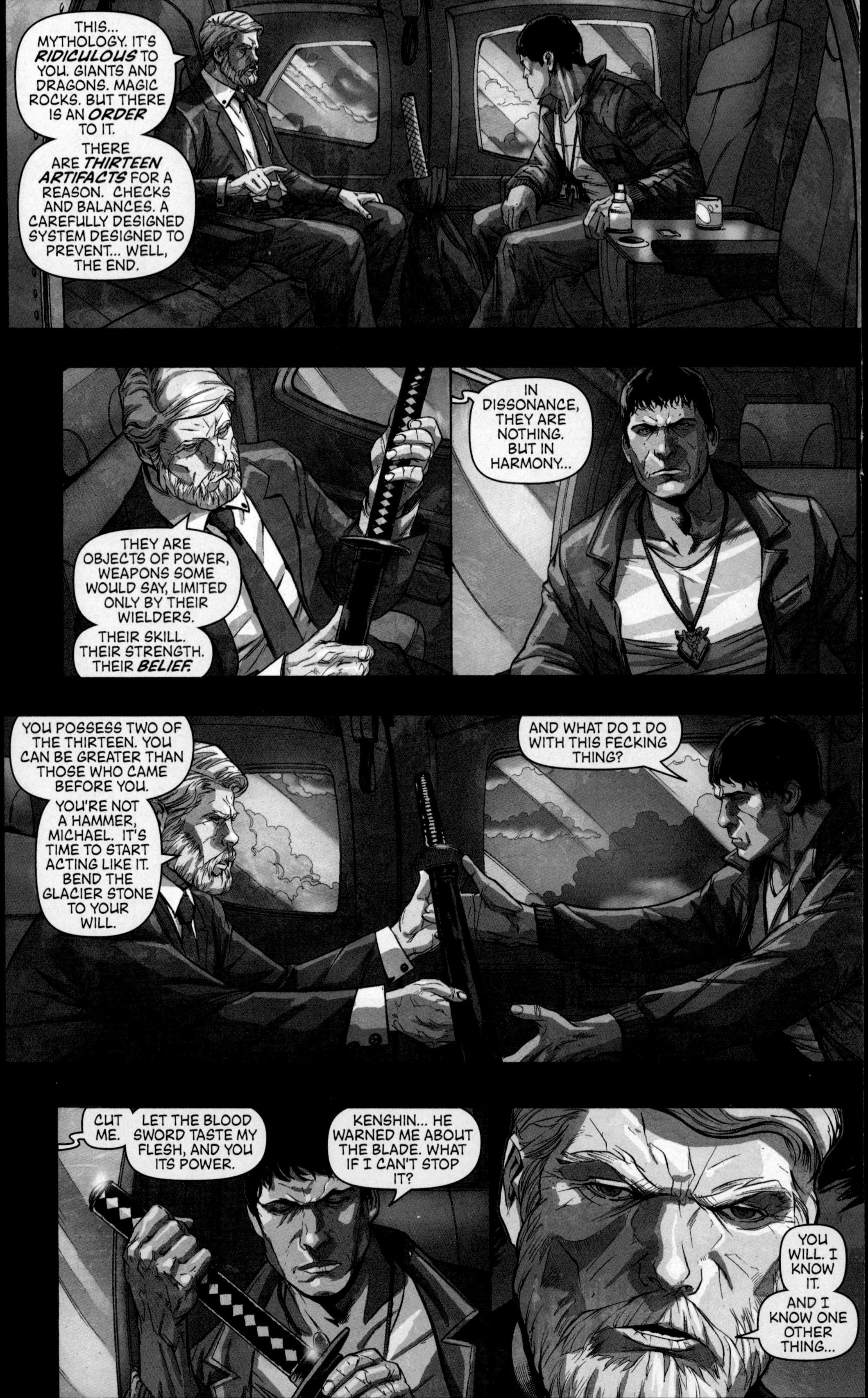
THIS... MYTHOLOGY. IT'S *RIDICULOUS* TO YOU. GIANTS AND DRAGONS. MAGIC ROCKS. BUT THERE IS AN *ORDER* TO IT.
THERE ARE *THIRTEEN ARTIFACTS* FOR A REASON. CHECKS AND BALANCES. A CAREFULLY DESIGNED SYSTEM DESIGNED TO PREVENT... WELL, THE END.
THEY ARE OBJECTS OF POWER, WEAPONS SOME WOULD SAY, LIMITED ONLY BY THEIR WIELDERS.
THEIR SKILL. THEIR STRENGTH. THEIR *BELIEF.*
IN DISSONANCE, THEY ARE NOTHING. BUT IN HARMONY...
YOU POSSESS TWO OF THE THIRTEEN. YOU CAN BE GREATER THAN THOSE WHO CAME BEFORE YOU.
YOU'RE NOT A HAMMER, MICHAEL. IT'S TIME TO START ACTING LIKE IT. BEND THE GLACIER STONE TO YOUR WILL.
AND WHAT DO I DO WITH THIS FECKING THING?
CUT ME.
LET THE BLOOD SWORD TASTE MY FLESH, AND YOU ITS POWER.
KENSHIN... HE WARNED ME ABOUT THE BLADE. WHAT IF I CAN'T STOP IT?
YOU WILL. I KNOW IT.
AND I KNOW ONE OTHER THING...

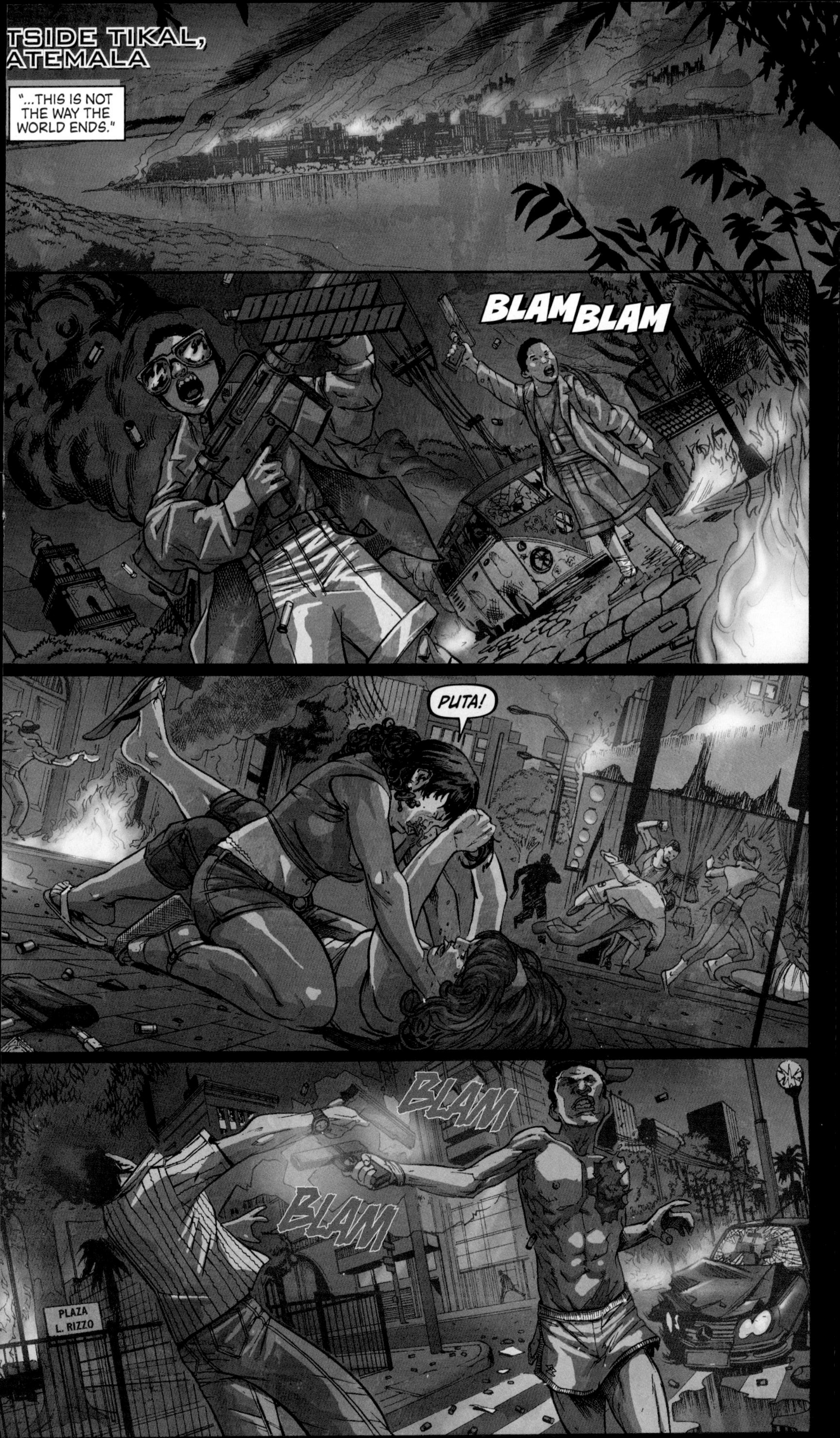
TSIDE TIKAL,
ATEMALA
"...THIS IS NOT THE WAY THE WORLD ENDS."
BRAKKA
BRAKKA
BLAM BLAM
PUTA!
BLAM
BLAM
PLAZA
L. RIZZO

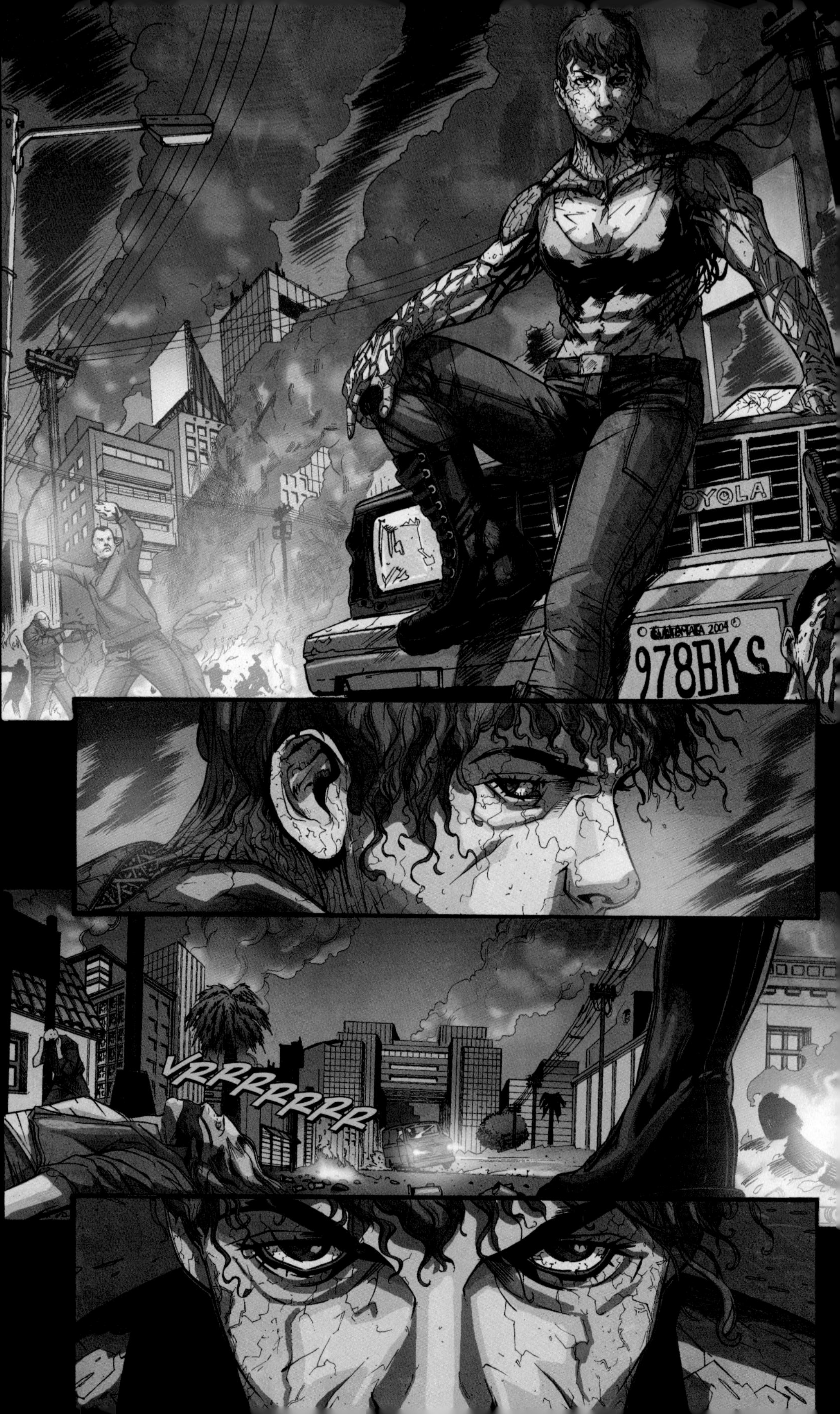
978BKS
VRRRRRRRR

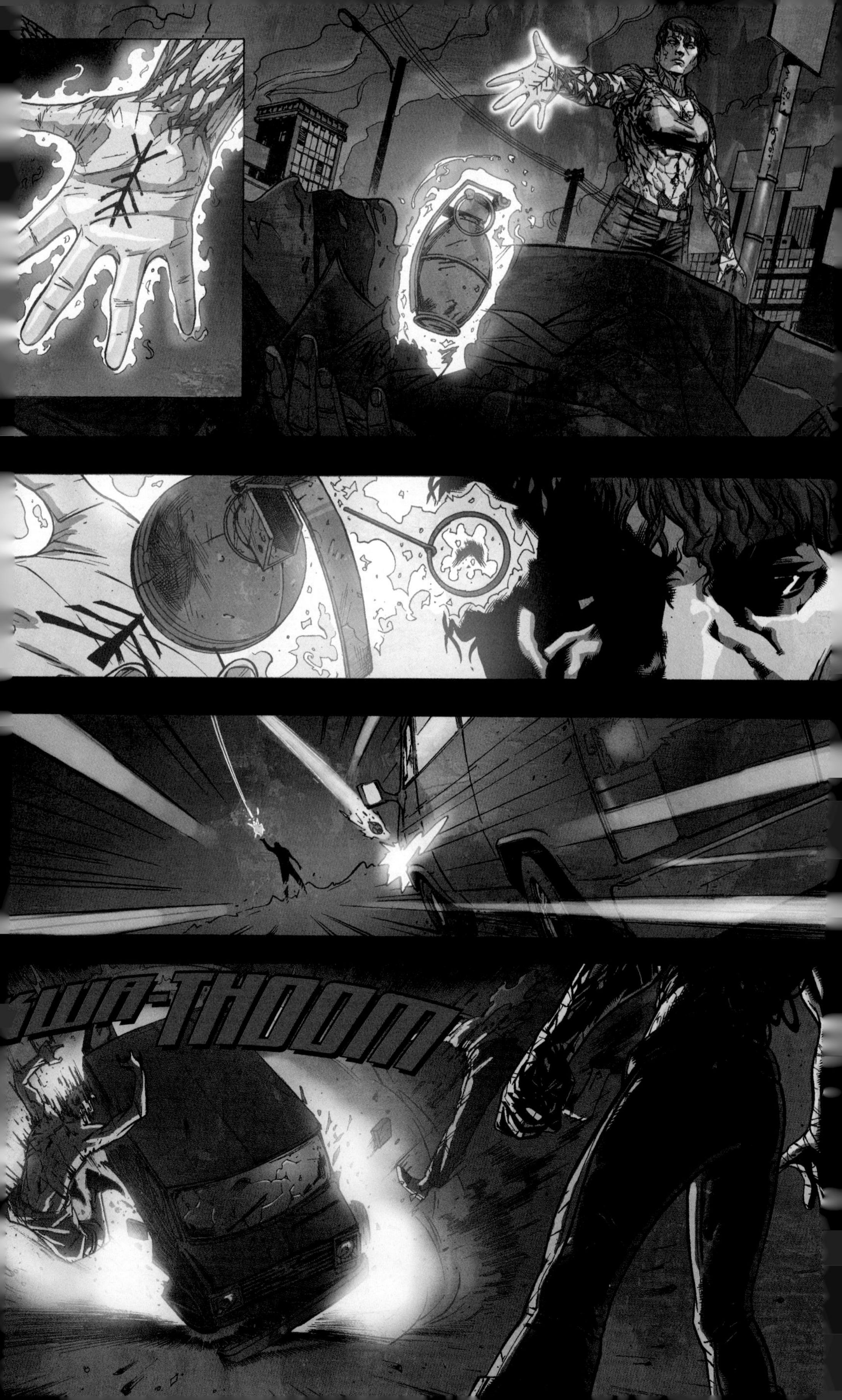
WA-THOOM

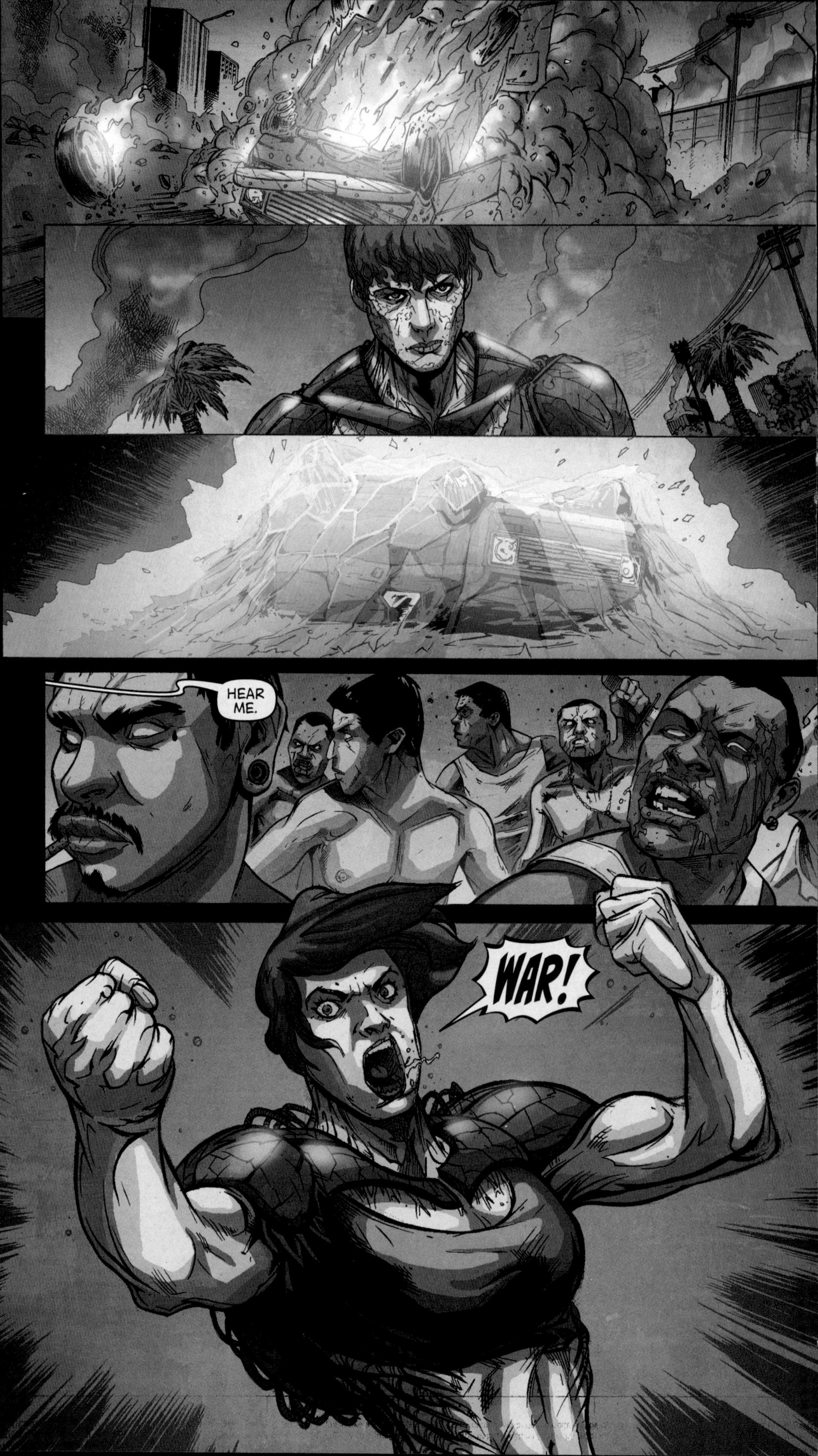
HEAR ME.
WAR!

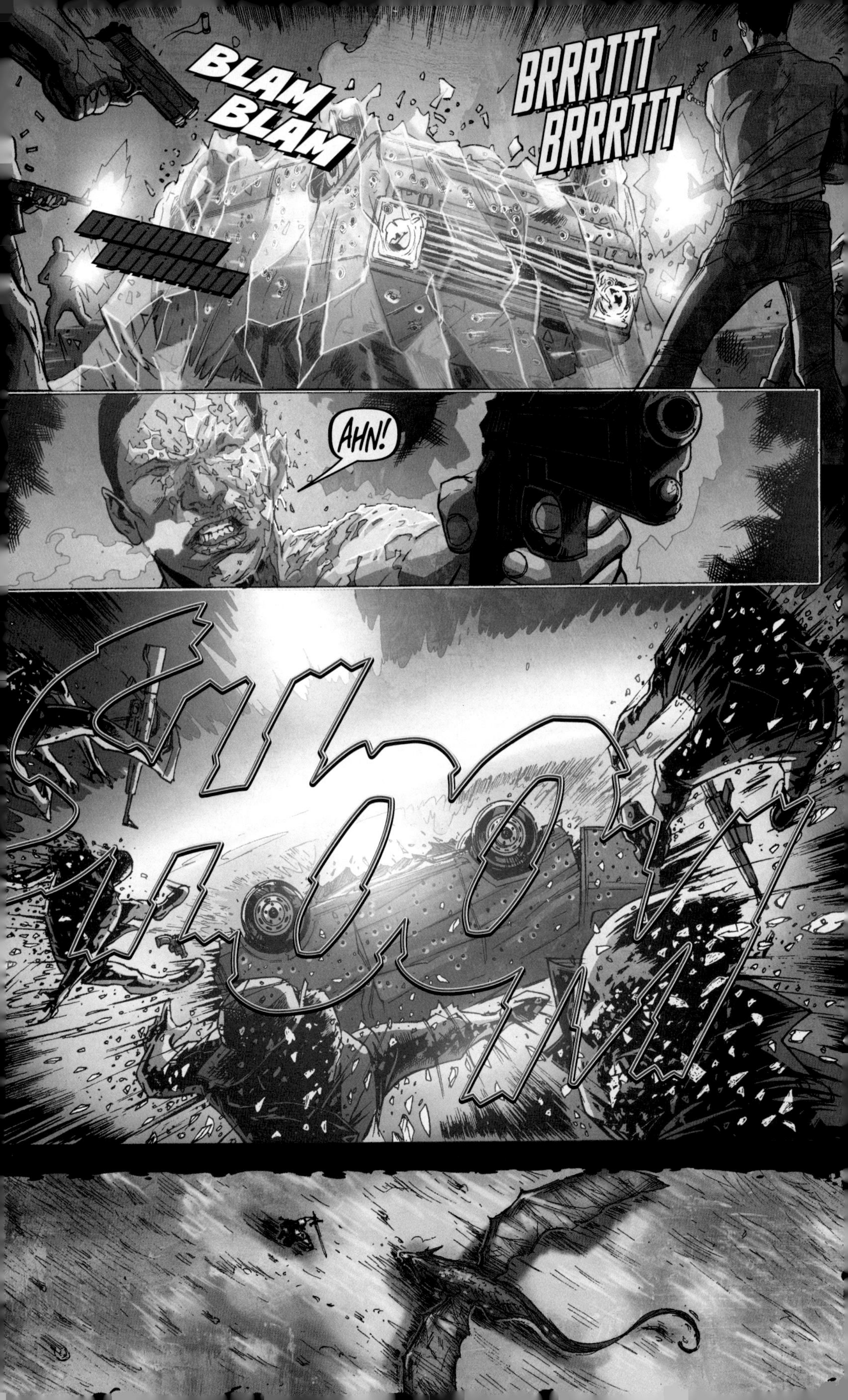
BLAM
BLAM
BRRRTTT
BRRRTTT
AHN!

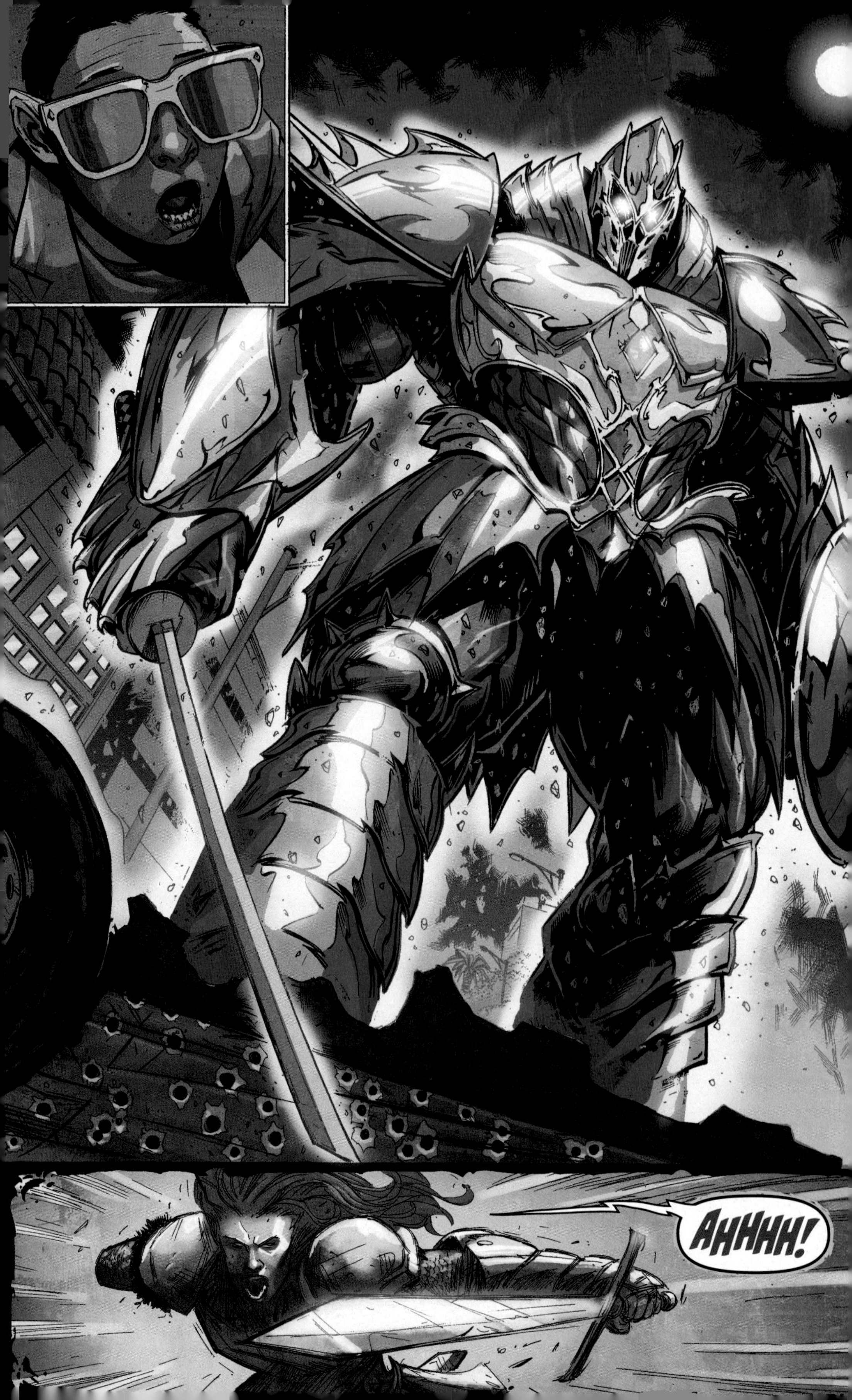
AHHHH!

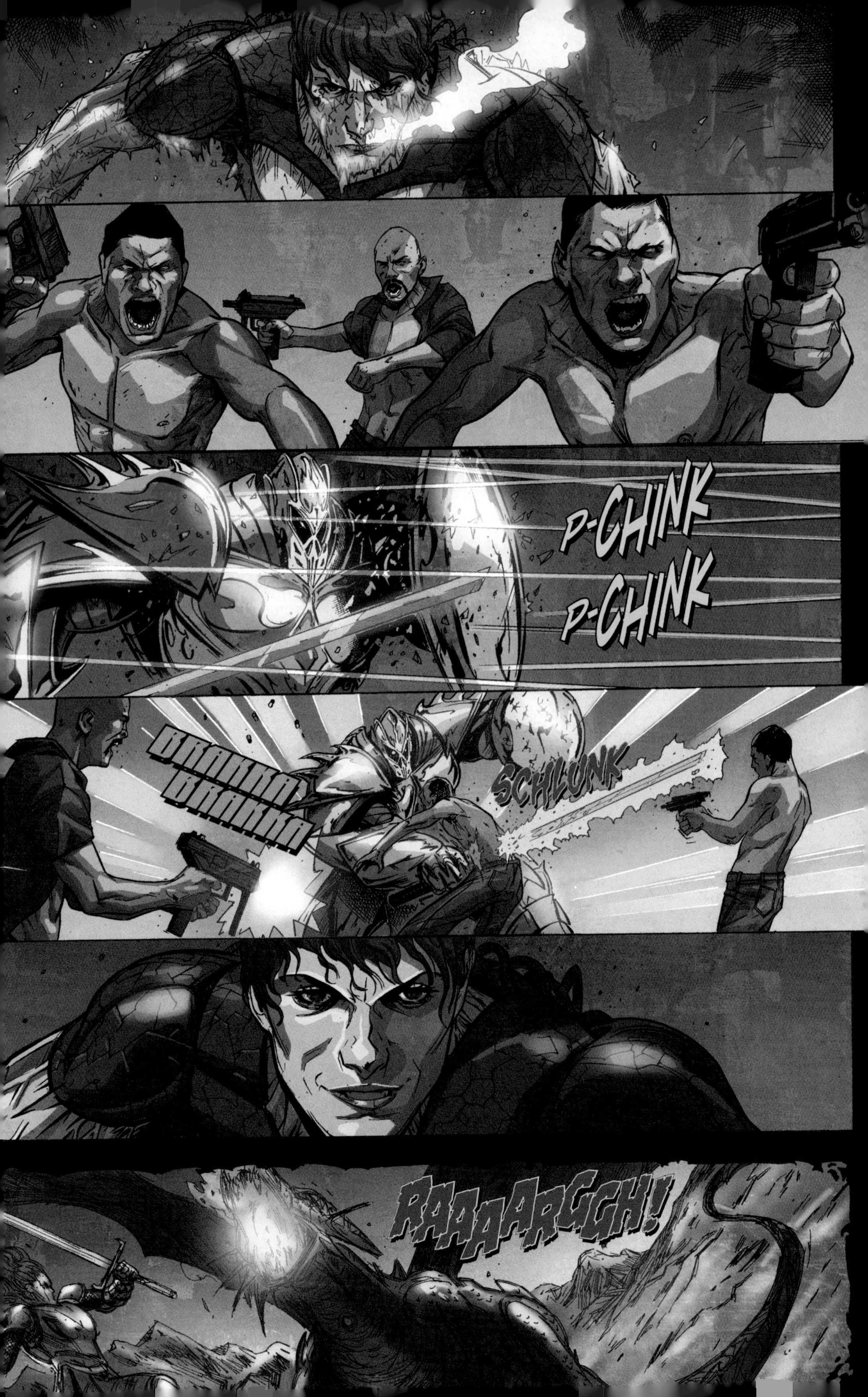
P-CHINK
P-CHINK
BRAKKA
BRAKKA
SCHLUNK
RAAAARGGH!

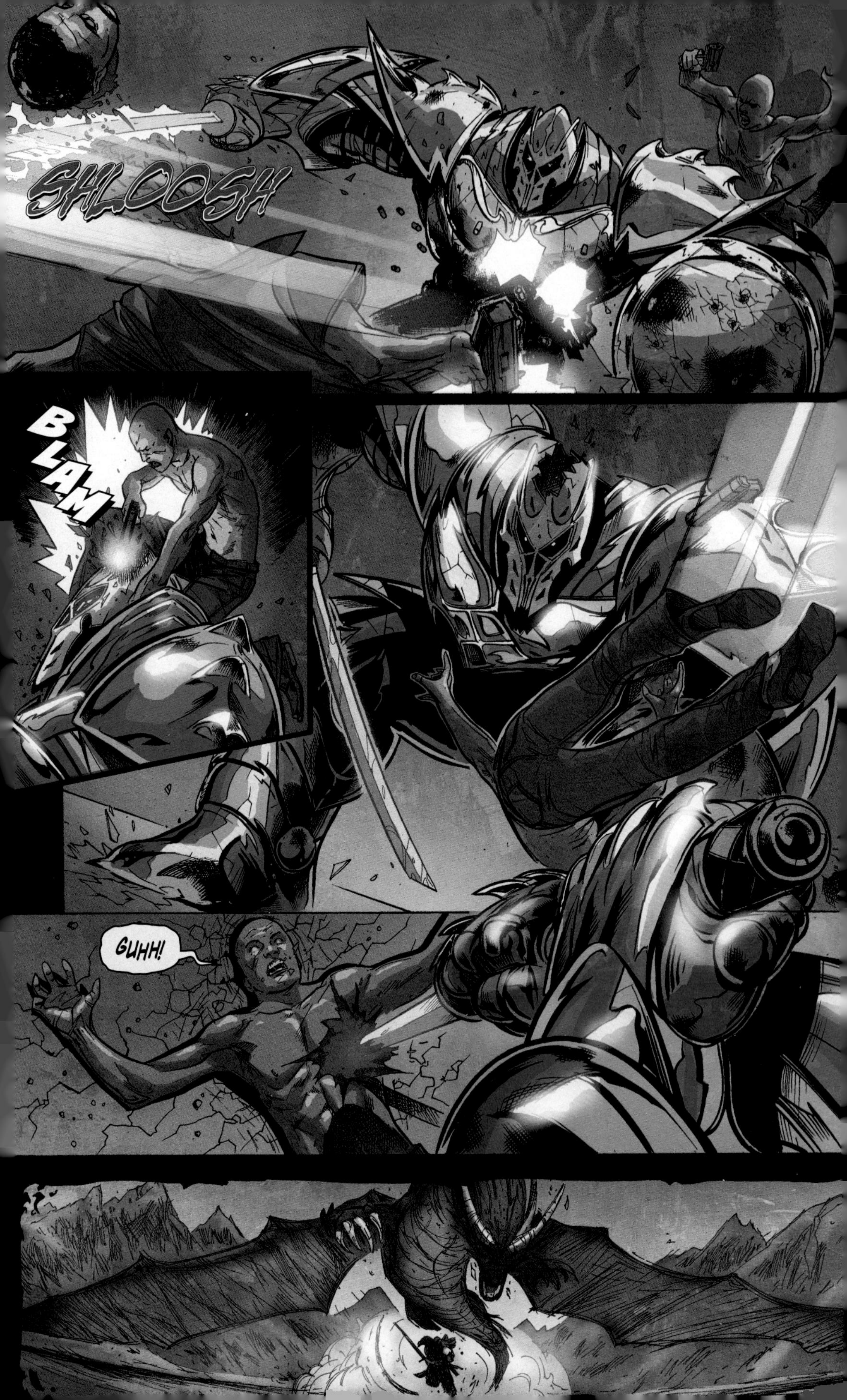
SHLOOSH
BLAM
GUHH!

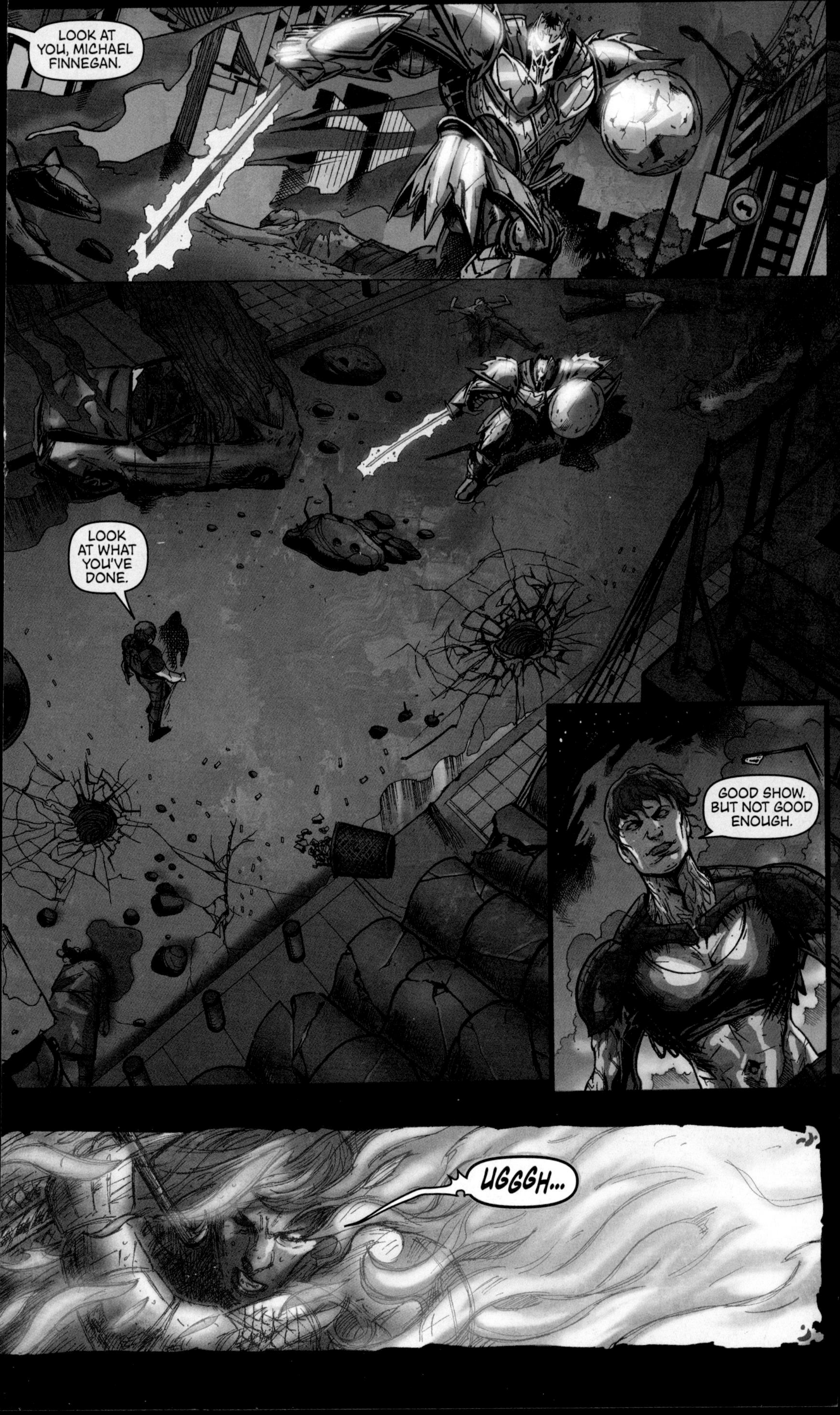
LOOK AT YOU, MICHAEL FINNEGAN.
LOOK AT WHAT YOU'VE DONE.
GOOD SHOW. BUT NOT GOOD ENOUGH.
UGGGH...

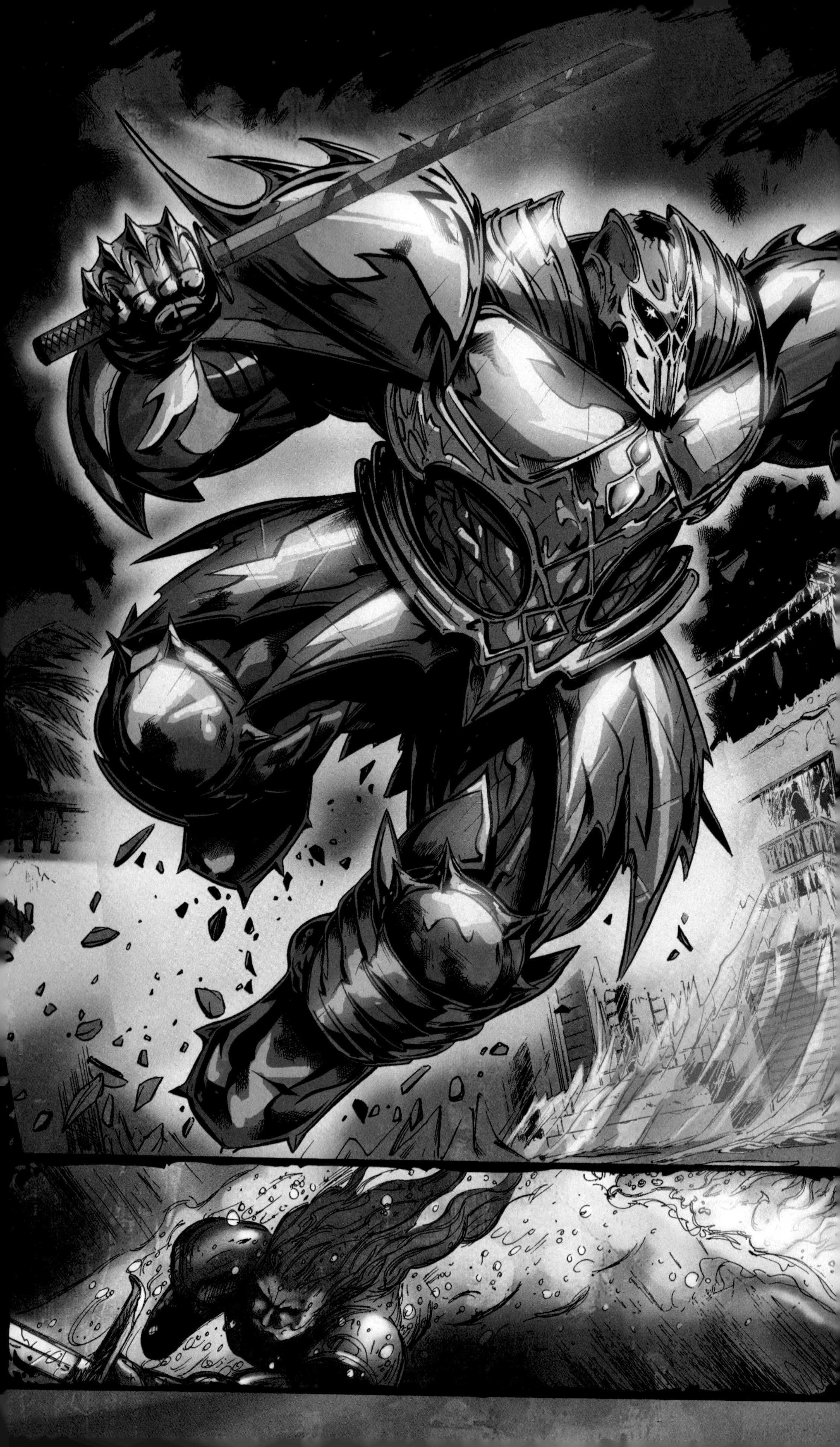

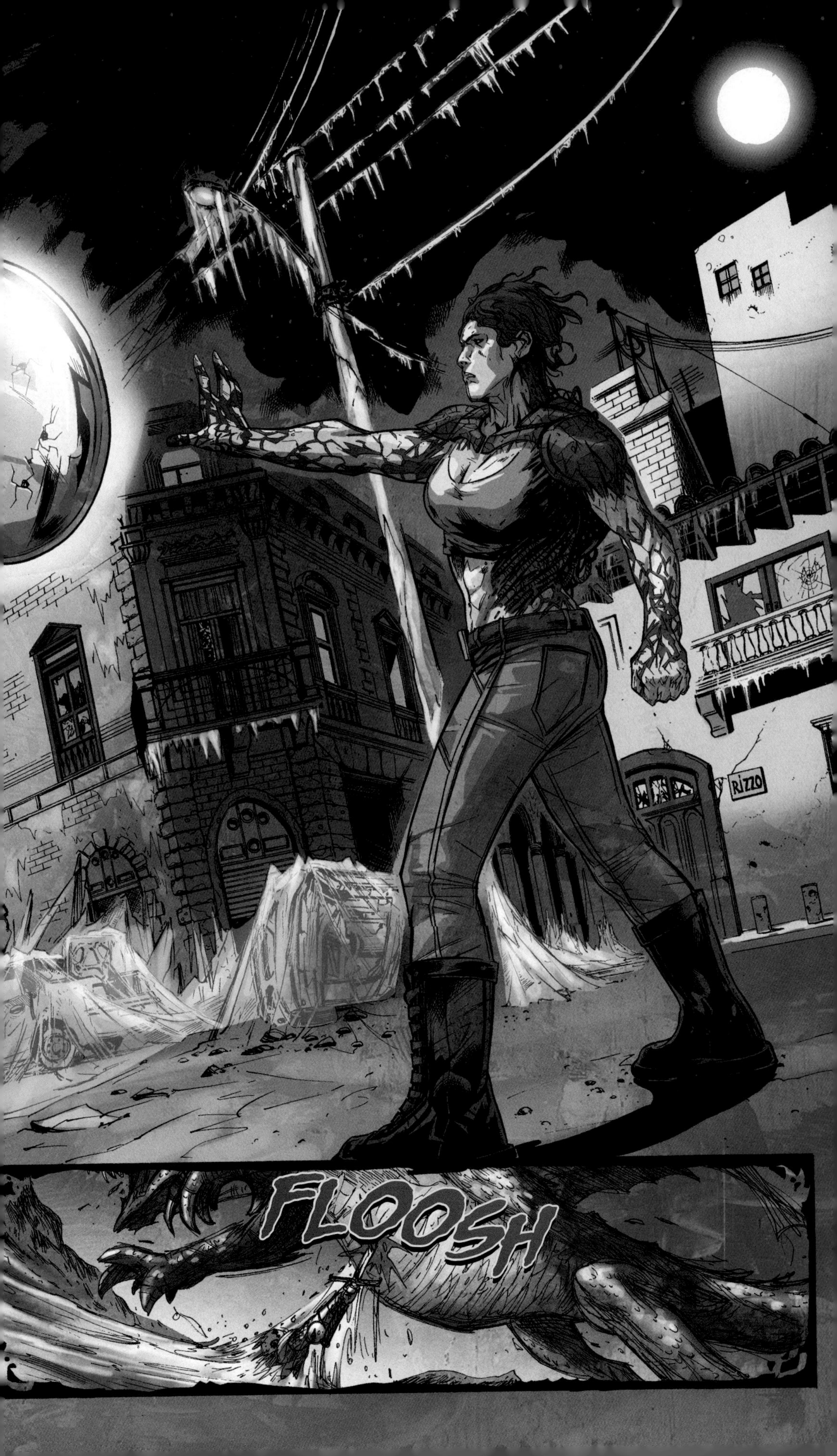
RIZZO
FLOOSH

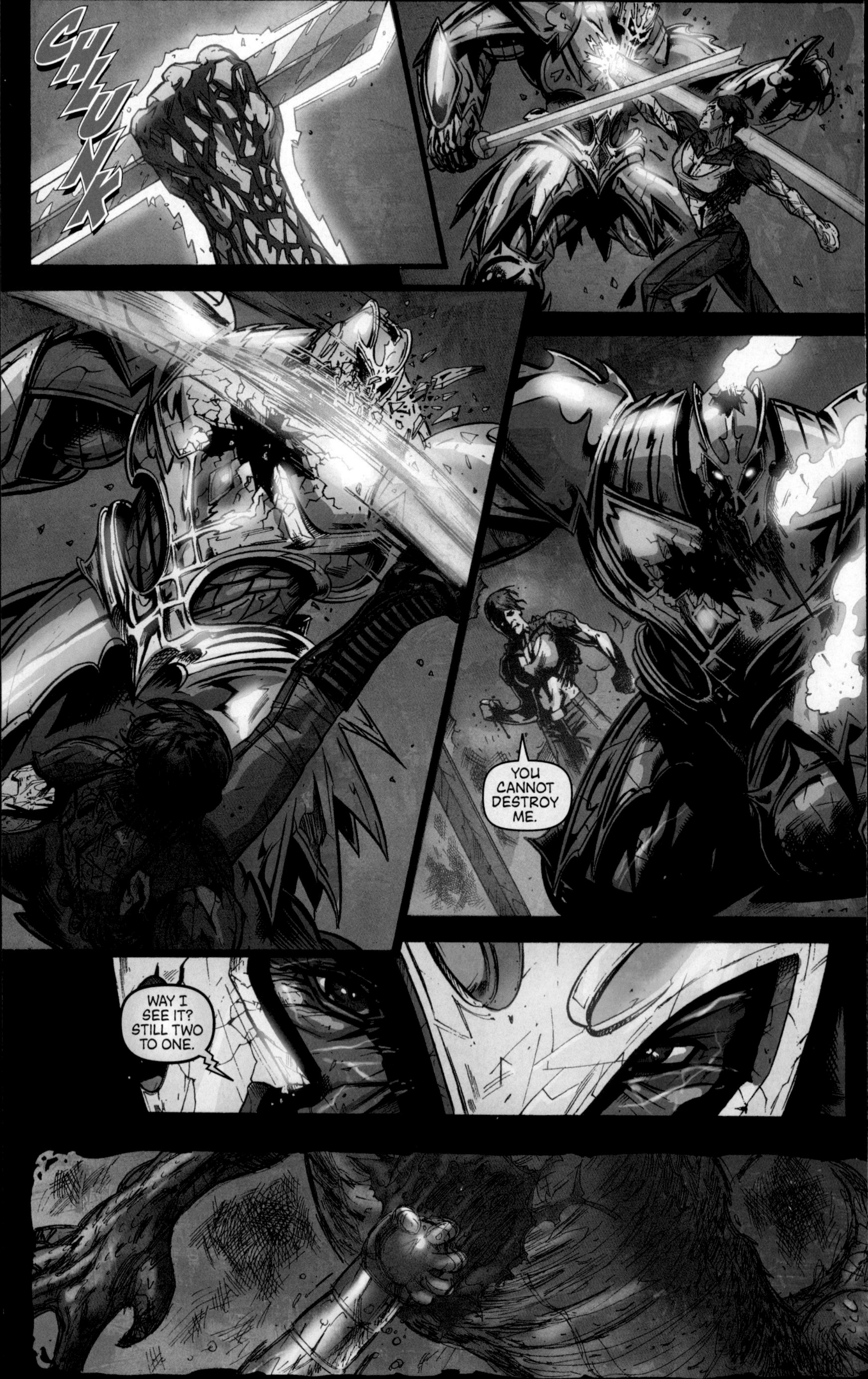
CHUNK
YOU CANNOT DESTROY ME.
WAY I SEE IT? STILL TWO TO ONE.

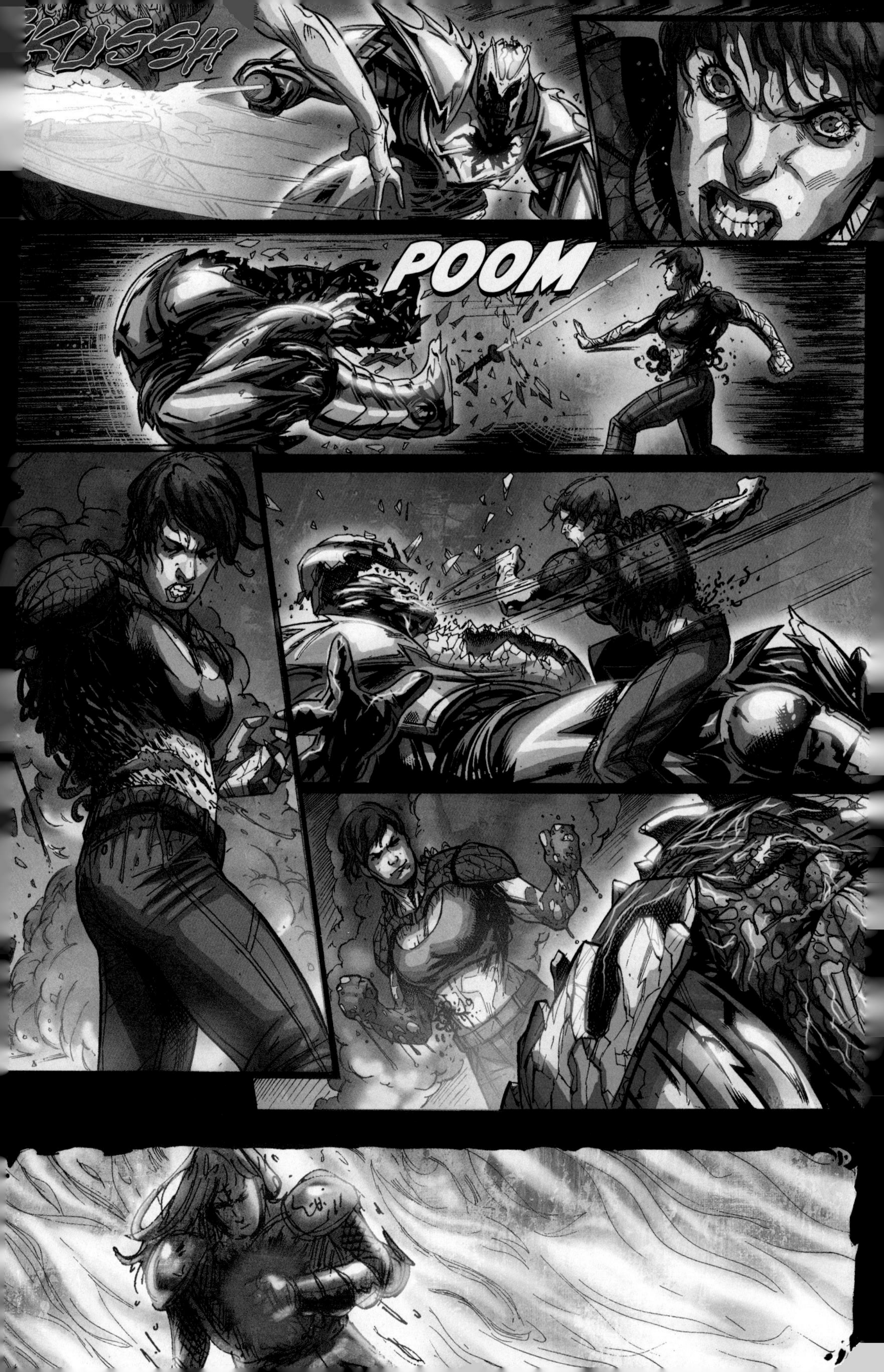
KUSSH
POOM

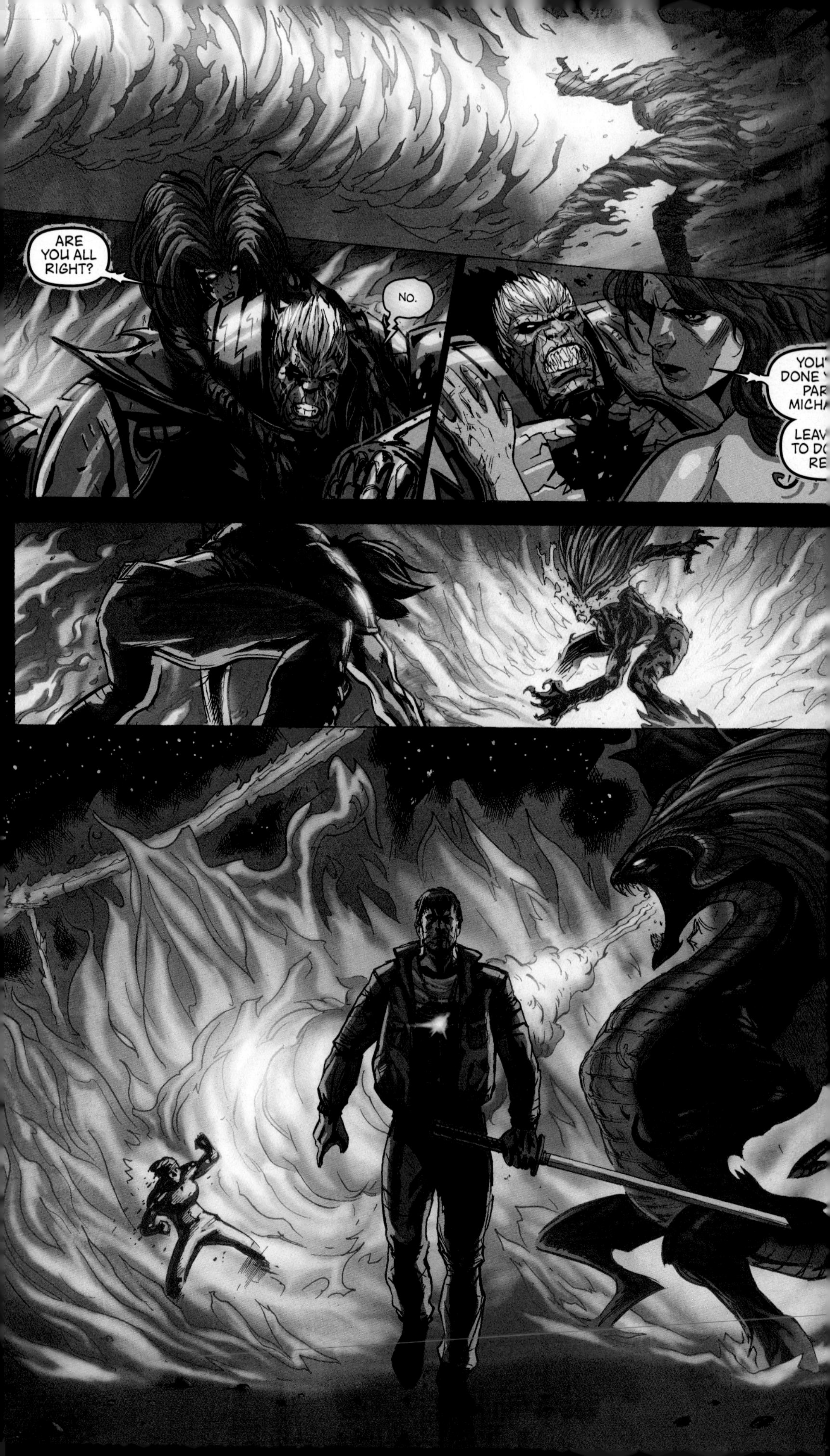
ARE YOU ALL RIGHT?
NO.
YOU' DONE PAR MICHA
LEAV TO DO RE

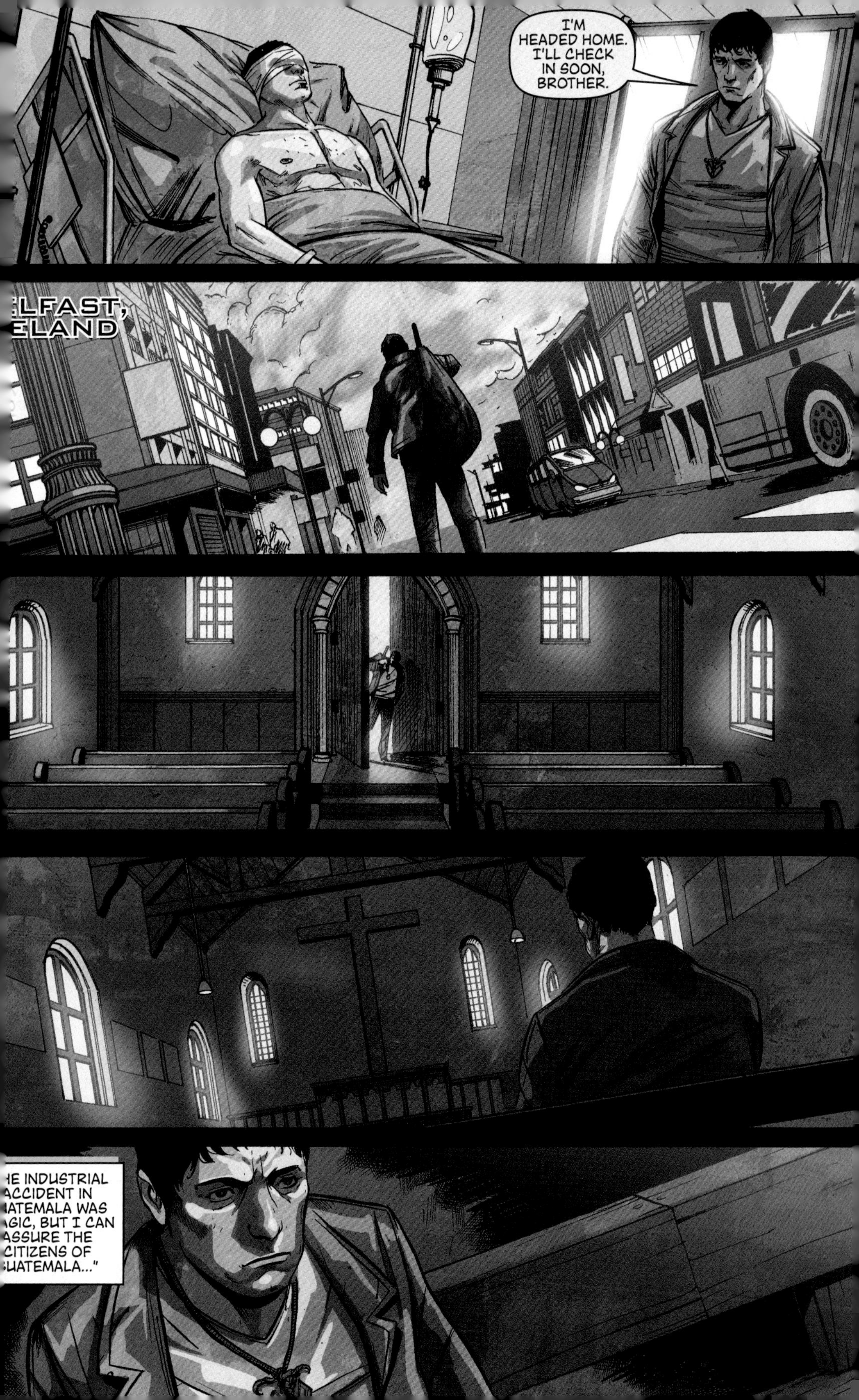
I'M HEADED HOME. I'LL CHECK IN SOON, BROTHER.
ELFAST, ELAND
HE INDUSTRIAL ACCIDENT IN ATEMALA WAS AGIC, BUT I CAN ASSURE THE CITIZENS OF UATEMALA..."

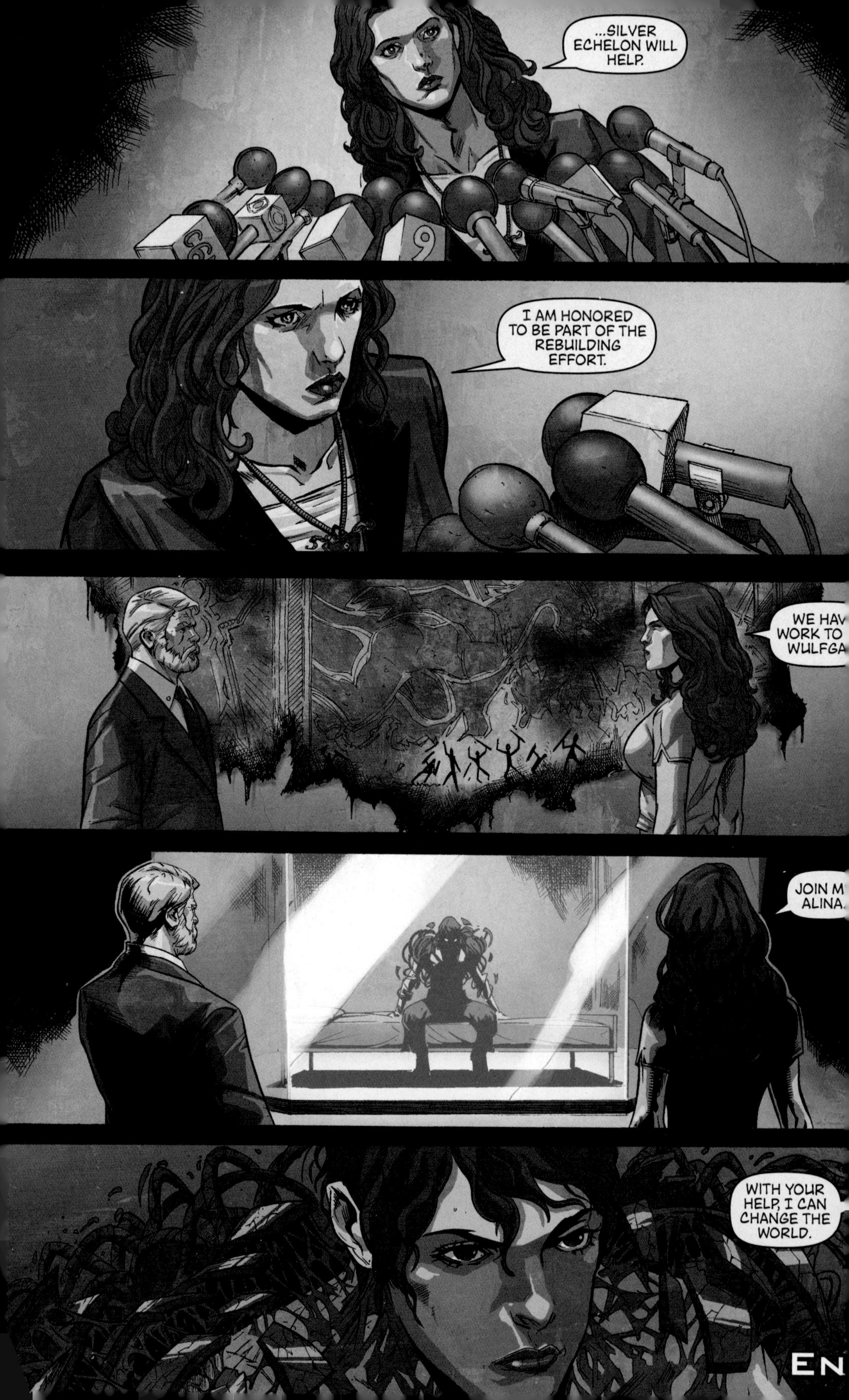
...SILVER ECHELON WILL HELP.
I AM HONORED TO BE PART OF THE REBUILDING EFFORT.
WE HAV WORK TO WULFGA
JOIN M ALINA.
WITH YOUR HELP, I CAN CHANGE THE WORLD.
EN

A letter from
Bryan Edward Hill
& Rob Levin

Long before JJ Abrams pushed the idea of the 'Mystery Box' into the cultural meme, people have asked the same question. From wrapped presents to the final scene of Se7en, we've all wondered, "What's in the box?"

In **Broken Trinity: Pandora's Box**, we tried to give you that answer. But we also aimed to give you an adrenaline pumping, edge of your seat, insert-hyperbole-here story that shows you a whole different corner of the Top Cow Universe. Because that's what we do. And that's what you, the reader, deserve.

Chances are, the book you're holding now isn't your first comic. That means you're familiar with the grammar and the tropes of mainstream comic books. You might even be familiar with Glorianna Silver and Michael Finnegan from *Broken Trinity*. That's good too. But you're likely not familiar with us or our collaborators on the project. And that's great.

Take everything you know and put it in a box. Label it "old stuff" and put it off to the side. It'll always be there for you if you need it. This story is an introduction to ourselves and our collaborators..

We're Bryan and Rob, and we've been your writers for the second chapter of the Broken Trinity epic. The pencils and inks are courtesy of the amazing Alessandro Vitti and Facundo Percio, and bringing it home on colors is the inimitable Sunny Gho and the crew at IFS Studios. And in case you wanted a familiar name, we were able to convince superstar Tommy Lee Edwards to put the proverbial lid on **Pandora's Box**.

Thanks for giving us a chance, and as always, we remind you to drink responsibly.

- Bryan Edward Hill & Rob Levin

THE CHARACTERS OF BROKEN TRINITY: PANDORA'S BOX

BY: BRYAN EDWARD HILL & ROB LEVIN

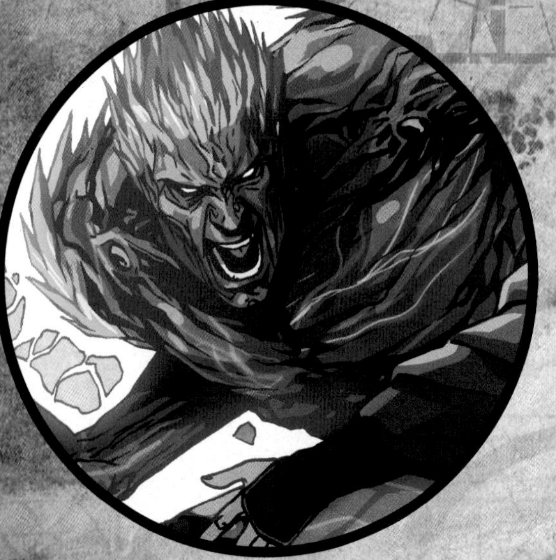

Michael "Finn" Finnegan - Ex-gun runner Michael Finnegan grew up on the coldest side of Northern Irelan learning from a young age that surviving meant combini violence, luck and charm into a way of life. Unaware of t legend of the Witchblade, Finn was hired to follow Sara Pezzini by Jackie Estcado a.k.a The Darkness. Finn quick found himself in a new world of magic and terror when The Curator gave him the Glacier Stone...and made him person responsible for serving its legacy in our time. Aft a violent confrontation with Glorianna Silver, Finnegan r struggles with the power of the Glacier Stone, half curio about its potential -- half resentful that his life was turn upside down because of it.

Glorianna "Glori" Silver - At seven years old, Glorianna Silver was orphaned when marauders invaded her poor Norwegian farmhouse. Just when it appeared she would be another statistic of poverty, she was found by Wulfgar Olafsson. On her eighth birthday, she was given a new purpose: Wulfgar told her it was her destiny to bear the power of the Ember Stone. Since that day, Wulfgar has trained Glori in everything from the highest-level academics to the most brutal fighting arts. Upon finding the Ember Stone, Glori claimed her legacy and set off to fulfill it...by taking the Glacier Stone, uniting the trinity and using its power to remake the world according to her vision. Now Glori commands a multi-million dollar empire given to her by Wulfgar's lineage. She has charities. Political contacts. Global influence...but she doesn't have the Glacier Stone, and that's where her obsession lies.

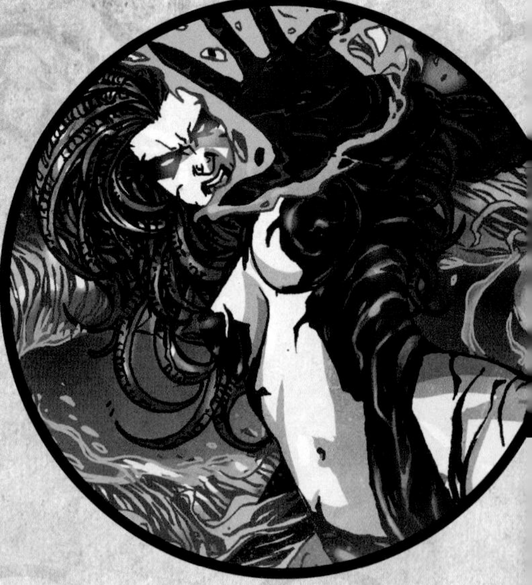

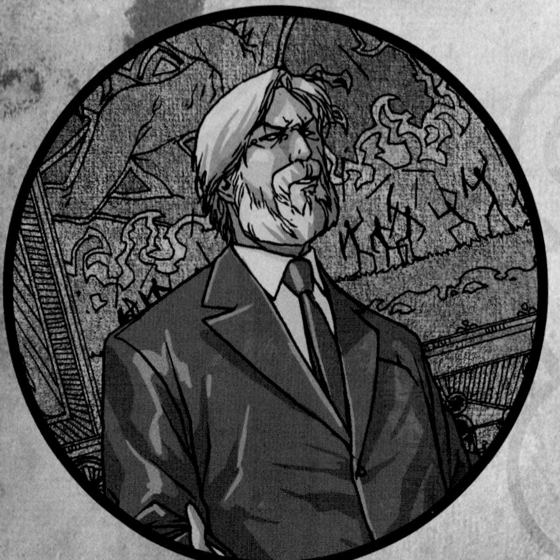

Wulfgar Olafsson - The Olafsson family line has exis for one purpose: to find and train the bearers of the Emb Stone. Stretching back to the dark ages, they have cultur a multi-million dollar fortune. In the modern day, Wulfg is the patriarch of the Olafsson's estate. Wulfgar created Sons of Ember, a group dedicated to protecting the Olafs Empire and the bearer of the Ember Stone, Wulfgar's ado daughter, Glorianna Silver. A lifetime student of history, literature and philosophy, Wulfgar has been Glori's teach mentor, trainer and protector. Now that Glori possesses the Ember Stone, it is through Wulfgar's counsel that Gl wages her war to unite the Broken Trinity.

enshin Kawakami - Kenshin is a former Japanese
ilitary man, but he never talks about it. Something bad
ppened when he was in the service. He bears the weight
this at all times. He's burdened by his past because he's
ed, seen, and endured terrible things. He's even done
me of them himself.

ter leaving the military, Kenshin retired to a hillside dojo
here he teaches philosophy and sword fighting in the same
anner as his ancestor, Miyamoto Musashi. At some point
his past, Kenshin wielded the Blood Sword, one of the
Artifacts. It's unclear how or why he gave it up, but the
arator trusts him enough to send Finnegan to study with
enshin and learn about the Blood Sword and the rest of the
tifacts.

Elias Legion - Elias is the charismatic prophet of the
Disciples of Adam. Born in the Middle East but educated
(socially and intellectually) in Europe. He's not a "warrior;"
he's a leader. A man of tradition. Purpose. He is constantly
moving forward.

His followers refer to him as 'Teacher Elias,' and he is the
only one known to have communicated with Disciple leader
Adam. Elias believes in Adam's wisdom and teachings above
all else, and he would bring the world to its knees, even
destroy it, if it accomplishes his goals. He's a zealot, and
that's what makes him so dangerous.

lina Enstrom - Elias' personal bodyguard/assassin and
cond-in-command. Born in a small town but raised in a
g city, she's a woman in a man's game (violence), so she
s precious little time for bullshit. She is, in all things,
ficient.

ina is the daughter of Pavel Enstrom, a black market
eapons manufacturer whose wife was murdered. He
entually found the Disciples and believed in Adam's
use, indoctrinating Alina at a young age. She is the
erfect weapon, unencumbered by a conscience because she
lieves that what she's doing is for a higher purpose.

The Disciples of Adam - Unlike most dangerous cults,
the Disciples aren't just armed; they're highly trained and
well-funded. The followers Elias has assembled may as well
be an elite special ops taskforce, not religious followers.
They come from all nations and many walks of life, though
most have military or private security backgrounds, and were
found by Elias when they fell from the grace of their nations
or their loved ones.

Their goal is to bring about the dawn of the New Eden,
cleansing the world and starting again without the mistakes
of the past. They believe themselves to be both pure and
righteous, and the rest of the world to be sinners. Every
disciple bears the Mark of Adam—a runic symbol tattooed
or branded into his or her flesh, usually on the right palm.
Some have added additional marks as a sign of loyalty.

FOR THE FULL STORY OF FINN AND GLORI'S ORIGIN, PICK UP THE
BROKEN TRINITY VOLUME 1 TRADE PAPERBACK IN STORES NOW!
– FILIP AND PHIL.

BROKEN TRINITY

• • • • •

COVER GALLERY

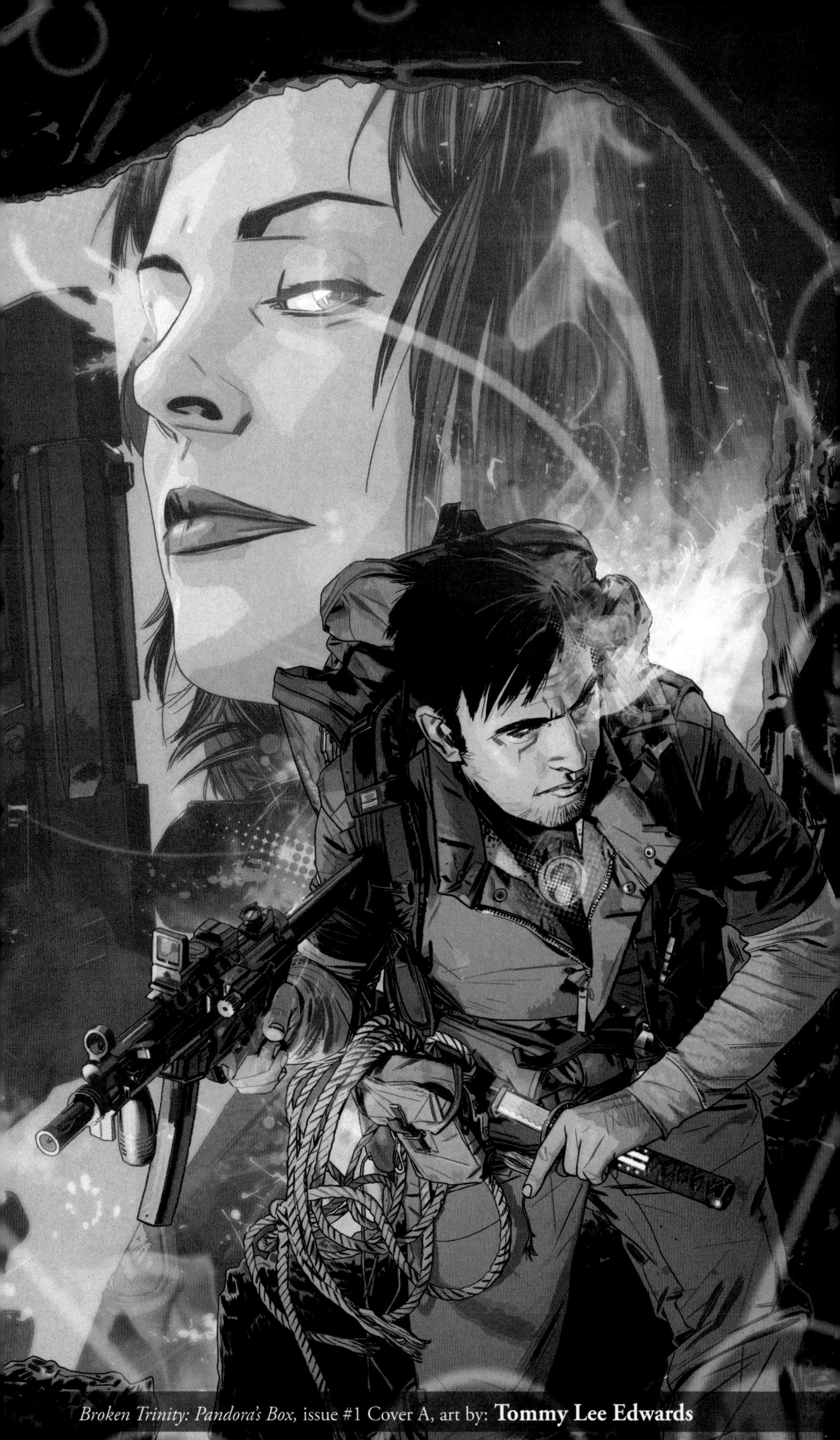

Broken Trinity: Pandora's Box, issue #1 Cover A, art by: **Tommy Lee Edwards**

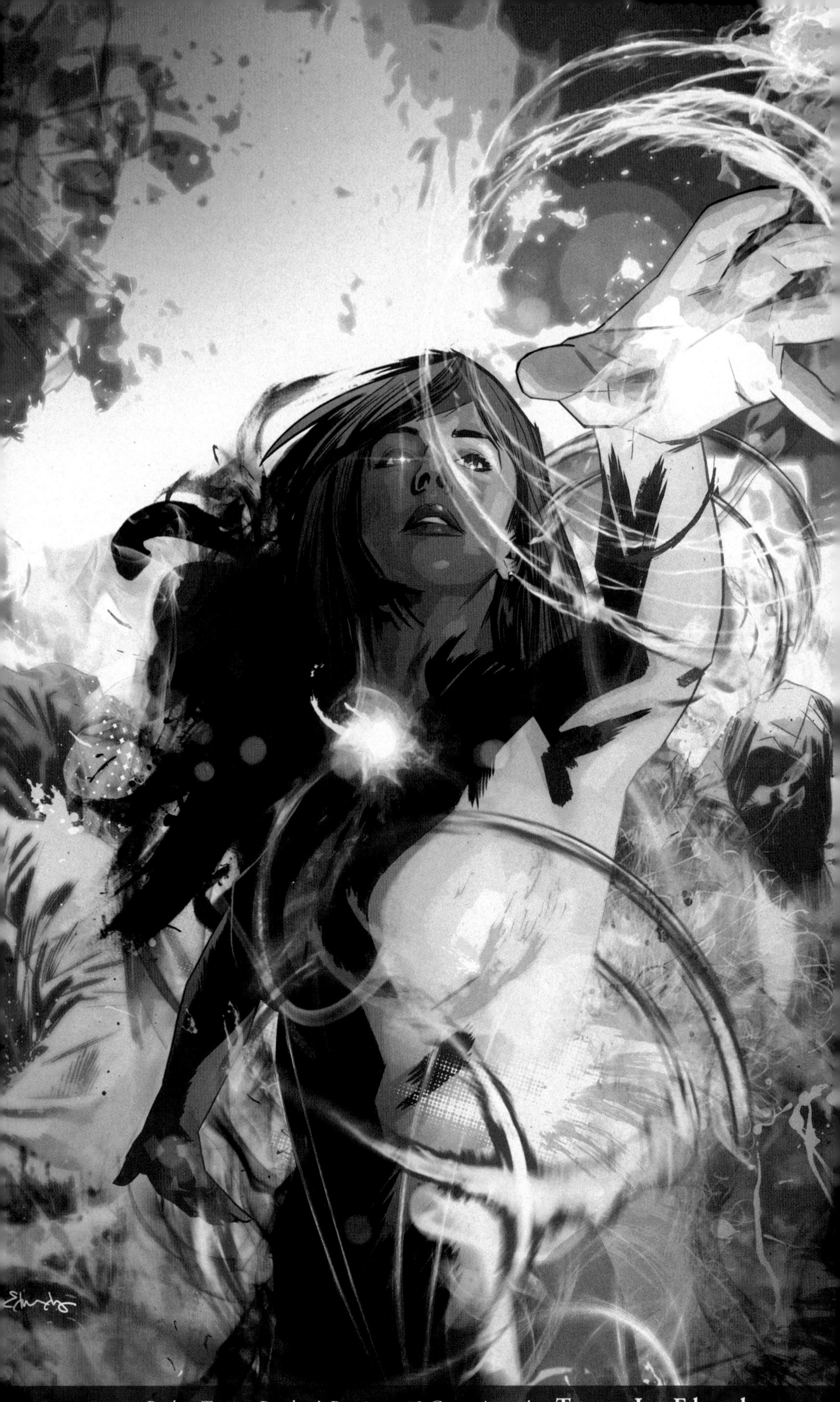

Broken Trinity: Pandora's Box, issue #2 Cover A, art by: **Tommy Lee Edwards**

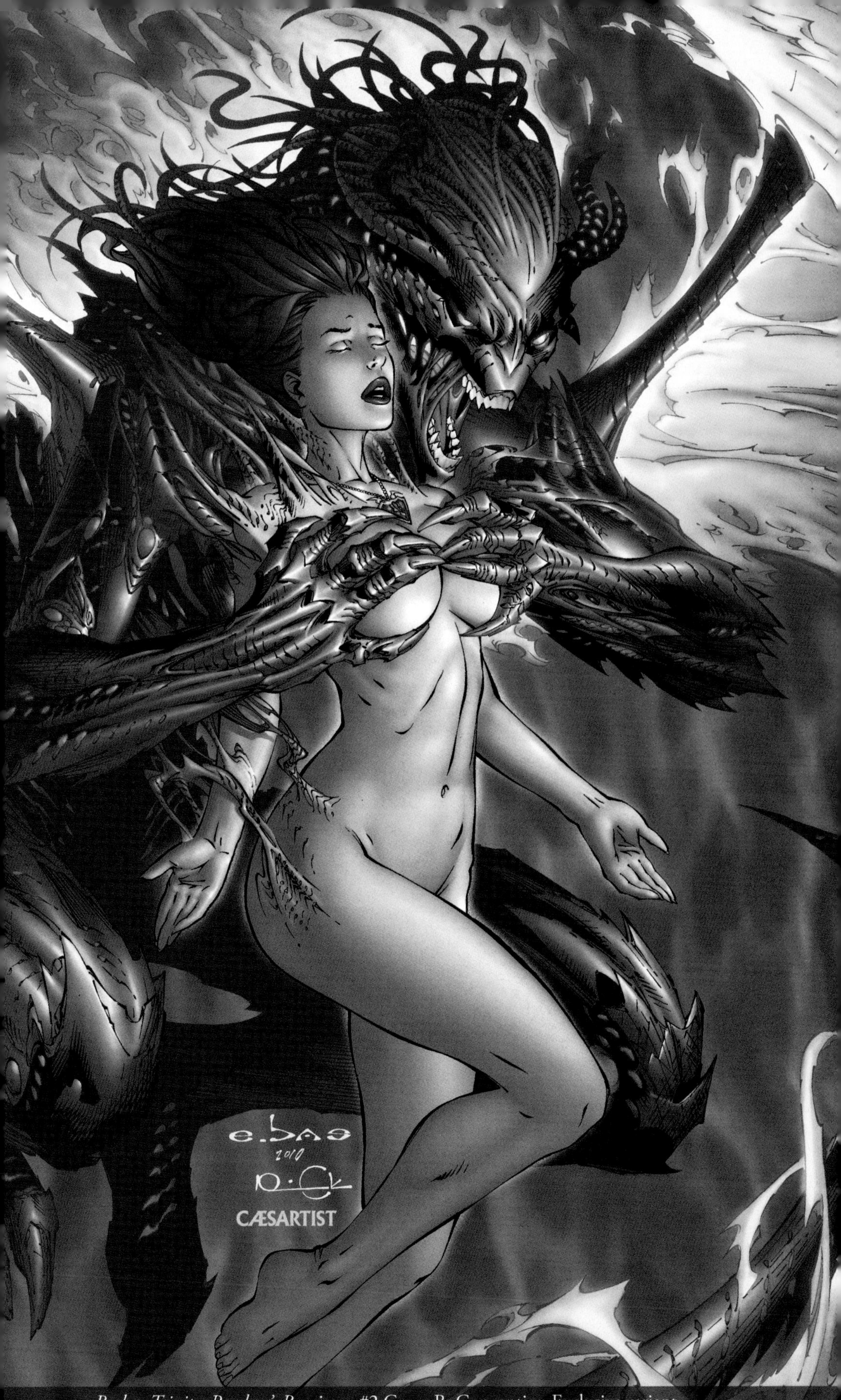
CÆSARTIST

Broken Trinity: Pandora's Box, issue #2 Cover B, Convention Exclusive variant,
art by: **Eric Basaldua, Rick Basaldua, Caesar Rodriguez**

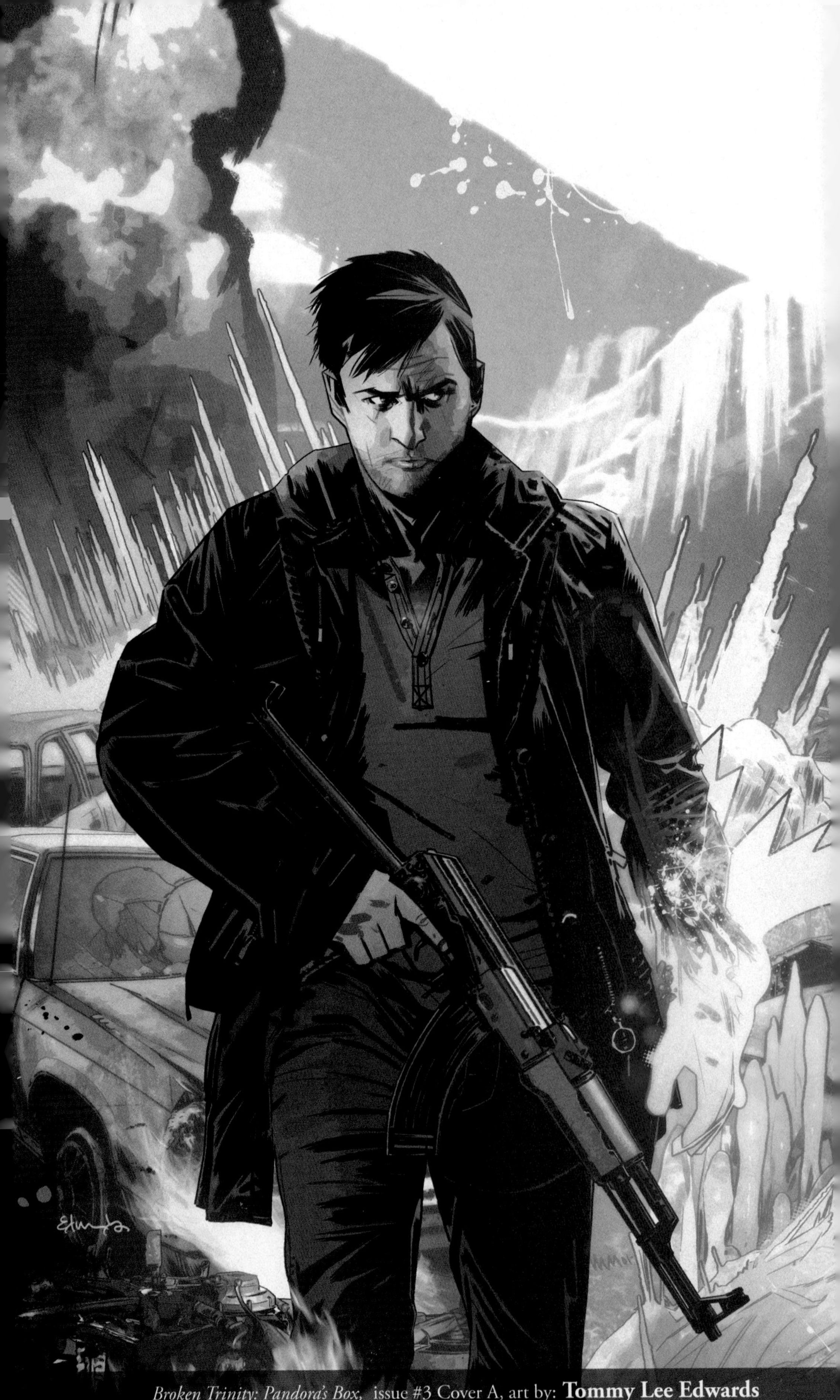

Broken Trinity: Pandora's Box, issue #3 Cover A, art by: **Tommy Lee Edwards**

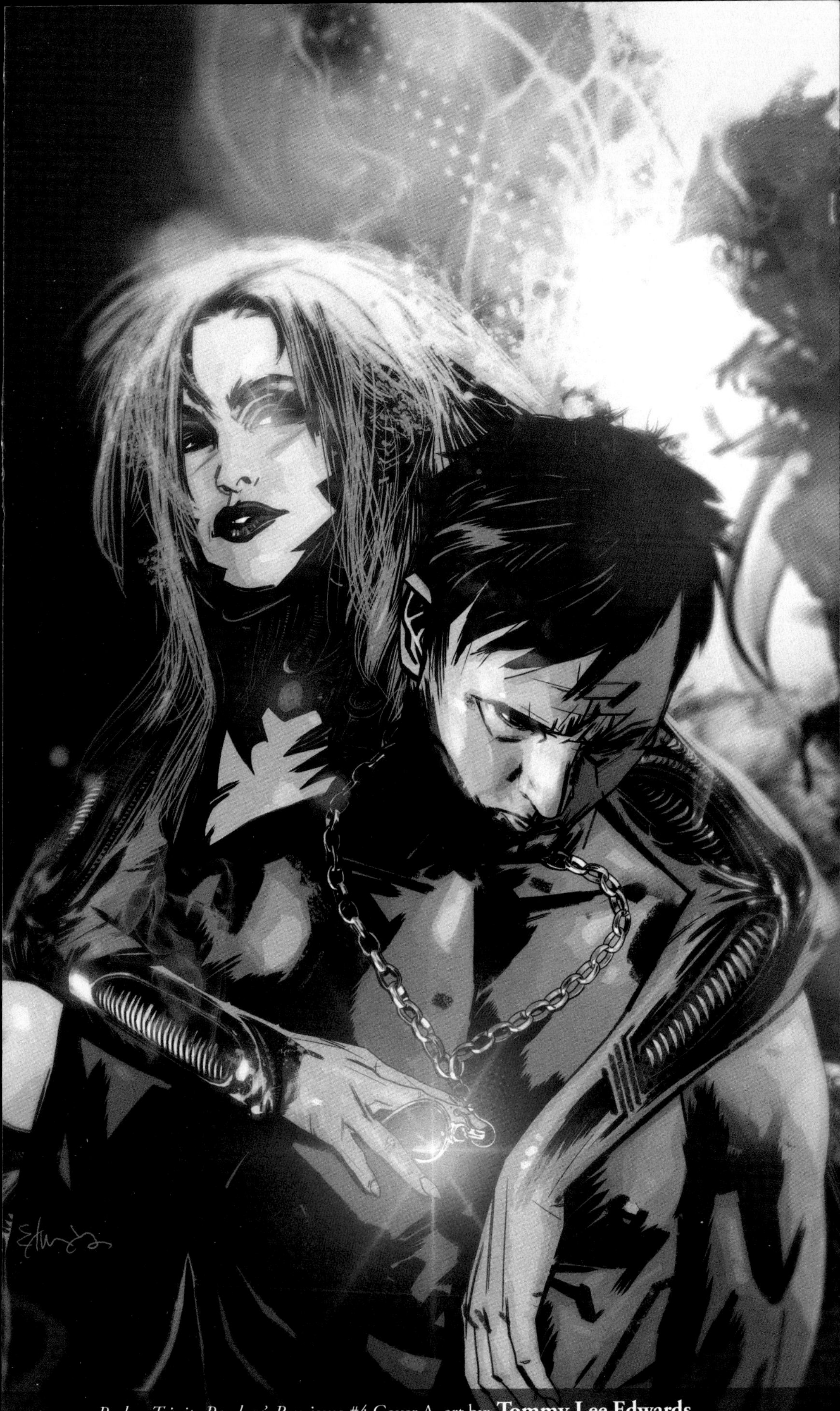

Broken Trinity:Pandora's Box, issue #4 Cover A, art by: **Tommy Lee Edwards**

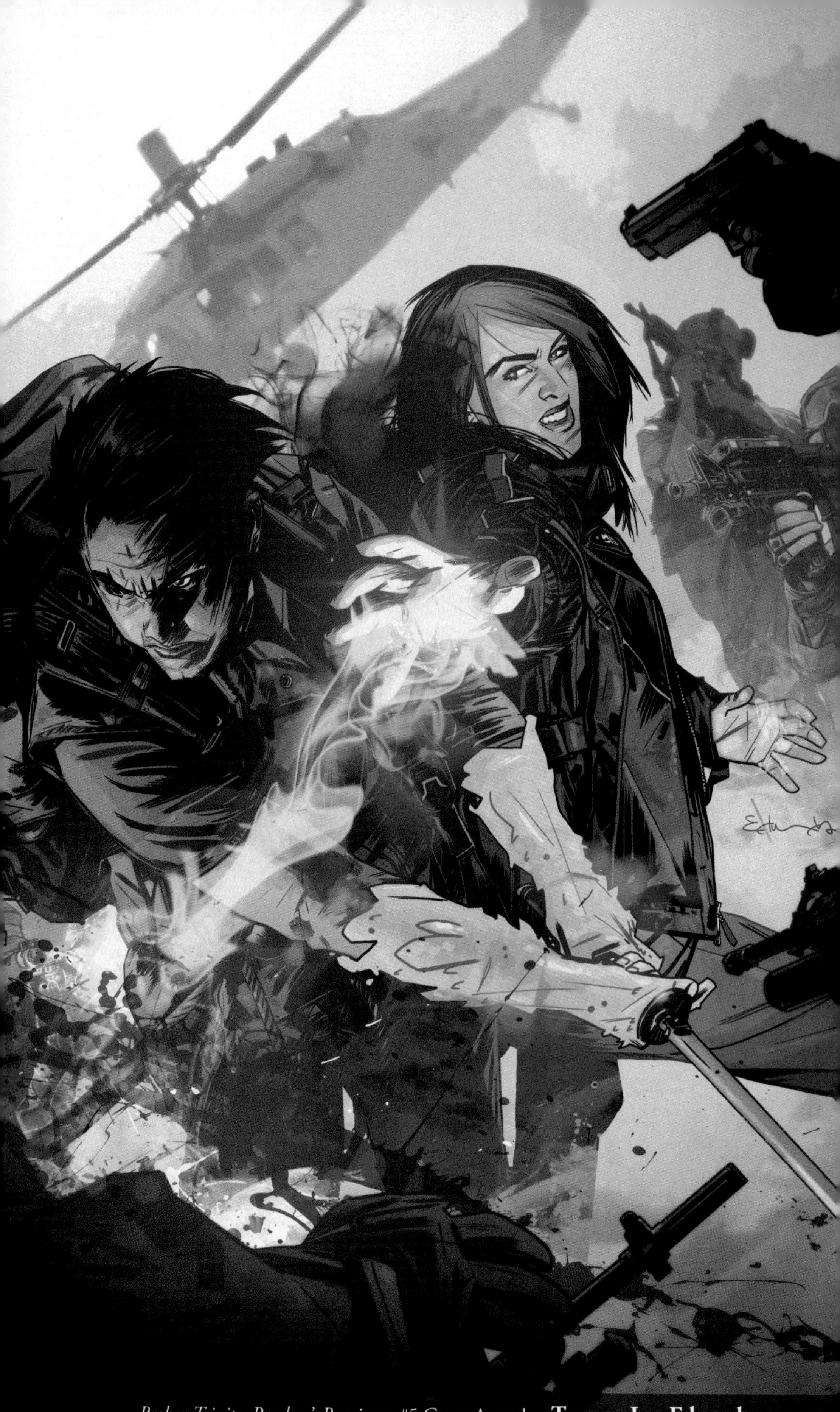

Broken Trinity: Pandora's Box, issue #5 Cover A, art by: **Tommy Lee Edwards**

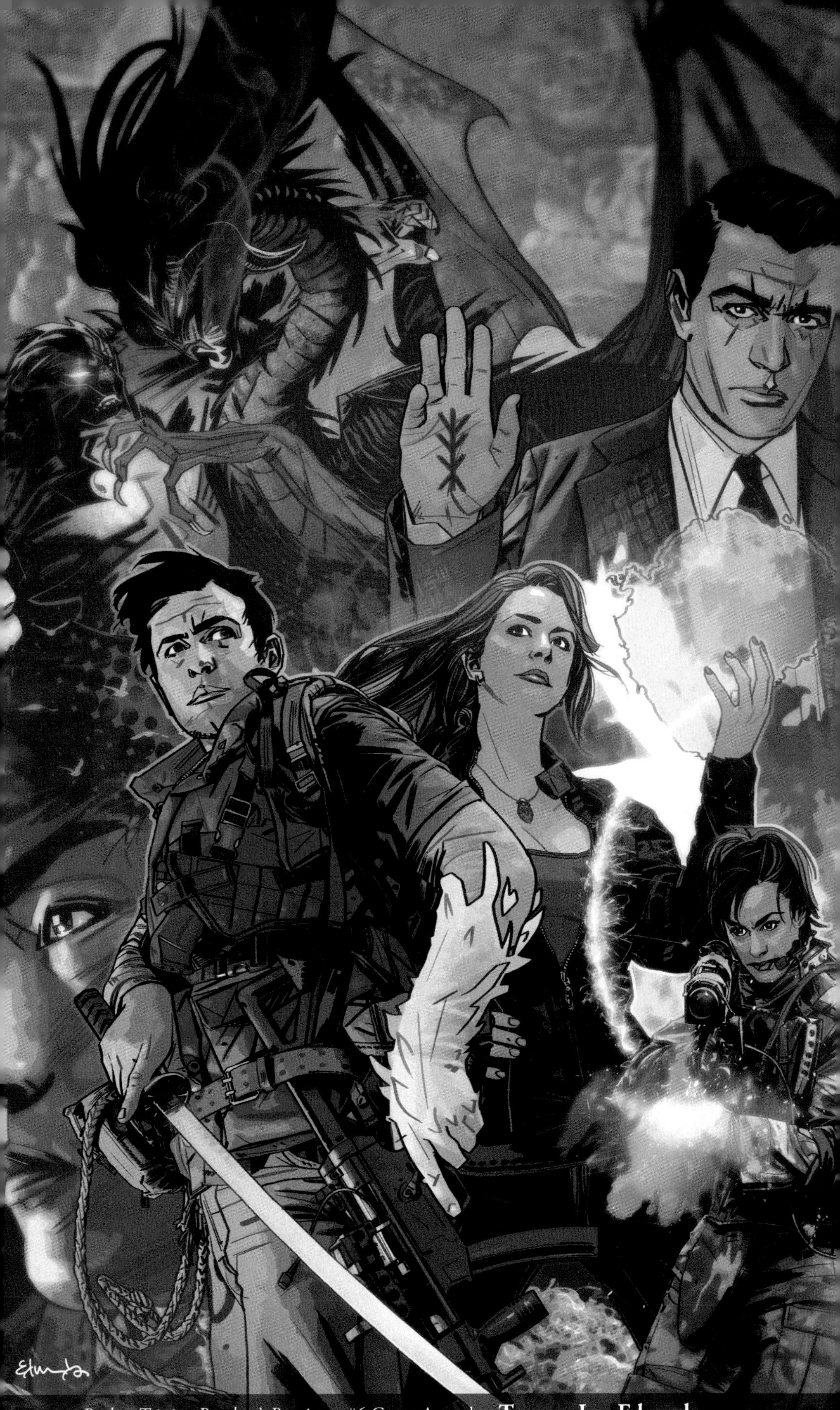

Broken Trinity: Pandora's Box, issue #6 Cover A, art by: **Tommy Lee Edwards**

BROKEN TRINITY
PANDORA'S BOX

Enjoy a look inside the sketchbooks of artists Alessandro Vitti and Facundo Percio with these never-before-seen character designs.

Kenshin   Alina

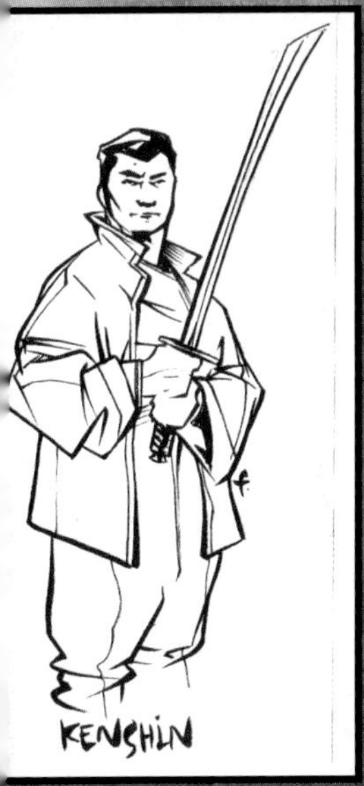
KENSHIN

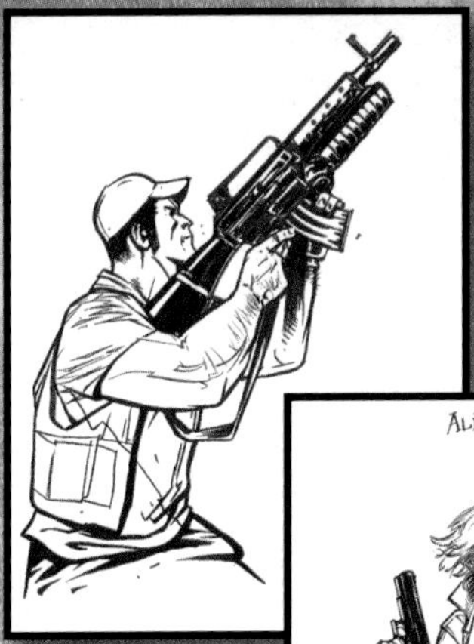

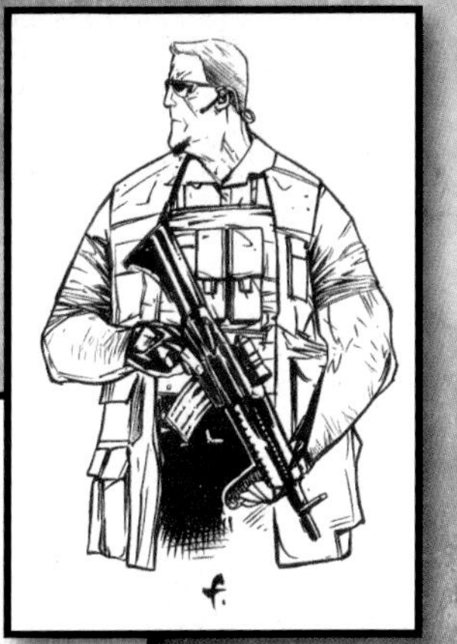

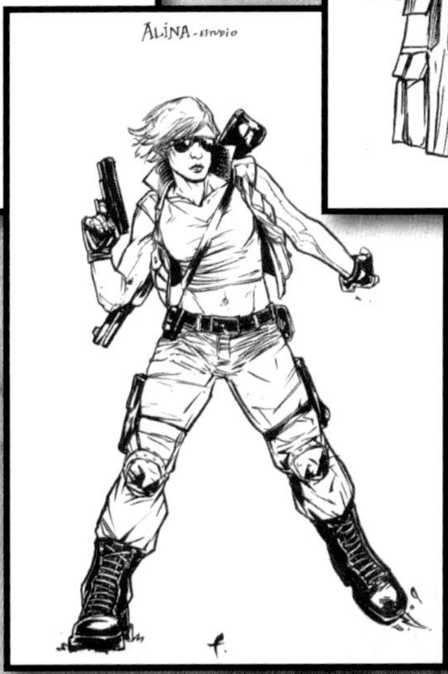
ALINA - ESTUDIO

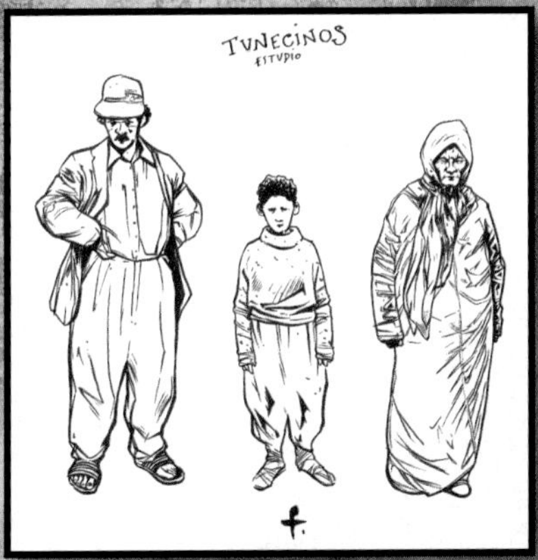
TUNECINOS
ESTUDIO

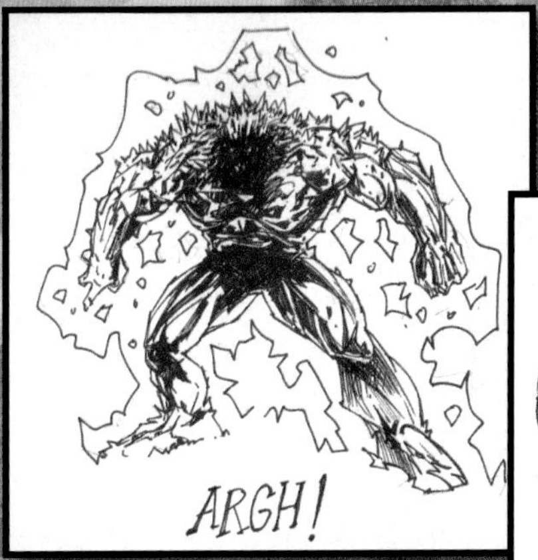
ARGH!

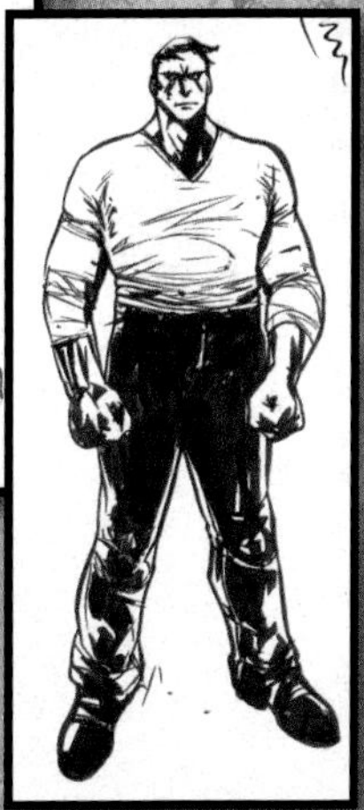

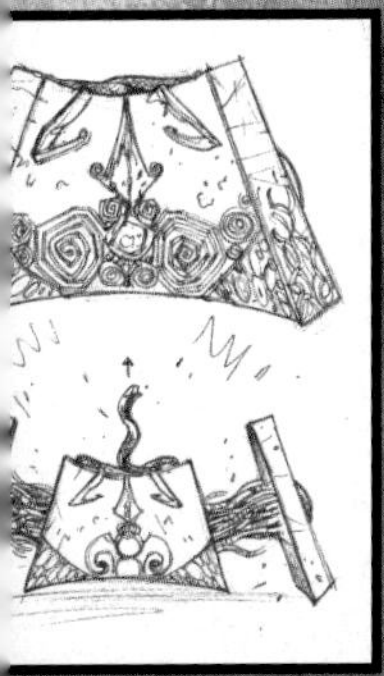

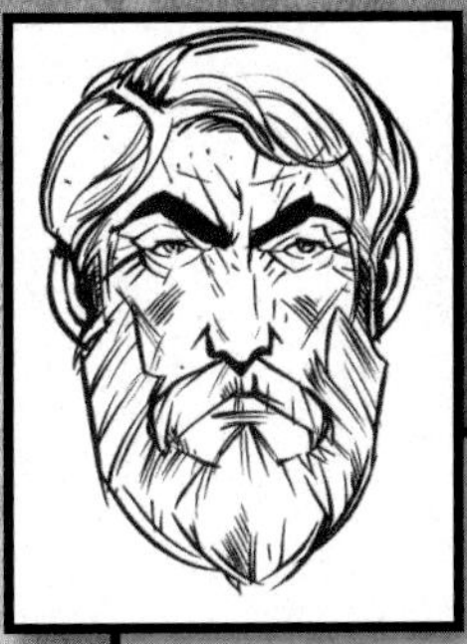

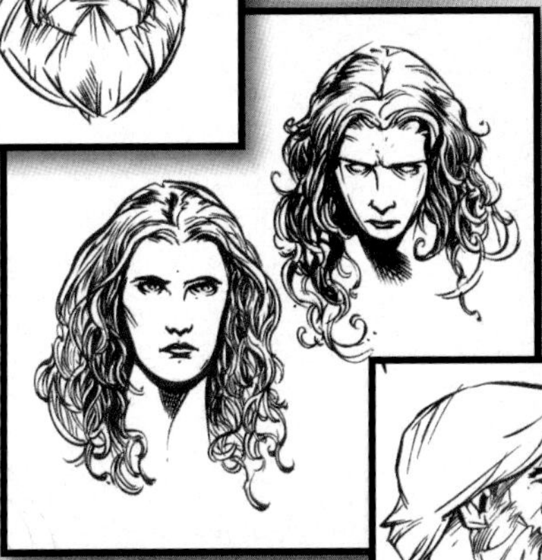

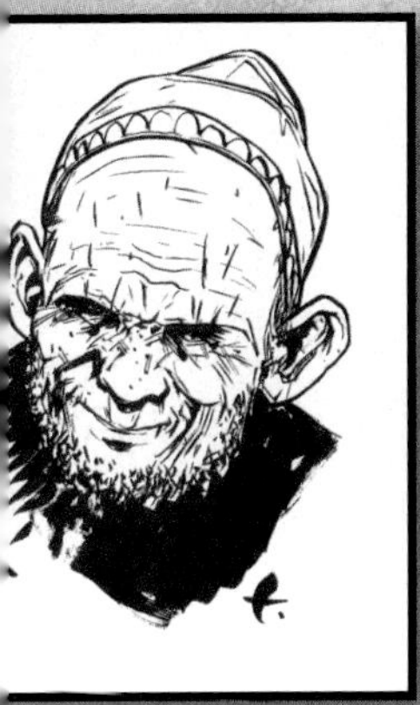

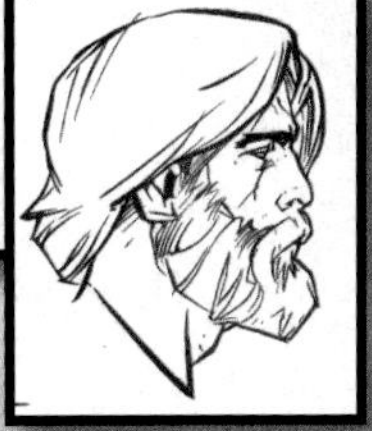

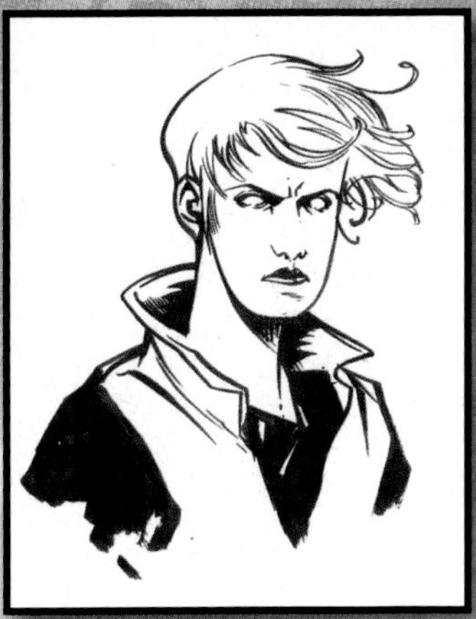

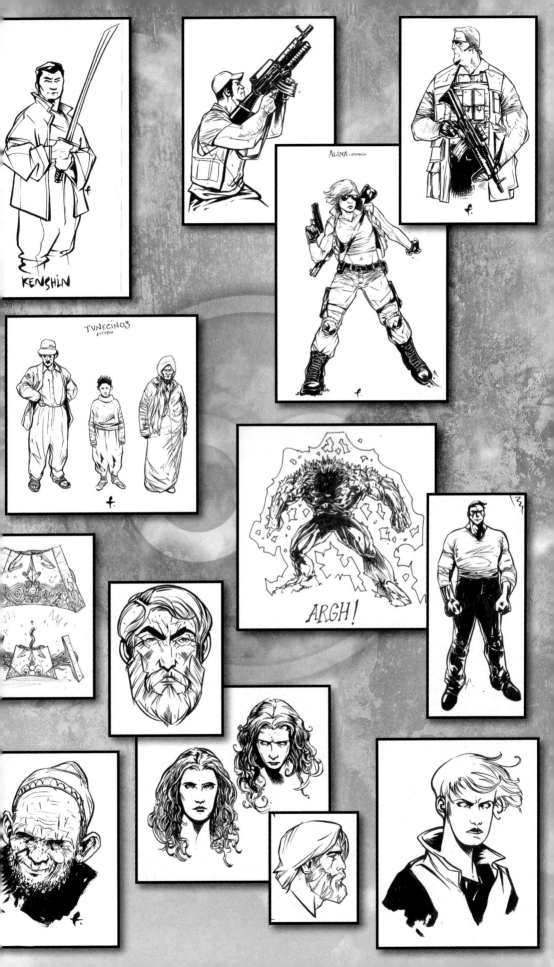

Top Cow presents a special bonus preview of its biggest event storyline:

ARTIFACTS

When a mysterious antagonist kidnaps Hope, the daughter of Sara Pezzini and Jackie Estacado, Armageddon is set in motion. Featuring virtually every character in the Top Cow Universe including Danielle Baptiste, *Artifacts* is an Epic story for longtime fans and new readers alike.

Volume 1 trade paperback available now!

ISBN 978-1-60706-201-4 • $9.99

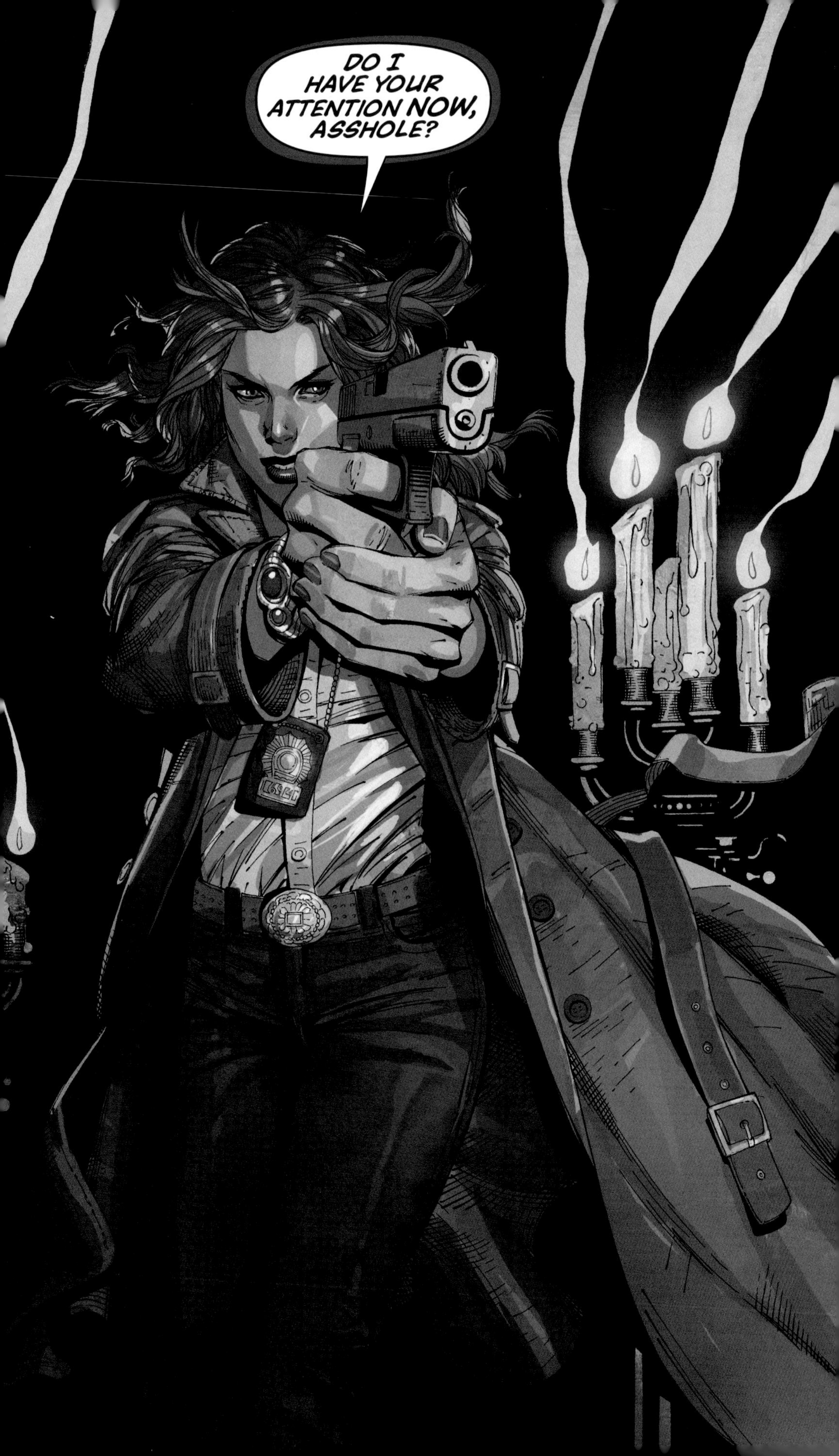
DO I HAVE YOUR ATTENTION NOW, ASSHOLE?

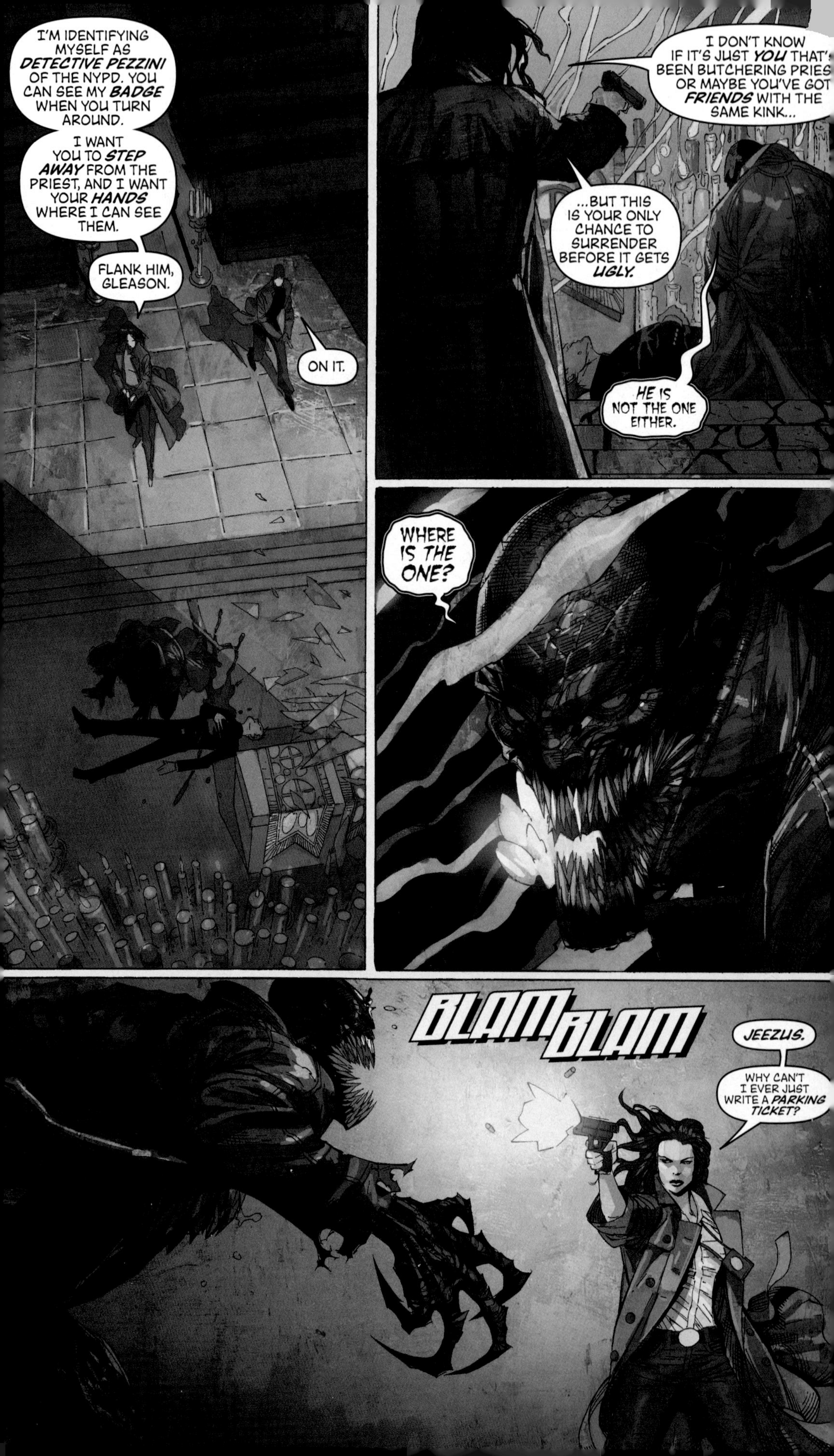
I'M IDENTIFYING MYSELF AS DETECTIVE PEZZINI OF THE NYPD. YOU CAN SEE MY BADGE WHEN YOU TURN AROUND.
I WANT YOU TO STEP AWAY FROM THE PRIEST, AND I WANT YOUR HANDS WHERE I CAN SEE THEM.
FLANK HIM, GLEASON.
ON IT.
I DON'T KNOW IF IT'S JUST YOU THAT'S BEEN BUTCHERING PRIES OR MAYBE YOU'VE GOT FRIENDS WITH THE SAME KINK...
...BUT THIS IS YOUR ONLY CHANCE TO SURRENDER BEFORE IT GETS UGLY.
HE IS NOT THE ONE EITHER.
WHERE IS THE ONE?
BLAM BLAM
JEEZUS.
WHY CAN'T I EVER JUST WRITE A PARKING TICKET?

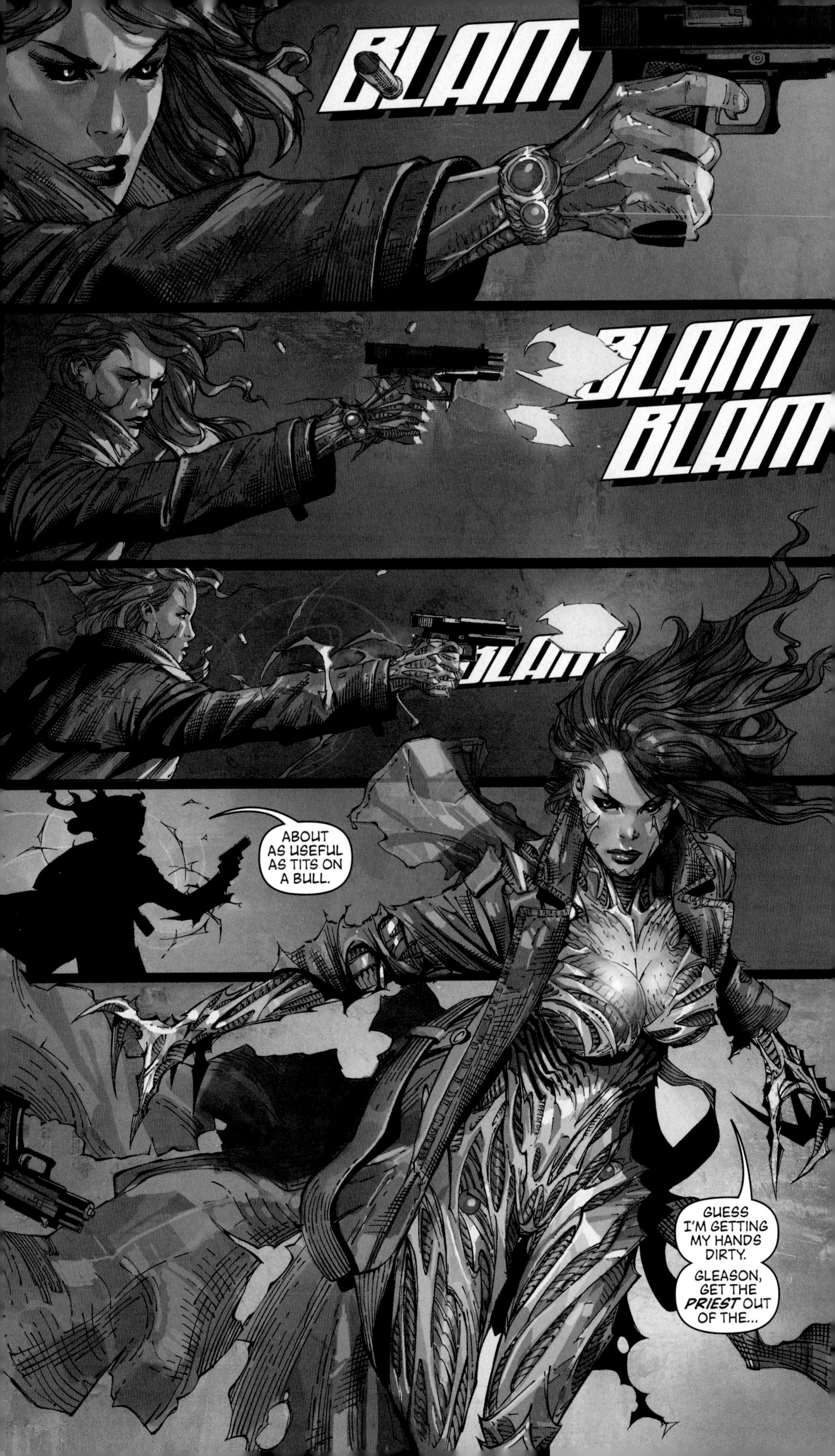
BLAM
BLAM
BLAM
BLAM
ABOUT AS USEFUL AS TITS ON A BULL.
GUESS I'M GETTING MY HANDS DIRTY.
GLEASON, GET THE *PRIEST* OUT OF THE...

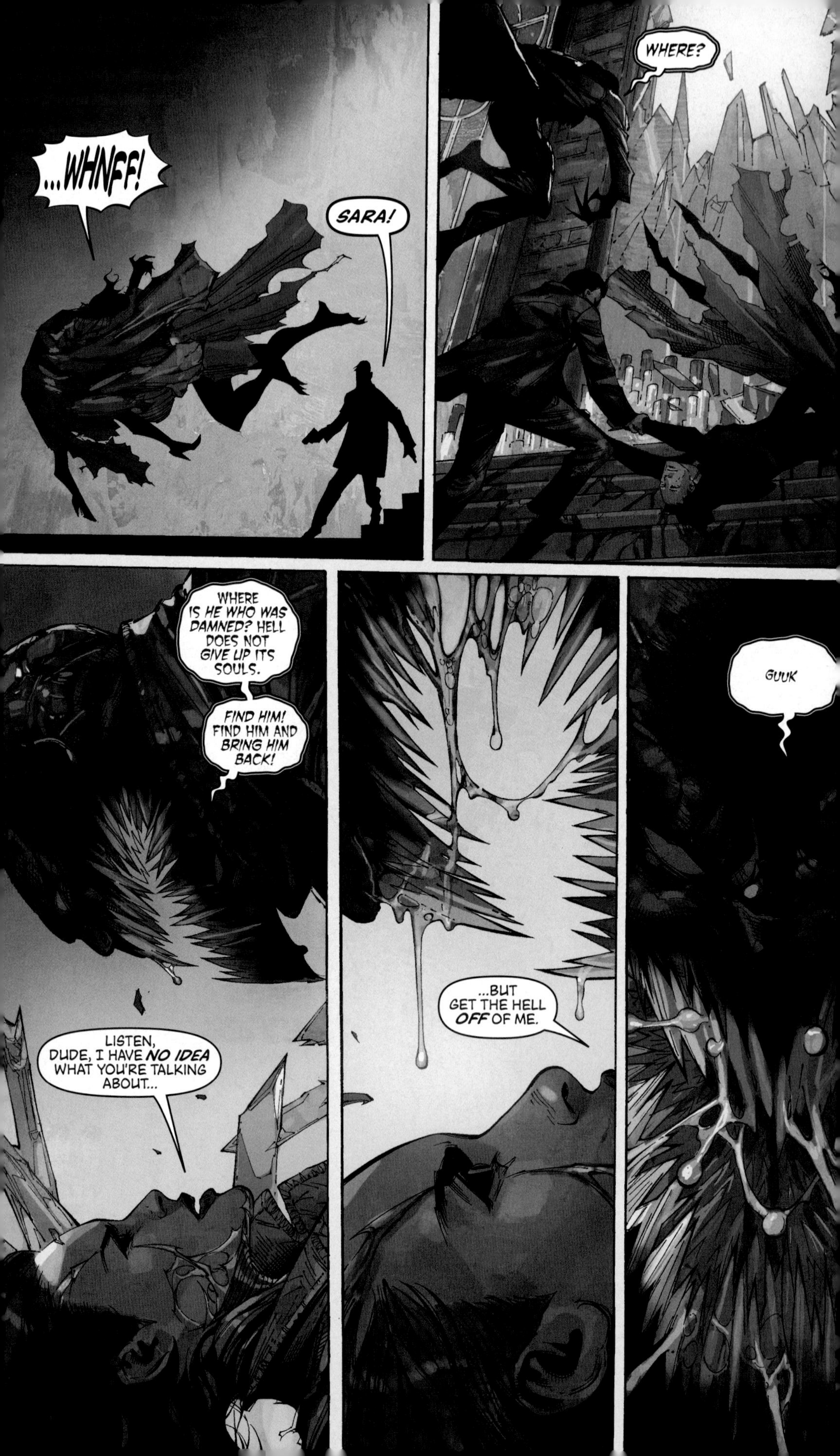
...WHNFF!
SARA!
WHERE?
WHERE IS HE WHO WAS DAMNED? HELL DOES NOT GIVE UP ITS SOULS.
FIND HIM! FIND HIM AND BRING HIM BACK!
LISTEN, DUDE, I HAVE NO IDEA WHAT YOU'RE TALKING ABOUT...
...BUT GET THE HELL OFF OF ME.
GUUK

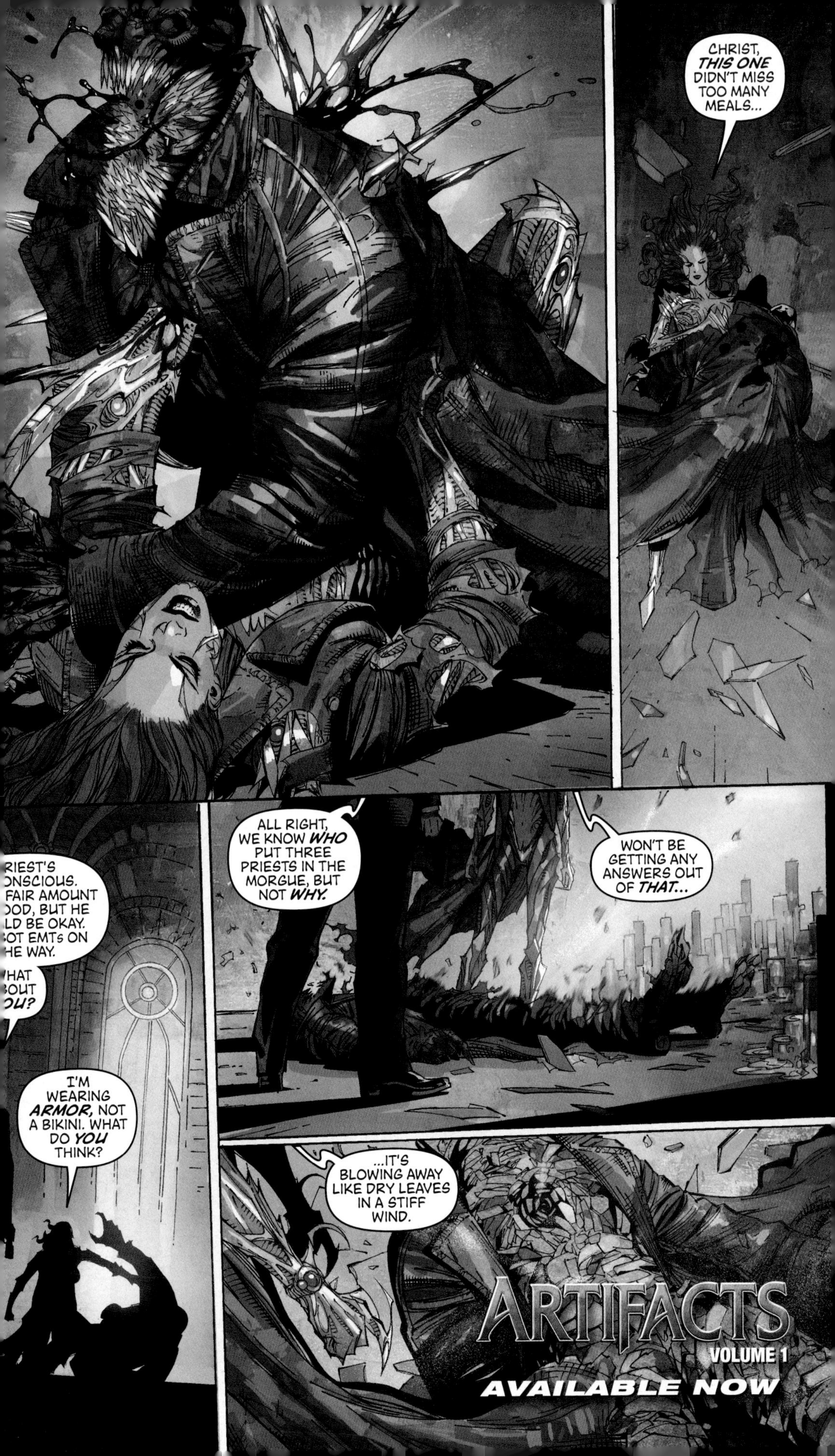
CHRIST, THIS ONE DIDN'T MISS TOO MANY MEALS...
RIEST'S ONSCIOUS. FAIR AMOUNT OOD, BUT HE LD BE OKAY. OT EMTs ON HE WAY.
HAT BOUT OU?
I'M WEARING ARMOR, NOT A BIKINI. WHAT DO YOU THINK?
ALL RIGHT, WE KNOW WHO PUT THREE PRIESTS IN THE MORGUE, BUT NOT WHY.
WON'T BE GETTING ANY ANSWERS OUT OF THAT...
...IT'S BLOWING AWAY LIKE DRY LEAVES IN A STIFF WIND.
ARTIFACTS
VOLUME 1
AVAILABLE NOW

Explore more of the Top Cow Univers

Ron Marz • Michael Broussard
ARTIFACTS
volume 1
FEATURING AN INTRODUCTION BY
MARC SILVESTRI

Artifacts
Volume 1

written by:
Ron Marz
pencils by:
Michael Broussard &
Stjepan Sejic

When a mysterious an
kidnaps Hope, the daughter of Sara
and Jackie Estacado, Armageddon
motion. Featuring virtually every c
in the Top Cow Universe, Artifact
epic story for longtime fans a
readers alike.

Collects issues #0-4

(ISBN 978-1-60706-201-1

From the pages of Witchblade
RON MARZ • STJEPAN SEJIC
ANGELUS
volume 1
FEATURING AN INTRODUCTION BY
ANGELA ROBINSON

Angelus
Volume 1

written by:
Ron Marz
art by:
Stjepan Sejic

Like so many other
somethings, Danielle Baptiste is t
find her place in the world. But f
that also means bearing up un
burden of acting as host for one
Universe's primal forces - The A
Returning to her hometown of New
with her friend and romantic interes
Dani must face an attack from her
enemy, the Darkness, as well as bet
the very warriors who pledged to se

Collects issues #1-6

(ISBN 978-1-60706-198-4)

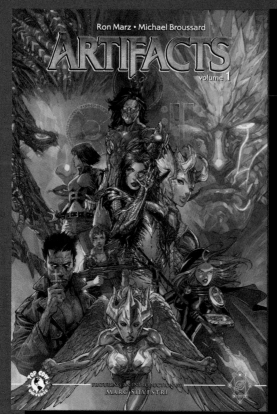

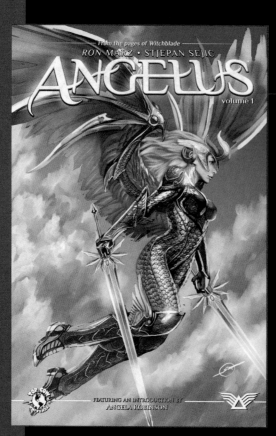

First Born
Volume 1

written by:
Ron Marz
art by:
Stjepan Sejic

Top Cow's stunning, epic crossover by writer Ron Marz (Witchblade, Green Lantern) and painter Stjepan Sejic (Witchblade, Angelus) is collected for the first time. Sara Pezzini prepares to give birth to her fi rst child, but the forces of Light and Dark both covet the offspring of the Witchblade bearer!

Collects First Born issues #0-3
and Witchblade issues #110-112

(ISBN 978-1-58240-864-5)

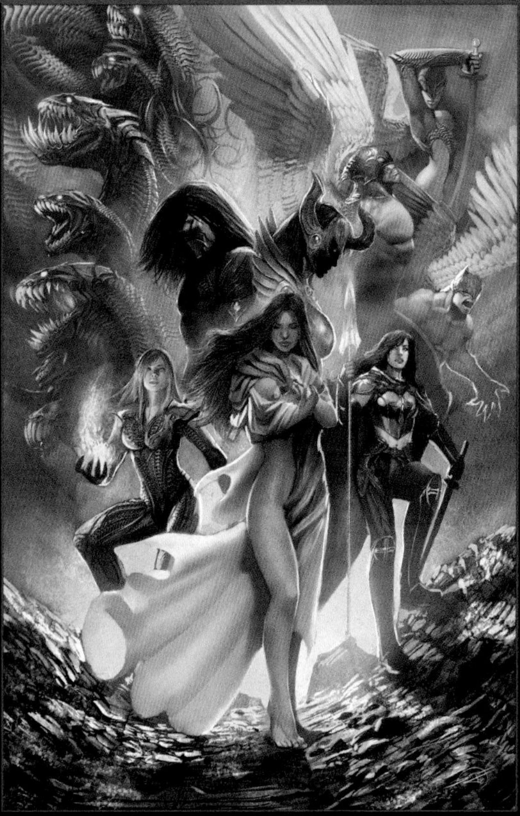

Broken Trinity
Volume 1

written by:
Ron Marz with Phil Hester
& Bryan Edward Hill
art by:
Stjepan Sejic, Phil Hester,
Jorge Lucas, Brian Stelfreeze,
Nelson Blake II & Tyler Kirkham

Broken Trinity brings together the Witchblade, The Darkness and Angelus once more, but this time the stakes are even higher as a new artifact is discovered, forever upsetting the balance of power. By the conclusion of the crossover, a major new player will be introduced into the Top Cow Universe, while at least one established character will be gone forever.

Collects issues #1-3, Broken Trinity: The Darkness #1, Broken Trinity: Witchblade #1, Broken Trinity: The Angelus #1 & Broken Trinity: Aftermath #1

(ISBN 978-1-60706-198-4)

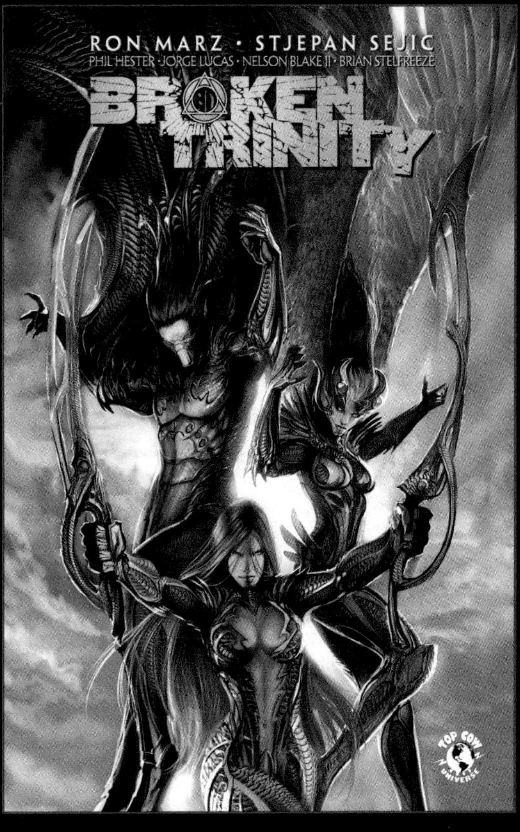
RON MARZ · STJEPAN SEJIC
PHIL HESTER · JORGE LUCAS · NELSON BLAKE II · BRIAN STELFREEZE
BROKEN TRINITY

Ready for more? Jump into the Top Cow Universe with *Witchblade*!

RON MARZ • MIKE CHOI
WITCHBLADE
VOLUME 1
FEATURING AN INTRODUCTION BY
RON MARZ

Witchblade

volume 1 - volume 8

written by:
Ron Marz
art by:
Mike Choi, Stephen Sadowski, Keu Cha, Chris Bachalo, Stjepan Sejic and more!

Get in on the ground floor of Top Cow's flagship title with these affordable trade paperback collections from Ron Marz's series-redefining run on Witchblade! Each volume collects a key story arc in the continuing adventures of Sara Pezzini and the Witchblade, culminating in the epic 'War of the Witchblades' storyline!

Book Market Edtion, volume 1
collects issues #80-#85
(ISBN: 13: 978-1-58240-885-9) $9.99

WITCHBLADE
PHIL HESTER

volume 2
collects issues #86-#92
(ISBN: 978-1-58240-886-6)
U.S.D. $14.99

WITCHBLADE
VOLUME 3

volume 3
collects issues #93-#100
(ISBN: 978-1-58240-887-3)
U.S.D. $14.99

WITCHBLADE
VOLUME 4
MARC BERNARDIN

volume 4
collects issues #101-109
(ISBN: 978-1-58240-898-9)
U.S.D. $17.99

FEATURING AN INTRODUCTION BY
ROBERT KIRKMAN

collects issues
First Born is
(ISBN: 978-1-582
U.S.

WITCHBLADE

volume 6
collects issues #116-#120
(ISBN: 978-1-60706-041-3)
U.S.D. $14.99

RON MARZ • STJEPAN SEJIC
WITCHBLADE
VOLUME 7

volume 7
collects issues #121-#124 &
Witchblade Annual #1
(ISBN: 978-1-60706-053-1)
U.S.D. $14.99

RON MARZ • STJEPAN SEJIC
WITCHBLADE
JIM STARLIN

volume 8
collects issues #125-#130
(ISBN: 978-1-60706-102-1)
U.S.D. $14.99

Join the Top Cow Universe with The Darkness!

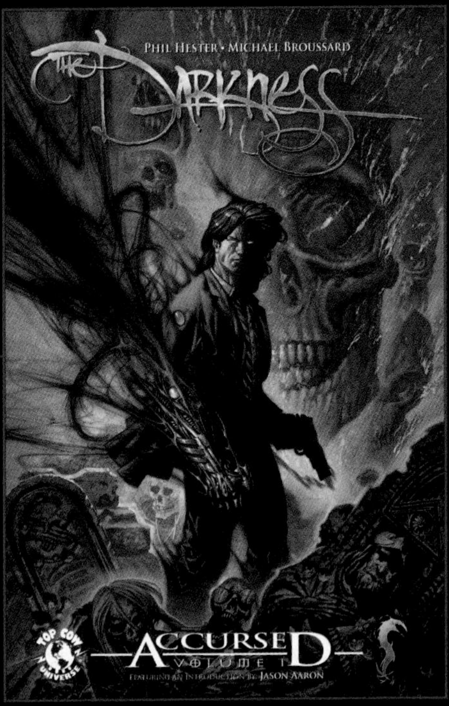

Phil Hester • Michael Broussard
The Darkness
Accursed
Volume 1
Featuring an Introduction by Jason Aaron

The Darkness
1 Accursed vol. 1

written by:
Phil Hester

pencils by:
Michael Broussard

Mafia hitman Jackie Estacado was both blessed and cursed on his 21st birthday when he became the bearer of The Darkness, an elemental force that allows those who wield it access to an otherwordly dimension and control over the demons who dwell there. Forces for good in the world rise up to face Jackie and the evil his gift represents, but there is one small problem. In this story... they are the bad guys.

Now's your chance to read "Empire," the first storyline by the new creative team of Phil Hester (Firebreather, Green Arrow) and Michael Broussard (Unholy Union) that marked the shocking return of The Darkness to the Top Cow Universe!

Book Market Edtion
ISBN 13: 978-1-58240-958-0
$9.99

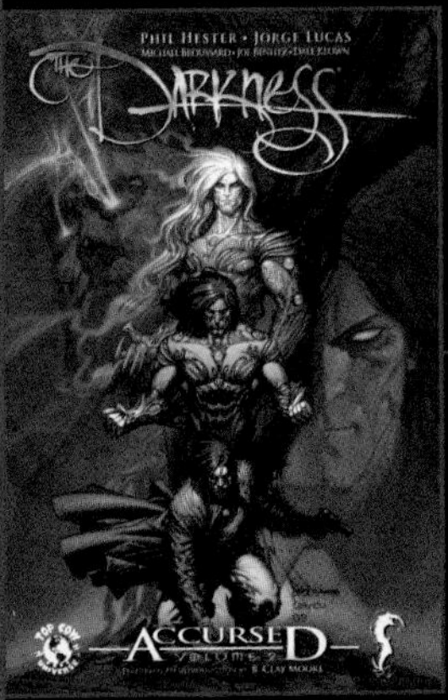

Phil Hester • Jorge Lucas
The Darkness
Accursed
Volume 2

The Darkness
Accursed vol.2
978-1-60706-0-444
$9.99

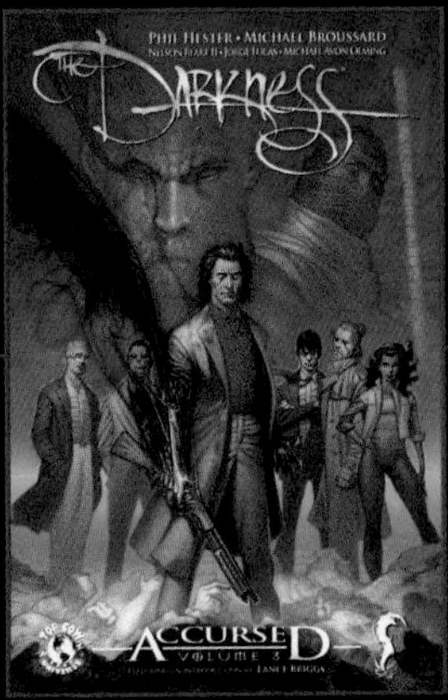

Phil Hester • Michael Broussard
The Darkness
Accursed
Volume 3

The Darkness
Accursed vol.3
978-1-60706-1-007
$12.99

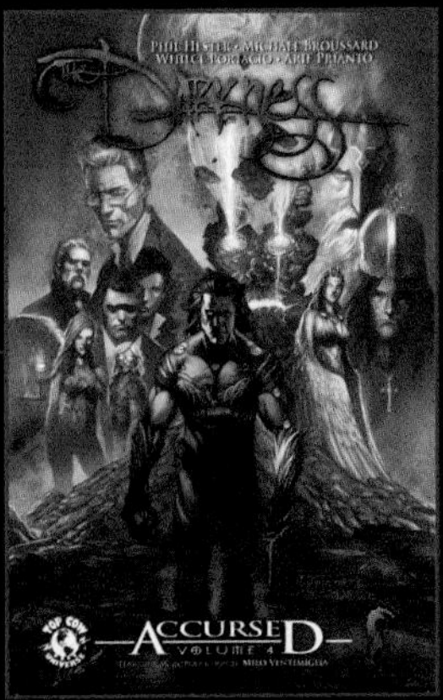

The Darkness
Accursed
Volume 4

The Darkness
Accursed vol.4
978-1-60706-1-946
$14.99

Premium collected editions

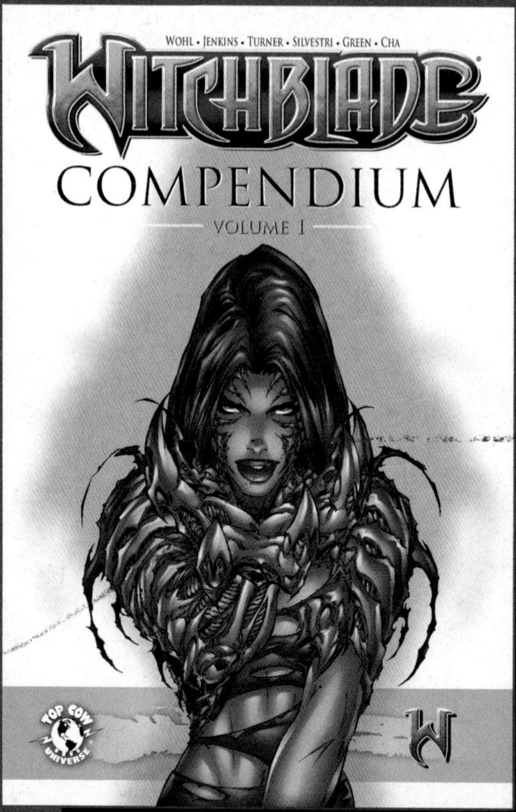
WOHL • JENKINS • TURNER • SILVESTRI • GREEN • CHA
WITCHBLADE
COMPENDIUM
VOLUME 1
TOP COW UNIVERSE

Witchblade

Compendium vol.1

written by:
David Wohl, Christina Z.,
Paul Jenkins
pencils by:
Michael Turner, Randy Gree
Keu Cha and more!

From the hit live-action telev series to the current Japanese a *Witchblade* has been Top Cow's flag title for over a decade. There's no like going back to the beginning reading it all over again. This ma collection houses issues #1-50 in a s edition for the first time. See how Witchblade chose Sara and threw her the chaotic world of the supernatural. the first appearances of Sara Pezzini Nottingham, Kenneth Irons and Ja Estacado in one handy tome!

SC (ISBN 13: 978-1-58240-634-3) $59
HC (ISBN 13: 978-1-58240-798-2) $99

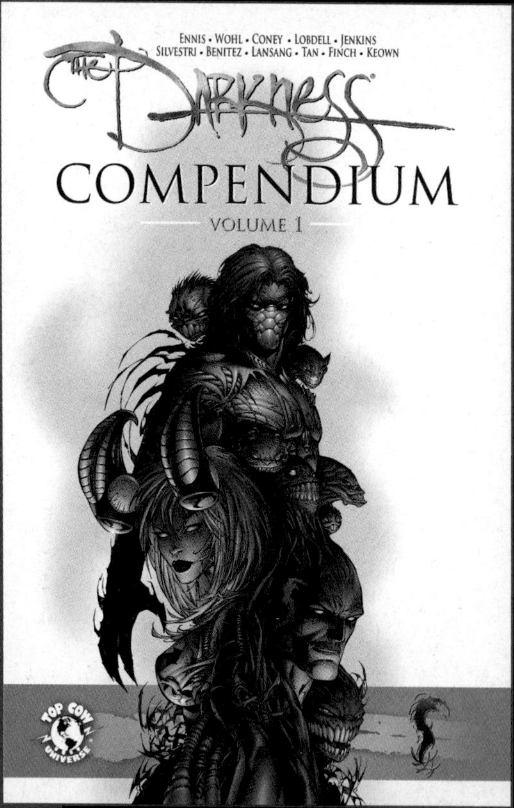
ENNIS • WOHL • CONEY • LOBDELL • JENKINS
SILVESTRI • BENITEZ • LANSANG • TAN • FINCH • KEOWN
THE DARKNESS
COMPENDIUM
VOLUME 1
TOP COW UNIVERSE

The Darkness

Compendium vol.1

written by:
Garth Ennis, Paul Jenkins,
Scott Lobdell
pencils by:
Marc Silvestri, Joe Benitez an
more!

On his 21st birthday, the awesome terrible powers of the Darkness aw within Jackie Estacado, a mafia hitman the Franchetti crime family. There's not like going back to the beginning and rea it all over again-- issues #1-40, plus complete run of the *Tales of the Dark* series collected into one trade paperb See how the Darkness first appeared threw Jackie into the chaotic world of supernatural. Get the first appearance The Magdalena and more!

SC (ISBN 13: 978-1-58240-643-5) $59
HC (ISBN 13: 978-1-58240-992-7) $99